Watching children learn is a beautiful and extraordinary experience. Their bodies transform, reflecting inner changes. Teeth fall out. Knees scab. Freckles multiply. Throughout the year they grow in endless ways and I can almost see their self-esteem rising, their confidence soaring, their small bodies now empowered. Given wings.

> *They fall in love with learning.*
> *It is a kind of magic, a kind of loving, a kind of art.*
> *It is teaching.*
> *Just teaching.*
> *Just what I do.*
> *What I did.*
> *Past tense.*

GABBIE STROUD was a dedicated teacher with over a decade of experience. But she resigned in frustration and despair because NAPLAN standardised testing and My School were preventing her from doing the very thing she was best at: teaching individual children according to their needs and talents.

This powerful memoir explores what it means to be a teacher: what makes a great teacher, and what our children need from their teachers. It tells the story of Gabbie's clear gift for teaching and what it was that finally broke her. Already being hailed as a work of national importance by educators, *Teacher* is a brilliant and heart-breaking memoir that cuts through the platitudes and statistics to show that our current education system is failing our children and destroying their teachers.

'Gabbie documents the inside story on the harm done to kids and teachers in our stressed-out, test-driven schools. Schools, especially primary schools, need to be based on relationship and a love of learning, yet we are doing the very opposite. Intense, personal, and impassioned but also crystal clear about what has gone wrong, and therefore how to fix it.'

STEVE BIDDULPH AM, bestselling author

'Moving. Insightful. Funny. Sad. Gabbie Stroud was a gifted teacher. She loved and nurtured her students, she was proud of their achievements, they made her laugh and cry. But the system ground her down, and teaching left her. She is a loss to the profession, and the children she might have taught. Her journey is a lesson for everyone who cares about education and the future of our children—and the country. How can the system be made to work better? How can we respect, recognise and reward the professionalism of teachers? Gabbie Stroud brings these questions to life . . . with a passionate insider's insight, from the classroom, staffroom and the principal's office.'

JULIANNE SCHULTZ AM FAHA,
professor, and founding editor of *The Griffith Review*

'What do we want for our children when they start school? What kind of teacher does any family want for their young ones? I want a teacher like Gabbie Stroud. PLEASE! Gabbie's story of a gifted teacher's experience shows what might be possible if we changed the policy settings to allow good teachers to do their job, attending to their students rather than documenting forever to demonstrate "standards" and "be accountable". Every citizen needs to read this book, feel the author's love for teaching and think about what would need to change to keep good teachers influencing our children.'

MARIE BRENNAN, Professor of Education

'*Teacher* is the story of one teacher's love of teaching and her ultimate heartbreak as the education system finally took everything she had to give and left her broken. Unfortunately, Gabbie's story is shared by many other teachers.

'The love and commitment she shows to her students, the guilt that she experiences as her students get the best of her, and her own daughters get the crumbs that are left, the overwhelming exhaustion she feels as her plate is piled higher, the frustration of spending so much time being forced to do what she knows does not benefit her students, all these things are palpable in Gabbie's story.

'This is such a valuable story to tell and to be heard. Gabbie was broken because the system is broken. Teachers all over the country are breaking and, even worse than that, students are breaking too. The joy has all but been sucked out of classrooms as standardised instruction and assessment have taken over from the creative art that once was teaching.

'Gabbie's story needs to be shouted from the rooftops. She very eloquently shows us why and how education needs to change. Teachers like Gabbie (once a teacher always a teacher) have so much to offer. Passion and wisdom are powerful things and she has them in abundance. *Teacher* made me laugh and cry. I loved it!'

KATHY MARGOLIS, education advocate

'In this powerful and poignant memoir, we share Gabbie Stroud's lived experience of what it really means to *be* a *Teacher*. Her wonderfully creative and compassionate teaching journey highlights each day's joys and challenges and increasing demands—until finally it all becomes too much. Beautifully crafted, honest and authentic, this memoir has the potential to help us understand—and potentially rescue— the profession. A must-read for all who care about the future of the teaching profession.'

ROBYN EWING AM, Professor of Teacher Education and the Arts, The University of Sydney

'Gabrielle Stroud details the minutiae of one teacher's life in a brutally honest individual account so well that it becomes a universal story. Her slow burn of passion, compassion, emerging skill, hope and dread, but above all the humanity of the most humanising professions, provides great insight into the costs and benefits, triumphs and tragedies of teachers' work. You'll laugh and cry. But you will really learn about life as a teacher. A must-read for all considering the profession.'

PHILIP RILEY, PhD, Associate Professor of Educational Leadership, Australian Catholic University

'*Teacher* by Gabrielle Stroud is a heartfelt and moving memoir about one woman who wanted nothing more than to teach our children and inspire them with her own big-hearted warmth, generosity and love of learning. Instead she finds herself broken by a system that cares more for data and demographies than young minds and spirits. She shines a penetrating light on all that is wrong with the Australian education system and how it fails both our children and our teachers. Impossible to read without choking up, this is an eloquent rallying cry for change and should be mandatory reading for all politicians and policy-makers. Luminous and heart-rending.'

KATE FORSYTH, bestselling author of *Bitter Greens*

'Gabbie Stroud has written a poignant book that explores her personal story of the good, the bad, the inspirational and inexplicable in the life of a classroom teacher. She was incredibly capable, passionate and committed—and yet she was eventually defeated by the forces of curriculum change, the pressure of incessant accountability and the sense of disempowerment and disrespect that has affected the teaching profession. Her story is becoming sadly all too common, and it is our children who suffer and who are missing out on a better education.'

MAGGIE DENT, bestselling author, parenting and resilience educator

TEACHER

One woman's struggle to keep the heart in teaching

GABBIE STROUD

ALLEN&UNWIN
SYDNEY·MELBOURNE·AUCKLAND·LONDON

*Certain names and details have been changed to protect
the innocent and guilty alike*

First published in 2018

Copyright © Gabrielle Stroud 2018

Allen & Unwin
83 Alexander Street
Crows Nest NSW 2065
Australia
Phone: (61 2) 8425 0100
Email: info@allenandunwin.com
Web: www.allenandunwin.com

A catalogue record for this
book is available from the
National Library of Australia

ISBN 978 1 76029 590 5

Set in 12.5/17.5 pt Fairfield LH by Midland Typesetters, Australia
Printed and bound in Australia by Griffin Press

10 9 8 7 6 5 4 3

For Yaya and the Boph

And Jess
Always Jess

Contents

Preface

The class sits in a circle. Little legs crossed, each rounded knee gently touching the person's next to them. Proximity doesn't bother them.

'So, today for Circle Time, our sentence is *When I grow up* . . . Let's think about that for a moment.' I demonstrate our 'thinking pose' and they join me—frowning and stroking their chin. 'Okay—when you're ready.' I nod at the first child.

'When I grow up I want to be a race car driver.'

'When I grow up I want to be a famous singer.'

'A builder.'

'A mummy.'

'An illustrator.'

Around they go, sharing their dreams.

And then it is Saphron's turn and we are all a little quieter. I find myself leaning forward. She's shy, softly spoken and from the Yuin Nation. She looks at me, eyes uncertain. I smile and gently hold her gaze. She takes a breath.

'When I grow up,' she says, still looking at me, 'I want to be like you.'

Thunk

The key to the door of my classroom is unreliable. I turn it once . . . twice . . . and each time I feel resistance, the impossible pressure of an obstructive lock. A thought twitches: *Maybe you shouldn't go in.*

The kids are in a jumble behind me. Week two, day three of Kindergarten and we still haven't quite got the knack of lining up. But that's okay. It's a small battle and I'm yet to be convinced that the straighter the line-up the better the learning.

It's forty degrees. Lunchtime is over. It had been a disappointment. The playground equipment had been too hot to touch—the bright-yellow slippery dip like a river of lava. The undercover area, although shaded, had been oppressive—the heat thick and heavy under a grey tin roof. And the Library had been overrun with bigger kids also seeking sanctuary.

Now my little ones are wilted and frustrated. They didn't get to play out their restless energy. Instead it was leached from them, absorbed by an unforgiving sun, like some strange kind of evaporation.

The key refuses to turn.

Two boys jostle at my legs, like pet dogs, anxious to be first inside.

'Line up,' I say. But they don't know what that means yet. It's a school language, a convention they are just beginning to experience.

'My shoelacer is too tight.' It is Grayson, hopping towards me, foot outstretched.

'When we get inside,' I tell him, 'I'll fix it for you.'

I twist the key again. No response.

'But my foot can't breathe,' he wails. He kicks at me. Twice. On the third attempt, he meets my shin.

'*Stop.*' I feel the twitch again. Grayson. The one whose name you learn first.

I slide the key out, then in, trying not to let it slip through my sweaty fingers. The sun bites at the back of my neck and a cicada starts up. It's loud and close and insistent, like the buzz of static on a radio. Some kids press their hands over their ears, while others imitate the sound, their voices competing with one another, with the cicada, with the heat.

Two of them run down into the garden, trying to locate the insect.

'This will shut him up,' one says, stamping his shiny new school shoes on the plants and shrubs. The other one is on all fours, pawing through the grass.

'Back to line,' I call. 'Come on.'

'Back to the lion!' shouts a child. I want to smile at the words, to laugh at the echo chamber. But Grayson has kicked me again and the two puppies are back underfoot, while three more kids have joined the hunt for cicadas.

I want the door to open. I want to be inside.

Click.

The door lunges forward and children surge inside like shoppers at the Boxing Day sales. They tumble onto the mat, rolling and lolling and flopping.

'My am just so tired,' says one and she pushes her sweaty fringe away from her eyes.

The room is old, large and stifling. The smell of wood glue saturates the air. I find the remote control for the air conditioner and frown, wondering why the screen is dead.

'Want me to turn it on?' asks The Helpful Little One. 'I know how.'

'I can do it.' I force a smile and slide the plastic panel off the back. I roll the batteries back and forth before replacing the panel and pressing the button again. I sit the remote on my in-tray and make a mental note—*change batteries.*

I pick my way through the pile of children, each of them deflated on the vibrant coloured mat. I watch for tiny fingers, like landmines that mustn't be detonated by my size-eight shoe.

Grayson is sitting in my seat and I let him stay there while I hang up my hat and sunnies and key and first-aid kit. *Choose your battles.*

The air conditioner bursts into life and a dull hum pervades the room. I remember the cicada and return to the door to see two students still outside, jumping and pawing at the earth.

'Come on, guys!' I call. 'Inside.' The lap-dogs circle me again.

'INSIDE!' one of them bellows.

The cicada hunters run towards us.

'Okay!' I say brightly, picking my way back to my seat. 'Everybody sitting on the mat.' I say it again, clapping my hands with each word.

I stand over Grayson, who is swivelling in my chair at the front of the room. He flicks out his foot and strikes my leg.

'Shoe,' he says and points.

'Yes!' I agree, but it is forced. 'I'm going to get everybody started on our next activity and then I'm going to do your shoe.' I tap the back of the chair. 'Quick sticks now, Grayson, sitting on the mat.'

He swivels, positioning the chair close to the shelves where scrapbooks and iPads are neatly stacked. He spins, knocking things to the floor before launching himself like a rock star into a mosh pit. One girl cops a kick to the head. There's a moment of hesitation before she decides to cut loose with a hearty and indignant cry. Grayson commando-crawls through the crowd to the edge of the mat.

'Come here,' I offer my hand into the writhing mass and extract the crying girl from the heap. I take her to my desk and offer her the tissue box. She takes one and scrunches it up. Her nose is streaming and she drags the balled-up tissue over the snot and then touches the tissue to her eyes. Before I can say *conjunctivitis*, she has done it again. I pluck several tissues from the box and glance at the door, hoping no one is watching. I wipe her eyes carefully, and hold the tissue while she blows into it. I feel the gooey softness swell between my fingers and try not to gag.

'You're alright,' I tell her. She burrows into me and hugs hard. I feel her neediness. Family trauma. Foster care. She is smiling up at me with tired eyes and tear-stained cheeks. A thought comes: *I don't have what you need.*

I bin the tissues and grab a sticky note. I scrawl—*Head kick, Martika, 2.14 p.m.*—and peel it off the pad. I stick it to my in-tray beside the remote. I'll have to fill in a form after school.

I take a breath and notice the feeling, the scratchy, anxious gnawing that has become the signature of my working days. I think for a moment about abandoning the lesson and calling for free play. I see myself filling out forms and changing batteries and sitting down while the children buzz around the room with dolls and Lego and jigsaws and dress-ups. But it's only Wednesday. There is so much to get through. And free play is a slippery slope—addictive for the children and me.

Instead, I start to sing. My voice is bright and jaunty and upbeat. 'Everybody sit down, sit down, sit down . . .'

The tune of the song has become familiar to them and now, like Pavlov's dogs, they straighten up and cross their legs, watching me. A few voices join in. 'Everybody sit down, just like me.'

I move to my seat and launch into the second verse, my hand cupped around my ear. 'Everybody listening, listening, listening . . .'

Their voices are lusty and loud. They love to sing and I'm glad. It's a crowd-pleaser and a crowd-controller. The verse rounds out and they're silent, eyes on me to see if we'll go again.

'Okay.' I reach into the tub at my feet, scrabbling for a book while not breaking eye contact.

Then a voice says, 'Jacob's bleeding.'

And we all stare at Jacob—the cicada hunter—who is standing in the doorway. He is indeed bleeding, one long stream from his knee down to his grey school sock. His buddy, The Stamper, has a proprietary arm around his shoulders.

'Jacob's bleeding,' The Stamper says again and he squats, pointing at the blood.

'It's like a arrow,' says a kid from the mat. 'See, like the blood is pointing to his sock.'

'Oh, yeah.' The Stamper rubs his finger in the blood and makes the arrowhead more obvious.

'No,' I bleat. 'No, no.' I stand up. 'Don't touch it. We don't touch other people's blood.' I move towards them and the lap-dogs follow. I usher Jacob further into the room and find the first-aid kit. The children watch in silence as I put on gloves.

I ask for tissues and there is a crush as three kids make a leap for the box. They carry it together, like it is a large piece of furniture. They offer it to me and I thrust my gloved hand inside.

'It's empty,' one of the children tells me solemnly.

I nod and leave my seat, edging around the mat to find the stash of tissue boxes. I pass Grayson, who isn't on the mat but curled up near the corner in a mad kind of yoga pose. His shoe is up near his face—he is chewing at the laces.

'One more minute, Gray,' I tell him. He eyeballs me and growls.

I find the tissues and bust open the pack. Assistants flank me as I wipe Jacob's leg with a medi-swab and then a tissue. The outline of blood is still visible. I take a moment to open a fresh swab and dab The Stamper's finger too. Then I find a bandaid and spend a futile minute trying to open it with rubber gloves on.

'You want me to do it?' asks The Helpful Little One. 'I know how.'

'You take these gloves,' I tell her, peeling them off and bundling them as an inside-out ball.

'Eww,' she says. 'They all sweaty.'

'Let me feel!' says The Stamper.

The sweaty gloves are passed around as I use my fingernails to peel the bandaid stickers apart. The children start calling the sweaty gloves 'the glubbers' and a chant starts up to 'rub the glubbers'.

'No chanting!' The words shoot out of me, rapid-fire. I raise my eyebrows, trying to somehow stretch my face. Inhale. 'We don't need chanting. Now put the glubbers in the bin.' A few kids laugh and I hear one say, 'The teacher said glubbers.'

I press the bandaid onto Jacob's knee and watch as it pops up, ineffectually covering his wound. The glubbers are still being rubbed so I take them from a nearby child and tiptoe the course back to my desk. I drop them into my handbag, sensing they might be foraged from the bin. I reach for a sticky note and scrawl—*Bandaid, Jacob, 2.25 p.m.* There is another form I will have to fill in—a form for bandaids. I sigh and then a flash of panic shoots through me. *Someone in the class is allergic to bandaids.*

I fumble through my program, past mission statements and duty rosters until I find the pages of allergies. I trail my finger down the list. Jacob is on page three. His face beams up at me from the photo. He is gluten and dairy intolerant. I read the few lines again carefully. No mention of bandaids. I slide the allergy pages out of their sleeve and add them to my in-tray. They need to be copied, laminated and pinned up where I can find them. Where everyone can find them.

The hypnotic magic of the medical emergency has passed. Children are rolling under the desks. Some are trying to burrow under the mat. Others are standing around my chair, spinning it faster and faster.

'Do my shoe,' Grayson demands. He is standing in front of me, his shoe now in his hand, the laces knotted up, black and tight.

I take the shoe and sing the song again. The Pavlovian effect has worn off: I have to call many of them by name. I get confused—using siblings' names and parents' names. And the children laugh at me, loud and raucous.

Eventually we are sitting, listening, looking. Still. Quiet. I have Grayson's shoe in my lap. I begin the lesson.

'This afternoon, Kindergarten, we are going to do something special.'

They stare up at me and a few of them take an excited breath.

'This afternoon we are going to be making a green sheep.'

Two little girls squeal with the absolute joy of it and hug each other, like they've just won a game show.

'Can you remember when we read the book about the green sheep?' I keep my eyes on them, sweeping my gaze around to create the climate of conversation. I try to feel warm and enthused so they might see it in my eyes. I pluck at Grayson's shoelace. It is wet and hard.

'Now,' I tell them, 'let me show you how we're going to make our green sheep.' I reach into the tub at my feet and pull out the sample I have made: pieces of green tissue paper torn and scrunched to create a fleece within a sheep-body template.

'That looks amazing!' one child exclaims.

'Did you make that?' asks Jacob.

'I did.' I try to smile as I remember the hasty gluing process that occurred late last night. 'Here's how we do it.' I clip a blank template onto the magnetic board and begin demonstrating, talking through each step like a celebrity chef. I move Grayson's shoe to the floor and immediately he stomps over and snatches it away. He growls at me again, but the class is mesmerised. My demonstration is like *Play School*—live.

'Now,' I say when the demo is complete, 'do we paint this glue on the table?' I use my most sensible voice.

'*Noooo*,' they chorus.

'Do we paint glue around here?' I gesture outside the template.

'*Noooo!*'

'Do we put glue on ourselves?' I remember an experience from last year.

'*Noooo!*'

One boy giggles. 'You don't glue yourself!' He is tickled by the idea and starts rolling around laughing.

I continue. 'On your desks you will find . . .'

They turn like meerkats, kneeling up and looking at their desks where I have laid out everything for the activity.

'Wait,' I say. 'I haven't told you to move yet.' But they are moving, creeping and shuffling towards their desks excited by the prospect of their very own green sheep.

There is a knock at the door and the students are lost to me, scattering to their desks to begin the project. I notice Grayson. He is hiding under my desk, swinging his shoe around—helicopter-style.

I move to the door where children have crowded like a welcoming committee. The sound of cicadas fills our room.

'Hi! I'm here to collect Daphne.'

The mother is young and I can see the Woolworths logo on her work shirt. I wonder how much she makes and if she ever takes work home.

'Sorry to be early.' She glances at her watch. 'I need to get Daph to the dentist. It's so hot, isn't it?'

Daphne rushes forward and clings to her mother's leg. The mum absently brushes her hand over the child's head. The welcoming committee wanders off, one of them announcing, 'Daphne's mum's here.'

'And while I'm here,' the mother continues, 'I've got that uniform order.' She fishes inside her handbag.

'Oh great,' I say. 'That one goes down to the office.' Behind me, I can hear the tearing of tissue paper. It's a muted, ripping sound.

'Oh, okay.' The mum produces more paperwork. 'And I've got this note about permission for walking around town?'

'Walking excursions,' I nod. 'Yep, that comes to me.'

'Great!' She flashes a smile and then says, 'How's Daph going, anyway?'

'Pretty good, I think, but let's make a better time to talk.' I can feel students circling around my legs. One child has slid into the space between me and the mother. He's holding up a green sheep that is heavy with too much glue.

'Of course.' The mother leans further into the room. 'You've got your hands full now!' She laughs and turns to leave, and then I remember and call her back.

'Excuse me,' I say, embarrassed that I can't remember her name. 'Before you can take Daphne, you need to pop down to the office and sign her out. I can't let her go with you until I have that slip.' There's a pause and I find myself adding, 'I'm sorry about that.'

'Oh, okay.' Her eyebrows are raised and I register her surprise. She can't see the apprehended violence orders and the custody battles and the court cases that hover over the school playground and infiltrate my classroom.

'Daphne just needs to stay here until then.'

'Oh.' Her voice is flat. She glances at her watch again.

I gently take Daphne's hand as the mother turns towards the office. More kids are clustered around me, and we watch her walk away. Daphne starts to cry, her face folding and crumpling at the bitter disappointment of being stuck here. I feel her pain and wish I could join her. But I haven't been able to cry for about six months. I'm not sure my face remembers how it's done.

I herd the children back to their desks, throwing out instructions to *hurry up and get those green sheep finished!* I glance at the clock and feel the urgency of the final twenty minutes. Children approach me in waves, a relentless ocean of need. They present their artworks to me: patchy sheep that look mangy and diseased. I encourage them to fill in the spaces and show them how to pull off the excess. 'We need to see his face,' I tell one child. Daphne trails beside me, howling.

I scan the room for Grayson. He is under his own desk now and his shoes and socks are off. He has his feet pressed against the bottom of the desk and is using all his strength to lift the table up before letting it drop with a *thunk*. I crouch and invite him to join the class. He pokes out his tongue and lets the desk drop again.

I stand up and move away, ushering Daphne along with me. Her mother returns to the door and several kids chorus *Daphne! Ya mum's here!* Daphne rushes into her mother's arms and The Helpful Little One receives the slip.

'Will I put this in your tray, Teacher?' she asks, and gestures to my desk.

I nod and swallow down a heavy feeling.

Thunk.

Thunk.

'Come on, Grayson,' I say, kneeling beside him again. 'Let's get your shoes sorted out.' I reach in for his shoes, but he rolls over them, making the foetal position. I press my hand against his back and feel his tiny spine. Just a little boy.

'Jacob's bleeding,' a child announces. 'Jacob's bleeding again.'

'Seriously?' I crawl out from under the desk and scan for Jacob. His nose is streaming blood all over a green sheep. His face is pale, eyes astonished. I feel something twinge in my chest and I push out a breath.

The lap-dogs have carried the first-aid kit over to Jacob's desk. I thank them and riffle through the box, searching for the rubber gloves while redirecting traffic.

'Go and sit down,' I tell each child. 'Go and finish making a beautiful green sheep.'

I call over The Helpful Little One as I plunder the tissue box.

'Do you know where the office is?' I ask.

Her chest puffs out as she nods.

'Do you think you could take Jacob down there?'

She nods again, her face sombre.

I show Jacob how to hold the tissues. I press his hand under the wet, bloody wadded mass. His eyes meet mine and I can see he is panicking.

'You're okay,' I tell him, and in his eyes something changes. The kid believes me. I turn to The Helpful Little One.

'So, you know what to do?'

'Take him to the office.' She jabs her thumb at Jacob.

It is my turn to nod and she smiles at me.

'I'm gonna be a teacher,' she tells me, 'when I get big.' She drags Jacob out the door.

Thunk.

Grayson's desk is still rising and falling as though it is breathing.

'Grayson? Come out now, mate.'

I move to the phone and call down to the office, asking them to watch for Jacob.

'Oh, hang on, Gab,' says the voice on the other end of the line. I press my hand against my ear; the room is growing loud behind me. Restless noise. 'James is telling me to remind you—bring your program to staff meeting this afternoon. You've got some new programming format or something.'

'Right.' I hang up and find my program still open on my desk. I flip it shut, the bright-orange folder already full and thick and heavy. I shift it and feel the weight of my summer break, the weight of organisation, the weight of me—trying to get ahead.

Thunk.

Thunk.

Thunk.

The room is in chaos. Paintbrushes are sticking to the desks, their soft new bristles already becoming brittle and hard. Glue drips from the edge of one desk. Balls of green tissue paper litter the floor. Three chairs are overturned. Shoes and socks are scattered everywhere. Most of the class are now lifting and dropping their desks with their feet—just like Grayson.

A child stands in front of me, his body so completely in my personal space that I almost can't see him.

'I go toilet,' he says urgently.

I nod. The desks thunk. And thunk. And thunk.

Thunk.

Thunk.

I take two steps, aimless. Lost in my classroom.

'Do. My. Shoe!' Grayson bellows—over all the thunking and chatter and laughter.

And then his shoe hurtles through the air. Hits my chest. Strikes my heart.

'ENOUGH!' I shout. It is louder and harsher than any sound I've ever made. It trumps Grayson and the thunking and the cicadas and all the other sounds. It covers my unsteady heartbeat and the blood rushing in my ears.

I snatch up the shoe. Stride across the room. Open the door. And I hurl that shoe as hard as I can into the world outside. I grunt with the effort of it.

Thunk

I slam the door and wheel around.
Breathe.
Their faces are filled with fear.
But, in that moment, nobody's more frightened than I am.

First teachers

I'm in the shower with Sophie, my youngest daughter. She is five, nearly six. Curious and hilarious. She notices that she's up to my belly button, that my belly is smaller than her daddy's, and that both of us have a faint birthmark on our abdomens.

Then, she asks what happens if you put a booger in your eye.

'A nose booger?' I ask, hoping I have misheard.

She nods.

'Snot? Into your eye?'

She nods again.

'No, you don't do that,' I say. 'It's not good for you.'

She thinks on this and I watch as water cloaks her scrawny frame.

She looks up at me through the sheen and asks, 'What kind of badness will happen if you do that?'

Where has this question come from? I think. Why isn't she picking her nose and eating it like a normal child?

I tell her she will get sick. I explain, as briefly as I can, the simple facts of conjunctivitis. Through the rush of water, I can see that she believes me. She is taking this in, these words I'm saying. Absorbing me. But I know it won't be long before I'm diminished, before my power as the 'all knower' is weakened. Because little Soph will soon be going to school.

Long before the knot of Grayson's shoe took up residence in my chest, long before I became a teacher, I stood up in the familiar comfort of my Kindergarten classroom to share my news. I took a breath and told the assembled circle of my peers that it was my dad's birthday.

'He's one hundred,' I announced.

'I don't think he'd be one hundred,' Teacher said.

'He is,' I insisted. 'And something else about my dad? His religion's Calathumpian.'

'Calathumpian?' A smile played at Teacher's lips, her eyebrows raised.

I nodded and sat down on the worn green carpet, ready to hear Bobby Hedger's news about how many kangaroos his father shot on the weekend. Next to me, my best friend Lauren had a Cabbage Patch doll stuffed up her jumper. I couldn't wait for her to reveal it.

That afternoon, Mum scuttled our car over the dirt road on the way home from school. Dust billowed as the car bumped and staggered over potholes.

'Is Dad one hundred?'

'No.' Mum didn't even glance at me, eyes fixed ahead for a kangaroo or, more likely, a rabbit.

'Is it Dad's birthday today?'

'No,' Mum scoffed. 'It's May. His birthday's not till July.'

Outside, the dust clouded around and made its way inside our car. Stifling yet familiar. I could feel dirt clinging to my nostrils.

We rattled over our cattle grid and along the most rutted stretch of road closest to home.

'What's Calathumpian?' I asked.

Mum negotiated the big rock that was set into the road, it's grey-blue face seeming to grow larger with each passing year.

'It's nothing,' she said. 'It's your father talking nonsense.'

She pulled into the carport, switched off the ignition and smiled at me. 'You know we're *Catholic*,' she said, patting my leg. And then she got out of the car and walked into the house.

Our white car was dusted dirt-brown. I pressed my finger against the duco and wrote: *GA*. That was all I had. *GABRIELLE* was such a long name, so many letters. I studied my writing, watched as some of the dust fell away and wondered how old my dad really was.

'That's nothing,' my sister Jacqui assures me now, many years later. We are all grown-up and gathered together for a family dinner. Most of us are home and seated around the dining table.

'When I was a kid, Dad told me that macaroni noodle shells were rare,' Jacqui says. 'He told me they cost a lot of money and we were a very lucky family to have them.'

I glance at Dad, slicing a roast while Mum hovers nearby. He's pretending he can't hear, but his eyebrows are raised—just so—and his mouth is set in such a way that I know he is listening, remembering and, inwardly, laughing.

'So,' Jacqui continues. 'I got all the packets of macaroni that we had in the house and I emptied them into an ice-cream container. I took it into school and I stood up for news and I told all the kids that we were a rich family because we had all these macaroni noodle shells. I can remember running my hands through them like this.' She demonstrates. 'And then I told the class'—here Jacqui pauses, catches her own laughter—'then I told the class that if they were nice to me I would let them touch my macaroni noodles at morning-tea time.'

We laugh and it is hearty and warming, like the meal we're about to share. We like to talk and laugh. It is the best of our family. I watch Dad as he shrugs and chuckles, all while slicing the meat. It has been a long time since he has tried to sell a yarn to us as a truth.

'What happened next?' My eldest daughter, Olivia, is eight. She listens with rapture whenever we tell stories. I can see her soaking up our history, our lore.

'What happened next?' Jacqui draws a breath, calms her laughter. 'I think Brian McFadden put up his hand and said, 'That's not rare as gold. We had macaroni for dinner last night.'

We laugh again and Anni, my eldest sister, pours more wine. She fills my glass to the brim and says, 'There you go,

kiddo.' She knows I'm feeling fragile. My husband is notice-
ably absent.

Anni is twenty years my senior, while Jacqui is ten years older
than me. My other sister, Cheryl, fits between them, as does
my brother Phillip. Mum was forty when I was born and Dad
was forty-four. They were already a complete family before
I came along, tacking myself to the end of our narrative like a
hasty exclamation mark.

My childhood felt quite solitary with my siblings so much
older than me. They were teenagers and young adults when
I was a child. They were forever moving away from me, growing
up into the world and into their future. I was never lonely,
though. I had an imaginary friend named Ankle who kept me
company. In my mind, he was an Indigenous boy with black
hair, a bare chest and grubby shorts. Ankle always wanted to
play what I was playing. He was a good listener and a gentle
friend and a very real presence in my childhood. I would strap
a seatbelt on him when we travelled in the car and consult
with him before I answered Mum on what we might have
for lunch.

Ankle would disappear when my siblings came visiting,
home from boarding school or taking a break from their
working lives. They would fill my quiet life with their noise
and their energy. Our farm house seemed to shrink with every
bedroom filled and every seat at the table occupied.

My brother, Phil, was my favourite. When I was little I had
a crush on him. He was thirteen years older than me. He was

tall and dark and handsome and fun to be around. Phil could flick a tea towel harder than anyone else in my family, which made drying up the dishes with him a dangerous but exciting experience. He was daring enough to try flicking Dad across the arse, which inevitably led to the pair of them sparring and shadow-boxing in the kitchen. I loved watching them dance like this, cuffing ears and stepping, ducking and dodging, laughing and grunting.

'Get out!' Mum would protest. 'Do that outside!'

And they would stop, mumbling apologies and making faces behind Mum's back.

'Where are you going?' I'd ask Phil from my swing as he crossed the front yard towards the ute or the motorbike or the 4WD.

'Timbuctoo,' he'd always say.

'Can I come?'

'Nah.'

'Please?' I would stop swinging and follow him. 'Please, Phil?' My voice thin.

'Oh, alright,' he'd say and make room for me to join in his adventure.

Like my sister Jacqui, Phil went off to boarding school for Years Eleven and Twelve. Goulburn was an impossibly long way from our house. Our family lore holds a story that the first time we dropped him off, I was so sad to say goodbye that I cried all the way home. Three hours of inconsolable sobbing. Two hundred and seventy kilometres of tears. True love will make you do things like that. It's a story still shared within my family—the day I cried all the way home from Goulburn. Like Ankle and precious macaroni and the Calathumpian, our memories live in the stories we tell, and so many of these are framed by the landscape of our farm.

It's the farm that holds our history and our secrets. Granite boulders and ribbon gums are painted on the backdrop of our youngest years. The sorry bleating of fattened sheep and the greasy smell of lanoline lurk in our earliest memories. There are snakes, too, and stinging nettles and roosters crowing and the stench of something dead rotting in the long grass. Working dogs. Shearing sheds. Cubby houses. Drought.

On our farm, the water tanks stood like sentinels on our hill. In the summer, when I was Soph's age, my dad would check on them every day, knocking the corrugated sides with enormous knuckles and listening carefully. *Three more days*, he might say, *and then we'll need to pump, won't we?* I would look up at him and nod, sliding my hand into his, confident that water would always come out of our tap because my dad knew to knock on the tanks. Sometimes, I would go to the tanks on my own and tap my fist against them. But I couldn't discern the sounds like Dad. The echoes I heard didn't tell me anything. I was secure in Dad's knowledge, secure in his judgement, and I had a sense— all yarns aside—that my dad knew pretty much everything.

And then I went to school.

In Year Two, Mrs Read was my teacher. Her name alone delighted me. She wore sensible sandals and smoothed her hair behind her ear with a slide comb. Mrs Read gave us spelling tests and read us books and challenged us with Maths games. She had a tidy desk and didn't tolerate students who wandered off task.

She had a small bronze tin filled with gold stars. If your work was very good or neat or worthy, Mrs Read would put her fingers into the tinned cosmos and pinch out a star. She would dab it on the tip of her tongue and press it against your page, lifting your work to celestial heights.

Mrs Read had an ageless quality, though she was younger than my mum (everyone was younger than *my* mum). My mother called her Jean, which worried me. It felt like Mum had no regard for the fact that Mrs Read was the tester of spelling and the keeper of stars. I was seven and already a conscientious student. I didn't want Mrs Read to judge me based on my mother's faux pas. Plus, I wanted Mum to respect Mrs Read just as much as I did.

I loved Mrs Read. I loved the security of her routines. I loved the stars she controlled. But the true moment when I fell madly and deeply in love with her was the day she gave me the whale song.

Along with Reading and Maths and Writing and Art and Projects and Music, Mrs Read used to teach us about animals. She was an advocate of something called The Gould League, which was a group of people who cared for animals and wanted all species to survive. Mrs Read came alive when she talked about the work of the League. She showed us pictures of all kinds of animals and helped us to understand the difference between native and introduced species. She showed pictures of the Tasmanian devil and the southern corroboree frog and the northern hairy-nosed wombat. The word *endangered* soon became part of my vocabulary.

Mrs Read also showed us pictures of a Tasmanian tiger. In one image, it was an angry-looking animal raging against the fences of his enclosure with his mouth wide open. In another picture, he seemed harmless and forlorn, standing alone and looking out at the world with miserable resignation. As I studied that Thylacine and learned the word *extinct*, a terrible sadness came over me. But Mrs Read gave me hope. She talked to us about protecting animals and their habitats so we could enjoy them in the future—even in the year 2000, which shimmered almost twenty years ahead of us like a mirage.

We were told about elephants, hunted for their ivory to make piano keys and dominoes. She told us how rat-like mammals, called minks, were killed so women could wear furry jackets and hairy stoles. She told us about whales, too, and how they had been hunted and harpooned in our beautiful oceans and slaughtered to make candles and soap and even hairbrushes and makeup. Mrs Read told us there weren't many blue whales left.

And then, one day, Mrs Read brought in her record-player, her *own* record-player from her house.

In her sensible sandals—and with two children helping— she lugged each speaker from the boot of her Fairlane, up the concrete steps to our classroom. She carried in the turntable and set it down on a desk. We watched as she crouched on all fours to plug it in. Her hair fell from its slide and she held the comb in her teeth until she stood up with a grunt and smoothed her hair back into place.

'Today we're going to listen to the sound of whales,' said Mrs Read.

'Whales?' It was William Former, our unofficial and self-appointed spokesperson. 'Whales don't make a noise.'

Mrs Read smiled. 'Yes, they do, William. Some people have found a way to hear the whales making noises underwater. And they've recorded them. We're going to hear them talking.'

'*Talking?*' Wendy Heinz, a blonde kid from the Year Three group, seemed alarmed. She stared at the record-player.

'Not with words,' Mrs Read said, 'but with their calls.' She carefully placed the record over the spindle and set the needle in place.

There was muted hush as the vinyl started circling. Then, the unsteady bleeps and blops that a record makes when it's starting up. And then there was whale song.

Trumpet-like notes filled our classroom and I grinned at Lauren. Her eyes were shining and I could feel something happening in my chest—a kind of lifting and filling as my sense of wonder was overwhelmed. We listened, transfixed, as the squeaks and echoes and *poetry* of whales—humpback whales—consumed every corner of our ordinary classroom. My affection for these animals was multiplying as the haunting *whoop whoop whooooops* soared around us.

After a time, we tried imitating the short, thready whistles. Our farming tongues were quite used to creating long, high-pitched notes just right for persuading dogs and directing cattle. But somehow our strong little tongues were not subtle enough to mimic a whale and we realised we were doomed never to replicate this peculiar sound.

We started laughing as the record went on and the whales made beefier, fart-like grunts. Mrs Read smiled, aware, perhaps, of the magic in the room; aware that she was opening up our world. That we were exhilarated.

I carried that whale song with me in my memory, in my mind and in my imagination. And with it I carried the horror that whales had been killed so that people like me could enjoy luxuries like cosmetics. I could have felt helpless, but the whale song revealed to me a part of myself that was braver and stronger and smarter than I knew. I stopped using soap the very day I listened to that record. There were ways of reacting to this world, I realised. There were ways I could express what I had learned and what I knew to be true.

So, when my dad asked me, some days later, if I had used soap to wash my hands after feeding the dogs, I told him I wasn't using soap anymore.

'We shouldn't use soap, Dad,' I went on. I had the same confidence he had when he knuckled his fist against those water tanks.

'Why not?'

'Because it's made of whale. They kill whales to make soap. I don't think that's right.'

I watched my dad's face, saw him frown and shake his head. 'That's a load of rubbish,' he told me. 'Now go and use some soap.'

I ran to the bathroom. Hot, fierce tears stung at my eyes and a quiet rage flamed in my chest. But I still knew that I was right and he was wrong. I had heard the whale song and so I knew. Mrs Read had told me. She had taught me.

I turned on the tap and scrubbed at my hands. But I didn't use the soap.

We don't have time
for that now

'Alright, everybody, sitting down ready to listen.'

It is my eldest daughter, Olivia, playing schools again in the lounge room. At her side is a chalkboard easel—it is nothing like the interactive whiteboards of her real classrooms—but on her other side is a toy computer that she consults and clicks at as her lessons progress. Her class of students, arranged in neat rows, watch her with rapt attention. Barbie is propped beside Ted, Baby Doll is gazing off to the side, and Ken isn't wearing any pants.

A few days ago I found a series of notebooks, stacked neatly in the area where Olivia likes to play schools. Each had a name written on the front. It was in Olivia's hand, but she had tried to convey different styles of writing in each book. Some sloped, others were cursive, another large and chunky. Inside each notebook she had created pages of work by the imagined student.

27

This work had been produced in pencil, and then she had written in red pen her 'teacher' corrections. She had ticked and crossed and adjusted spelling. Pages had been stamped. She had even written comments:

Well Done!!!
Good Try!
More detail, Gloria.
Try harder with your writing, Luke.

There were ten books in total, and as I leafed through each of them I wondered at the work and the patience and the care it had taken to create these elaborate props for play. Maybe, I thought, she has what it takes to be a teacher.

Now I watch as she calls out the roll, naming each student and reprimanding one called Cam who didn't answer clearly.

'We have a lot to get through today, boys and girls,' she says, clicking at the mouse of her computer. 'First up, literacy groups.' She taps the blackboard where she has written Litterarcy Gropes. 'Then fruit break, then story writing and then, if we've got time, fitness.'

'If we've got time!' I think as I move to the laundry. She sounds like a real teacher. Part of me is hoping that Olivia will become intrigued with some other profession in the years to come. I find myself wanting to sit her down and tell her, quite firmly, that teaching isn't just interactive whiteboards and public announcements. But I hush those voices inside me. They are my own demons and my little girl doesn't need to hear from them.

I am tired of this fragile feeling, these cracks that show I have been broken. My marriage is limping along and, as I reach deep *within to work on it, I'm painfully aware that my cup is empty. How much has teaching taken from me?*

I take a deep breath and then several more, thinking of my psychologist as I do so. I've been seeing her—on and off— for a few years now, my first appointment just months after 'Grayson's shoe'.

Inhale.

Exhale.

Take fifty deep breaths if you have to, *my shrink says with* a smile.

I bring my mind into the present—practise mindfulness— and watch the creases subside as I iron navy school shorts.

And then, very carefully, I let my memories slide.

In primary school when class photographs were taken I was always in the second row or, if the class was large enough, the third. Tall for my age. And I was always squinting. My eyes were reduced to slits partly because of my chubby cheeks and partly because we were always asked to stare into the sun. Every year the photographer said the same thing: *Those in the front, knees together and hands like this.* He would demonstrate, with fingers laced, like my mum's hands when she prayed in church. I wanted to be in the front row with my friends but I was always up the back, with the boys.

It was a small public school in the town just north of our farm. We were a rural bunch—sons and daughters of farmers. We weren't transient families. We stayed together from Kindergarten all the way through primary.

Our uniform didn't change, either. The T-shirt was yellow with a big green image emblazoned across it. There was nothing symbolic about it; we were each wearing a picture of the main street with poplar trees stretched across our bellies and the town name squarely over our chest. The motto—*Towards a Better World*—underscored the picture. We also wore green trackies and most of us wore sneakers, except for some of the boys in riding boots.

In 1986 I was nine years old. Adjoining my Year Four classroom was a bag room. There were hooks for bags, and after a time the teacher added a table. It was *The News Table*, a dedicated place for us to leave the things we had brought in for *show and tell*. It was *my* table, really, because aside from the occasional bird's nest, snake skin or sheep's skull, nobody else was bringing in news like mine. After my news debut in Kindergarten, where my dad's age and religious status was met with a patronising smile from the teacher, I became a news broadcaster of a different kind.

Each news day I arrived with a big sturdy box, the kind that was made from thick, waxy cardboard. An expanse of cling wrap would be stretched over the top, punctuated with a smattering of biro-made holes. Inside, there would be a habitat of questionable quality, pebbles, rocks and dirt rattling sadly around the base. A few pieces of bark or broken-up sticks wedged in the corners; tufts of grass fading to brown and curling in clumps; an upturned jar lid acting as a makeshift watering hole. A small branch might be included, held roughly in place with a wad of play-doh or masking tape. Sometimes there would be dry dog food or chicken pellets or a blob of meat in a separate lid.

Tenants of the box would vary each week:

A skink.

A mouse.

A spider.

A lady beetle.

A stick insect.

A blue-tongue lizard.

And, once, a cloud of grasshoppers.

My teacher, Mrs B, was always interested in my offerings on news day. She would look into the box and exclaim loudly when she caught sight of the creature enclosed. Then she would tactfully remind me to leave the box on *The News Table*.

My friends peered through the plastic and tried to enlarge the holes with their fingers. I would answer their questions, telling them what I knew about the animal, which was a regurgitation of everything I had read in our *Encyclopaedia Britannica* and all the stuff my dad had told me.

I had found my niche as a news presenter and quickly became the resident expert on all things creepy, crawly and catchable. And it turns out I was a trendsetter, too.

We were well into our morning Maths lesson, working through twenty mentals with competitive fervour, when Mrs B broke the silence, cocking her head to one side.

'Can anybody hear that?'

I watched her and thought again how beautiful she was. Like Princess Diana, but with red hair and wrinkles. I stopped writing and listened as hard as I could.

'Nuh,' said William Former.

We went back to our mentals: *$16 shared between four students*. I pencilled my answer into my Maths book and glanced at Lauren. She smiled at me and mouthed, 'Four?' I nodded and lifted my fingers so she could see my answer.

The next question was $163 + 44 =$

I folded my pages and started making a sum in the back of my book. I was never confident doing these in my head. Mrs B moved past my desk, her yellow dress wisping against my pencil case. I glanced up, saw her frown.

I added the four and the three, moved to the next column and then heard the thump.

'What was that?' asked William Former.

We had all stopped working, paused like student statues in a tableau.

Thump. Bump.

We all looked towards the bag room.

Thump. Thump.

Then another sound. Like something crying or growling or maybe both.

'Does anybody know what that is?' Mrs B's eyes were wide.

We shook our heads, listening as we heard a long, low moan. We leaped from our seats and rushed to the bag room. Jim Guardian was there first—a fearless cowboy from way back— but his Blundstone boots stopped dead the moment he stepped into the room. We pressed up behind him, craning to see.

A schoolbag had come to life. It had broken free of its hook and was lurching around the floor. It rolled into the corner, moaned, then rolled away. It changed shape, morphing from flat and low to tall and round. The bag was thrashing through the space, the straps flicking while a loose pocket flapped on the front. Dark, growling sounds filled the room. I stood on tiptoes and watched as the bag bashed against the wall.

'That's mine!' exclaimed Wendy Heinz.

I glanced at her before looking at the bag, which was now trying to climb the wall.

'What's *in* it?' Mrs B asked, her voice shaky.

'It's my cat,' Wendy said. 'I brung it in for news.'

We glanced at Mrs B then, waiting to see what she would do, watching her like a barometer. Mrs B would know what to do when a cat came to school . . . in a schoolbag . . . for news.

'Your cat!' Mrs B exclaimed and her face softened as she laughed. 'Your cat!' She reached out to Wendy and touched her face. 'Well, then,' she went on. 'You better go and bring him in and we'll have news right away.'

Wendy's face glowed and she stepped forward, approaching her bag and saying, 'Here Puss, Puss, Puss!'

At recess, Wendy's dad arrived to take the cat home. I saw him laughing with Mrs B as they walked towards his car, the cat now secured in a travelling crate.

'Bye, Smokey,' Wendy shouted, waving from her place atop the monkey bars. 'See ya when I get home!'

I laugh at the memory, all these years later as I'm ironing. I can still see that crazy schoolbag dancing around the bag room. But I can also remember the relief I felt that day: I was so glad that Wendy didn't get into trouble. The thing she had done was innocent—a kid-thing that hadn't been thought through. I was glad Mrs B made room for the cat that day.

'Alright, packing up now!'

From the lounge room I hear Olivia's voice brim with authority. She has the intonation just right.

'No,' she's saying. 'No, Cam, we don't have time for that now. We don't have time for toys. Put that away in your bag.'

The iron hisses and steams over their uniforms, polo shirts with logos that seem small and irrelevant.

'We don't have time for that now,' Olivia says again.

You're right, I think sadly. There's never any time. No time for the cat.

Gift

'*Is this the book I ate?*'

Olivia holds up a Golden Book that is ripped and tattered. We are packing, preparing to move house. I have finally admitted defeat—my marriage is over. Another personal failure. It's three years since Grayson threw that shoe at my chest but I can still feel it. It's a bruised kind of feeling, like my heart has been punched. The pain of divorce blends into that bruise. Bleeds into it.

I'm grieving and overwhelmed, but handling these books with Olivia is like therapy. Each book is a friend. I can remember where I bought it from, where I was when I read it, what was happening in my life at that time. Although each book contains a story, it holds my story too.

'No,' I say to Liv as I reach for the book and inspect the pages. 'To be honest, I think I had to throw that book out.'

'Tell me again,' she asks and crosses her legs, settling in for a tale with books and boxes surrounding her like treasure. Her face seems to have changed a little in recent months. There's sadness around her eyes and a wariness when she smiles. I hate the idea that my failures affect her, and little Soph too.

'When you were a baby,' I say, 'maybe nine months old, you woke up one day and ate a book! Instead of crying or calling out, you slotted one chubby arm through the rails of your cot until your fingers found a Little Golden Book called The Very Best Home for Me. *When I came in to check on you, you had already eaten about one-third of the book—including the cover. It was as though Cookie Monster had taken a bite.' I smile at her.*

Olivia's been devouring books ever since that day—eating them up with a passion that makes me feel proud and somehow less worried for her future. Judy Blume is a new favourite, with so many stories about loss and divorce.

I have always known how to read, and in knowing how to read I have always known that I can *know*. From a young age, even before I started school, I had been able to decipher the squiggles on the page and make meaning from them. It had given me a kind of power, a feeling that knowledge was mine—I just had to find the right book.

Writing was also a gift. I was always writing and wanting to put my mark on things. Back in the eighties, many homes had a telephone table and ours was a reliable place to find pens and paper. I would fill up entire notepads with marks of my own making. I loved to imitate cursive writing and would race the biro across the pages, filling them with steep and wavy shapes while I spoke aloud the story that went with my scribble.

I was always compelled to inscribe my name on things and I graffitied the letters GA wherever I could; I even labelled an ancient and very beautiful timber dresser that stood in my room. With permanent marker I wrote GA and drew a line and then a picture of a person—me, with curly hair.

It was serendipity that placed me in primary school just as the theory of process writing was implemented as an effective method for teaching children to write. I still have my large plastic folder that was issued to every child in our class. It was a place to keep our drafts because *real writers* make drafts before they publish. And we were encouraged to believe that we were *real writers*.

In the junior grades, my stories were simple. They revolved around witches and ghosts, friends and family. *Once there was a ghost and it was bad and it grabbed me and Lauren and we screamed a lot and Dad came out. The ghost grabbed Dad and Dad screamed* . . . But as I got older and read more, my own stories became more sophisticated. My classmates and I would settle down to writing sessions with quiet enthusiasm, stopping only to read our stories aloud or talk about new ideas. We wrote about robots and animals that could talk and girls who rode horses and children who were spies and had adventures of various dimensions. Inspiration was all around us. We retold the books we were reading. We meshed together known stories. We collaborated. We invented. We imagined. We wrote things that were kind of like other stories, but kind of new, too.

My school embraced process writing and our stories were commissioned for publication. Mothers were invited to type our stories so they could be bound up with cardboard covers, just like real books. We created classroom libraries where we could share the books we had written and read our friends' writing.

Of course, when the call for typing mothers was mentioned in my classroom, my hand shot into the air. My mum had a typewriter. She could type stories, and if she didn't want to *I could do it for her!* I'd been wanting to get my hands on that pale-blue Hermes 3000 for years.

I brought home four stories in a manila folder and gave Mum her instructions. She was not the most enthusiastic publisher, but I helped her by reading each story aloud. Mum plugged away on the clunky white keys and I watched with satisfaction as she swiped the metal handle that shifted the paper carriage onto the next line. The *clickety-clack* of each key was fulfilling and uplifting, as was the impressive speed with which Mum could churn through each sentence. As chief dictator, I felt I was something of a literary agent representing each writer, and I started adding to and embellishing my friends' stories.

'Chapter Two!' I would announce with a flourish.

'Does it really say that?' Mum would frown and lean towards the book, wanting to see the draft.

'Yes,' I would insist. 'See, here.' I would wave the page in front of her, knowing her eyesight wasn't excellent and my friend's handwriting almost illegible. 'Let's go, Mum. Come on. Chapter Two!'

I would make up chapters, add things, decorate and invent. And my peers liked what I had done. They started demanding postscripts to their stories as I stepped onto the bus each afternoon with my manila folder peeking out from my bag.

'Put something extra in at the end,' they would shout. 'Put something with an *explosion*.' I would nod and wave as the bus doors swivelled shut behind me.

From a young age, I understood something about writing. I knew that it was a powerful and empowering activity—like reading. The production of words on a page could make people react and respond. I could create notes on the shopping list that told Mum to buy chips. And I could stick up signs that said BEWARE and cause my tired old Dad to pause before he opened the hall door. I gave out 'tickets' when my siblings were home, fining them for being too loud, too fast or too annoying.

Soon I discovered letter writing. I had several penfriends that I wrote to using pretty stationery that was creamy yellow and bordered with pastel roses. I liked nothing more than sliding a letter into a perfectly matching envelope. Chain letters filled me with excitement and every day I nagged at Mum to drive the kilometre down the dirt road so that we could check the mailbox.

I wrote—regularly—to the prime minister. I didn't use my pretty stationery for those letters. On plain white paper, I would write long, passionate and sometimes scathing letters to Bob Hawke about woodchipping and whales and world peace. I told Bob all the things I thought were going wrong in our world. I also offered clever and insightful solutions, pointing out just how simply these major problems could be solved. *There should be laws*, I told Bob, *about using both sides of a page to reduce paper waste. Australia should tell other countries to stop killing whales. And we should encourage everyone to be nice because that's the first step to world peace.*

After I had written these letters, I would proofread them first to myself, pausing with pen in hand to add an extra *very* or to underline an *absolutely*, then I would find Mum and read the letter to her. She might be outside feeding the chooks or watering the garden, or she may have been slogging through a basket of ironing or adjusting the hem of my school uniform on her old Singer sewing machine. It didn't matter: I would launch into my reading, making my voice sound grown-up and serious like the presenters on TV. I loved that part of the process—reading my writing out loud. My ideas were given breath. My ideas were coming to life in the chook yard and the garden and the laundry and the sewing room. And, after each impassioned reading, I would give these letters to Mum and ask that she would post them to Bob.

He never replied to my letters. At the time, I thought he was too busy, but I understand now that it was Mum who was too busy. Posting letters to Canberra would be low on her list of things to do. As I reflect on it now, I suspect she used those letters to light the fire.

After seven happy years at the public primary school, my Catholic mother wanted me to go to the Catholic high school. All my friends—including my beloved Lauren—were going on to the *public* high school. I was twelve and thought that a minor rebellion might be the best way to change Mum's mind. Just days before starting at the Catholic school I tried to create a hostage situation in the local uniform shop.

'I'm not going to wear it,' I told Mum, folding my arms against my chest and refusing the necktie she was handing me. 'So don't bother buying it.'

'Alright,' Mum said.

'I'm not going to the Catholic school,' I told her, 'and I'm never going to wear a tie.' I felt my stomach flood with fear.

'Alright,' Mum said again, gathering up the bags of uniform. The tie was left, snaked along the counter

Outside on the street, I trailed behind her, strangely unfulfilled and certainly defeated.

The next day I watched her stitching name tags into the collars of my new clothes. I cringed. Surely I would be the only kid with labelled clothes.

'Why didn't you make me get a tie?' I asked her.

'I can't make you do anything.' She snipped off the thread and reached for another shirt.

'But what will happen if I don't wear the tie?' I wanted to sound nonchalant, but I was raw with nerves—new bus, a new school, a new uniform, new people.

'Not sure.' Mum snipped.

'I want to wear a tie,' I said, and tears came without warning. 'I'll need to wear a tie.'

'Well,' Mum didn't even look up, 'I'll finish this and find you one.'

Later, she called me into her bedroom and instructed me to try on my new school uniform.

'Now, here's the tie.' She produced a strip of green that was only half as long as it should have been. It was tattered on the end, like it had been chewed up and spat out. And it was

41

so faded that it didn't even come close to matching the solid bottle-green of my school skirt.

'But . . . what?' I stumbled as Mum threaded the slip of dull-green fabric around my neck.

'I think this was your brother's,' she said. 'I think he ripped it up the last time he had to wear it.' Mum completed the knots and I glanced in the mirror. I looked like I'd leaned over a paper shredder.

'Mum, I can't . . .' The tears threatened again and I set my jaw.

'If you wear your jumper, you won't see a thing.' She offered me the woollen top, which was, mercifully, not hand-knitted. I put it on and smoothed it down. The tie looked perfect. I took a breath and eyeballed Mum.

'I've raised four teenagers now, love,' she told me, 'and I've already decided: I'm not going to fight with you.'

She left me standing in her bedroom, sweating in my almost-perfect school uniform. *Damn Mum*, I thought. *And damn Phil with his bloody stupid ripped-up tie.* I tried for a moment to be mad at him, but he was my favourite so I couldn't.

At the Catholic school I met Mrs Dee. She was the first teacher to tell me I was a good writer. 'Gift' was the word she used. I was in Year Eight and she was my English teacher, my favourite teacher.

Mrs Dee would always arrive late to class, bursting in the door with an enthusiasm that was both daggy and endearing. Mrs Dee always had news.

'Did you guys see this in the paper?' she would ask (as though *we* read the paper). 'I'm outraged. You will be, too—listen to this.'

'I'm so excited today!' she would say. 'Somebody's going to die!' And she would wave her copy of *Romeo and Juliet* in the air.

'I've found a writing competition,' she would announce. 'And I just know that someone in this room is going to win it!' Entry forms fluttered to our desks.

'Our drama unit begins today!' Kicking off her shoes and moving furniture. 'Get up! Get up! Don't sit there like an amorphous blob!'

She brought energy and knowledge and praise to every lesson. And she sat on the teacher's desk and let her legs swing like she was a kid. She talked with us, listened to us, joined our ideas together and joined *those* ideas to the set texts. Her classes felt effortless and I grew to love English and books and reading and writing even more than I did before. I loved her.

Without knowing it, we worked hard in Mrs Dee's class. She taught us, explicitly, how to write an essay, how to analyse a poem and how to deconstruct a text. She gave us opportunities to write, to read aloud, to edit and to rewrite.

'Where's Nathaniel?' she might say as we pulled out our notebooks and prepared to begin a writing task. 'Oh, there you are! Hey, Nate, do you think you could read out that section from your work yesterday? That funny part about the Houses of Parliament? Listen to this everyone, Nate's work is a terrific example of a parody.'

So Nate would stand up and read his work. Somehow, Mrs Dee had us so engaged that we forgot our adolescent awkwardness and our embarrassment at the idea of contributing in class. Her feedback was so encouraging and specific that we could almost feel ourselves improving. My own writing became stronger and I was more courageous with my written expression.

'You're a writer!' Mrs Dee would grin at me as she handed back my essay: *10/10* with a paragraph of comments, scribbled in Mrs Dee's bouncy, rounded handwriting.

Being a small regional school, Mrs Dee was my English teacher again in Year Ten. Throughout that year she often delivered what I came to think of as a Teacher Speech. It might be a story from her own life or from a book that would segue into an issue that was going down at school. It was always candid and earnest and layered with meaning. Mrs Dee spoke to us as though we were equals, capable of considering big ideas about the world and about life. She wasn't afraid of taking us into territory that other adults tried to steer us away from. Drugs. Sex. Relationships. Mrs Dee canvassed them all. Her 'Teacher Speeches' were a gift in themselves and many of them stayed with me.

'The thing we should always remember,' Mrs Dee said one Monday as my friends nursed hangovers and coddled regrets, 'is that we are in control of our life. Nothing is an accident. With each decision you make, you are choosing the life that you want. You are choosing the kind of person you want to become.'

As I listened, I felt my chest expanding. It was like the whale's song in Mrs Read's classroom all those years ago. A revelation, a feeling of hope. It was empowering. *I can choose my life*. The idea filled me up and made the whales sing inside me.

It was around this time I started thinking about what I might like to do 'when I grew up'. The senior high school years of Eleven and Twelve were on the horizon and people had begun to ask me what I would do when I finished school. Even though Mrs Dee had fostered my talent as a writer, I knew that I didn't want to be a journalist or copywriter or even a novelist. I wanted to be like Mrs Dee. I wanted to be the giver of gifts. I wanted to be a teacher.

I'm making spaghetti bolognaise and feeling virtuous. It's a nutritious meal and I'm grateful I have the energy to make it. Dinner-guilt is something I've struggled with over the years, but now I have the time to think about our meals and cook things that we can enjoy together.

As I make the dinner, my daughter Sophie scours the book club catalogue with pen in hand. It's her first book club catalogue and she's circling everything she would like to buy. In another room, we can hear Olivia playing schools. A student named Cam is being told off—he hasn't done his homework.

'And I want this one, Mum,' Sophie says, flattening the cata- logue so she can draw her circle. 'It's science. I love experiences.'

'Do you mean experiments?' I smile.

'Hmm, I'm not sure,' she says. 'Can I get it, Mum?'

I tell her that I'll think about it, but she knows I will buy them. I'm a reader. And a sucker. She continues to circle.

'This looks good,' she announces. 'It's Org Army.'

I leave the bolognaise and move over to the bench. I look where her grubby finger is pointing.

'Origami,' I say.

'Origami,' she repeats. 'That's what we did with Aunty Anni.'

'Hey!' I say, remembering. 'Did you borrow from the Library today?' Just last week she had borrowed Homer's The Odyssey. (She's in Kindergarten.)

'Yeah,' she says, flipping the flimsy page. 'I got another book today. Find Willy or something.'

'Where's Wally?'

'Yeah, that. Can we read it together tonight, Mum?'

'Yes,' I tell her. 'I can't wait.'

And later that night, with our bellies full of pasta, we snuggle on the lounge to read together. Sophie tugs the oversize Wally book out from her library bag and we spend a while searching for the stripy man until eventually she pulls a second book from the bag. It's The Odyssey.

'I thought you would have returned this,' I say, handling the large, illustrated text.

'No, Mum, I renewed it,' Sophie says and I'm surprised she knows the word and has remembered it.

'Wow,' I laugh. 'That's a great word: renewed. Why did you do that?'

'Because we haven't finished reading it.'

And as I read to her about sirens and storms at sea, I find a moment of peace. I am handing on my gift.

How to teach

The Catholic school only went to Year Ten and Mum had promised me I could shift to the public high school for Years Eleven and Twelve. I was sixteen and fiercely committed to the idea of becoming a teacher. I saw school as the stepping stone to university and university as the stepping stone to teaching. To gain entry into a Bachelor of Education degree I would need a Tertiary Entrance Rank (TER) of 52 (out of a possible 100) on my final Higher School Certificate (HSC) exams.

Fifty-two would be an easy reach for me, but even so I threw myself into assignments and essays with a fervour that I now recognise as nerdy and somewhat needy. I waited for test results with the same excitement I had waited for Santa Claus. I was *that* student who hassled the teachers with questions like *Have you marked our essays?* and *Will we need to know this for the calculus exam?*

I perceived myself as a clever, high-achieving student, but when I look back on my school reports I realise that I wasn't as smart as I thought I was. I did well on things I could control, like bookwork, homework, behaviour and participation. In areas of understanding or knowledge I was consistently average (except for English). It's clear that while I loved school, loved learning and loved many of my teachers, I wasn't always *getting it*. I didn't have a deep conceptual understanding of the concepts being covered.

I was disappointed to score just 72 on my HSC TER. When I opened the envelope containing my results I was overcome with regret: subject choices, the time and energy I had devoted to my role as school captain and those nights when I'd watched TV instead of studying. I spent ages thinking about the exams and the things I had done wrong: the ridiculous outfit I had designed in the textiles paper and the last question on the second Maths paper that I just hadn't been able to solve.

The night we got our results, a friend rang me from the pub.

'Gab! Why aren't you here?' She was drunk.

'Hey,' I said, looking out the window to the pitch black of our paddocks.

'You should be here.' I could hear the slurred voices of friends filtering down the phone. *Who ya talkin' too? Get off the phone!*

'So?' Her voice became urgent, almost aggressive. 'Whadya get?'

'Seventy-two,' I said, my voice flat. The number still didn't seem right.

'Oh, fuck you!' she said. 'I knew you'd get something like that. Fuck!'

I kept staring at the paddocks, heard a lone plover give an angry, late-night *pip pip pip*. I could feel something shifting, something was happening down that phone line. My friendship, slipping away.

'I hate you,' she said and her voice was calm and matter-of-fact. 'I hate you so much.'

'Why?' My voice desperate. 'What did you get?'

'Twenty-five,' she said and hung up.

Twenty-five. My friend was so much more than that. She was creative and funny and she wrote beautifully and she was generous. She thought about things, she could turn an idea inside out just to be sure of where she stood. Twenty-five. No wonder she was angry. And drunk.

I set the phone back down and watched the coils of cord loop around themselves and back into their familiar tangle. Seventy-two was better than twenty-five. But ninety was better than seventy-two. And at the end of the day, especially at the end of that day, they were all just numbers, just manufactured things that tried to quantify something that could never be measured.

I pulled the curtains shut, sat in the chair and let darkness swarm around me. I cried. Stupid seventy-two. It had cost me a good friend.

I met Matthew at my Year Twelve formal. He sidled up to me at the bar, squeezed himself into an impossible space and tried to look casual.

'Oh!' I said, shifting away.

'Did I frighten you?' he asked.

I laughed. 'No,' I told him. 'You didn't frighten me.' He was a few years older than me, a bit drunk and kind of cute.

'Can I buy you a drink?'

'No thanks,' I said. 'I've just ordered.'

'I liked your speech, School Captain.' He was slurring his words. 'It was funny.'

'Thanks,' I edged away from him. He was wilting into my personal space.

'And I like your suit.'

'Thanks,' I said again and felt myself blush. I'd been so busy preparing for exams that I'd left the dress selection to the last minute. I ended up hiring a tuxedo and pairing it with a ruffled white shirt, thinking I might look cool and chic like Julia Roberts when she accepted her Golden Globe in 1990. As I'd left the house that evening I realised I looked less like Julia and more like a pirate; there was too much ruffle in the front and too much tail in the back, but it was too late to make a change.

'You're different, aren't ya?' He was almost leaning against me now and I wasn't sure he would remain upright when I moved away.

'Maybe,' I said, grateful that the bartender had arrived with my drink.

'My name's Matthew.' He offered me his hand.

'I'm Gabrielle,' I said.

'Yeah, I know. I'll buy you a drink one day.'

Matthew kept turning up in my small-town life during that funny transition space between finishing school and waiting for whatever was coming next. He started calling me and I found myself stretching the phone cord into our hallway so I could talk to him without Mum and Dad listening.

'I want to be a teacher,' I told him one night. 'I'm going to university next year.'

'A teacher?' He was a cabinet-maker and worked at a local joinery.

'Yeah.'

'Great pay,' he said. 'And good holidays too.'

'Hmm,' I said, twisting the phone cord around my finger. 'I've never even thought of that.'

'Can I visit you at uni?'

'Maybe.'

It was 1995 and 72 was enough. I opted for the Catholic University in Canberra that had once been a dedicated teachers' college before it amalgamated with the Australian Catholic University and was rebranded in the early nineties. A course at the Catholic University would open up the range of schools I could later apply to as I would be required to complete units of Religious Study. This degree would enable me to apply for jobs in independent, Catholic *and* public schools. It felt like a smart move. Bachelor of Education specialising in Primary. Four years. Full time. I left the farm and all that was familiar and moved into a bedsit in Canberra.

I felt immediate kinship with the other education students. We shared a certain lairy creativity and a disproportionate appreciation of the ridiculous. We were childish I guess, or maybe playful is a better word, always ready to laugh and joke around. Paramount to our constitution was a love of children, and our desire to become teachers threaded itself through our lives. We were filled with almost utopian ideals of what our teaching lives would be like—a sort of starry-eyed romantic speculation fuelled by the energy we gained during our blocks of prac teaching and lively tutorial presentations. Our conversations were always glinting with hopeful statements like *Once I'm teaching* and *When I've got a class of my own*.

Matthew called me regularly and visited every weekend. He became part of the group at uni and we went to house warmings and twenty-firsts, pretending to be grown-ups although we still felt like kids. We talked about him moving to Canberra and living together while I studied, but my focus was single-minded. *Not until I've got my degree,* I told him. I wanted to be a teacher more than anything and I had a sense that my degree would become my greatest asset. Once I had achieved it, nobody could take it from me.

It's hard to pinpoint precisely what I learned at university and what I learned out in the real world. But I can remember some moments of enlightenment from my university days: things that challenged me and made me think. Often these gems came from tutors who were real-life teachers with real-life jobs in real-life classrooms. They would turn up to tutorials scheduled around five or six in the evening after their day of teaching was done. We would watch them with reverence and awe.

'She teaches out at Wanniassa,' someone would whisper as the teacher–tutor unloaded her swag of resources. 'Shannon in fourth year did prac with her. Said she was brilliant.'

Their tutorials were always fun and engaging. They shared practical ideas and useful resources. We hung on their every word and enticed them off-task by asking about their day, their class or something else relating to the real world of teaching. At times we challenged them, told them some nugget of information from our lectures and watched with satisfaction as they rolled their eyes and said something like: *Yes, in theory, but in a real classroom* . . .

After one PE class, the lesson degenerated. We had been skidding around the hall on pages ripped from a telephone book, discovering games to keep kids active during wet weather. Duster hockey, tail tag, fruit salad . . . The games had called out our inner child and we were breathless with the joy of it all. The tutors, both of them teachers, had been packing away their gear while we fired questions at them.

'What do you do with the bad kids?' someone asked. 'Like, how do you deal with them? Do you use lollies and stickers as rewards? Or do you try for intrinsic motivation?'

One of the tutors snorted. '*Intrinsic motivation*,' she said. 'I haven't heard that since I was at uni. Hey, do you guys call it peda*dodgy* instead of peda*gogy*?' She laughed and turned to her partner, who was waiting with a high-five.

'Seriously, though,' someone else insisted. 'What do *you* do with bad kids?'

They stopped their laughing. The guy squatted down and sat his arse on a basketball. He made an effort to look us each in the eye. 'Here's something you need to know,' he said. 'There's no such thing as bad kids. There's <u>only bad behaviour</u>.'

It was a small thing; just two sentences, really. But it forced me to think. Mind expanding. I filed that one away on a mental shelf and labelled it <u>*IMPORTANT*</u>.

★

My last day of uni had an unexpected edge to it: all the energy and excitement I had been carrying around in my heart for four years had suddenly metastasised into liquid anxiety sloshing around in my guts. I had finished my degree, but I was still doubtful and hesitant—surely there was more to know? Surely I couldn't possibly be qualified to be a teacher?

I didn't *feel* like a teacher.

A few lecturers corralled us into the largest of the tutorial rooms. We didn't care about being crammed in. We'd just done four years together. We had endured stressful all-nighter assignments, shared the ups and downs of *Beverly Hills 90210*, argued about the difference between phonics and whole language, painted each other's faces for drama tutorials and borne witness to hangovers of disgusting proportions. We were one big, happy family about to be scattered all over the place.

The meeting was mainly about graduation in March and the final assessments we had to submit if we wanted to receive a graduation certificate.

'Now,' said the lecturer up the front of the room, 'if you're hoping to teach and be paid for it, *and* if you're applying for permanent jobs, you need to have your police checks done.

If you didn't attend the first-aid course we ran last session you should make sure you get to one somewhere out in the community. And your CVs: I wanted to mention those. You can add any of us here as referees and you should ask your supervising teacher from your last prac.'

She paused and glanced at the other lecturers. 'I think that's it?' They shrugged and nodded. Nothing more to discuss. Apparently, we were now teachers. I felt panic swelling in my throat.

'So,' said the lecturer, smiling, perhaps glad to see the back of us, 'any questions?'

My hand was up.

'Yes, Gab?'

'I don't know how to teach a kid to read.' The words came out fast. I was barely containing the desire to scream: *I don't know anything.*

The lecturer chuckled. 'Any other questions?'

'Me neither.'

It was my friend Cathy—dear, sweet, beautiful Cathy, who had matched me box for box every time we had needed a Chicken Crimpy binge. My assignment-partner Cathy, who thought nothing of an 11 p.m. run to the shops for vanilla choc-chip ice cream. Nerdy Cathy, who had driven with nerdy me to the outer suburbs late one afternoon so we could have our teaching folios professionally printed and bound.

'I don't know how to teach a kid to read,' she said. 'Or write, for that matter.' She laughed her nervous laugh and looked over at me. 'I really don't.'

'Me neither,' someone else said.

Suddenly they were everywhere: hands up and voices saying, *I'm not sure.*

'Now, that's not true,' said another of the lecturers. She sighed as she turned to the whiteboard and took a marker from the tray. She scribbled *Reading & Writing.*

'Just start by saying what you *think* you know.'

'Immersion?' I called out. 'Immerse them in print and language.'

'Whole language,' Cathy added. 'Read real texts.'

'High expectations,' someone called.

'Bit of phonics,' Davo said.

'Assess where they're at, plan for where they're going.'

'Let them write. Let them choose their topics.'

'Reading groups and book talk.'

'Publish their stories.'

'Explicitly teach the skills they need, like grammar and spelling and punctuation.'

We filled the board and it gave me a sense of satisfaction to see it all set out there.

'See?' the lecturer said. 'You do know some stuff.' She set the marker back on the tray. 'You'll be okay.'

I picked up my bag and checked with Cathy on the details of where we would be going to celebrate. But something still felt unsettled inside me. I wanted to say one last thing.

'Okay,' I wanted to say. 'You've taught me *how* to teach. Now show me how to be a teacher.'

Joy

For my final block of prac, I was placed with a teacher named Miss Jenny.

'Now there are some things you need to know about me,' she said at our first meeting. 'My husband says I can talk underwater with a mouth full of marbles, so you'd better let me know if I'm talking too much and interrupt me when you want to speak. Don't wait to get a word in because you might never get to!

'You're going to love this class—there are some characters in here and they give me a laugh, but they're generally good little learners, you know? Now, love, I thought you might like to observe for the first week and get the lay of the land, and each day you can slot into something like the reading groups or the Maths activities. Take my program home with you and have a good look at it—copy anything you think is useful.

'That reminds me: I'm planning on retiring soon so you should go through my storeroom there and start pulling out any resources you might like. I've made so many over the years, before we had laminators and all that, you know? I used to put clear contact over my posters and all the games I made. My husband thought I was mad, but I've still got them. I'd love them to go to you, Gab, so that they'll keep on being used.

'I've got a little present for you. I like to bake so I've made you a piece of slice—do you eat slice? Probably not—look at you, you're so fit and slim. But you need to have something sweet so here's a treat to say welcome. Oh, love, I'm so glad you're here. We're going to have such a good time together.'

She handed me a parcel of foil and I opened it to find a perfect rectangle of chocolate slice.

'You do like chocolate, don't you, love?'

I smiled and nodded and wondered how I could be so lucky.

The school was in a northern suburb of Canberra, close to where I was living. The families were friendly, working-class folk. On my first day, Miss Jenny presented me with a clipboard and the Year One class list duplicated twenty times.

'Now, I like to keep lists.' She squeezed my arm. 'I can't seem to help myself, Gab. I find everything goes more smoothly when I'm organised. So, I run off lots of class lists and every time I mark the children's work, I put a tick next to their name. See here.' She showed me her own clipboard and a page already filled with ticks and dashes and annotations. 'And look here.' She pointed to a few random letters next to a child's name. 'See, I write down if they had trouble with the work, or if I had to help them, or if they worked with a buddy.'

'What's "N.I." mean?' I asked, pointing to another annotation.

'No idea.' Miss Jenny laughed, a bright and hearty sound that would certainly be heard in Class 1M next door. 'It really means "No Idea". That poor little one had no idea when I presented that concept to him. He'd never even seen it before. It reminds me: I've got to teach it to him again. Nobody will see this list, except for me—so I just use my own kind of shorthand, you know? But, my goodness, when it comes time to prepare for parent–teacher interviews, or write reports, these lists are my best friend. It reminds me of what's going on for each of the kids.'

Watching Miss Jenny that first week, I knew that when I grew up—when I evolved into a teacher—I wanted to be just like her. Some forty years into her teaching career, Miss Jenny made it seem effortless. She was super organised and every Friday morning before school she sent me down to the photocopier to run off all the sheets we would need for the following week.

'Oh, you don't want to be in here on your weekends doing photocopying,' she explained, handing over a pile of books marked with Post-its. 'Friday morning, all the teachers are in the staffroom, sucking up coffee, so it's a perfect time to nab the photocopier. Oh, and here's your morning tea, love.' She added a foil-wrapped pack to the stack of books. 'Pop that in your lunch box for later.' Her smile was wide. I could feel myself falling in love again.

It was clear that the students in Miss Jenny's class were also in love with her. She began every activity with a song and the children knew exactly how to transition from one activity to another without Miss Jenny having to tell them.

'Ahh wanny wanny gee ahh wanny,' she would call out. It was a nonsense song with rhythmic arm actions. The children would stop work immediately and start folding their arms in imitation. Their voices would swell and fill the room until they were eventually all sitting on the mat, singing lustily and watching Miss Jenny with shining eyes. Soon enough the song would end and a perfect, attentive silence would remain. Miss Jenny would smile and begin giving the next lesson.

Her energy and enthusiasm were beyond infectious. She must have been in her sixties and I struggled most days to keep up. Other teachers dropped into Miss Jenny's classroom throughout the day and it seemed to me that they were just stopping by for an energy hit or an emotional pick-me-up. Whatever it was that Miss Jenny had, she had it in abundance, and she wasn't stingy in sharing it around. Like her foil-wrapped gifts of sweetness, Miss Jenny nourished your soul. She made you feel good to be alive.

Miss Jenny was always ready to laugh, too. She would defer to humour over drama every time.

'Thank goodness for that storeroom,' she told me one day. 'Sometimes I get the giggles so badly I just have to take a moment in there on my own, especially if it's over something one of the kids has said. I mean, you can laugh *with* them about some things, but other times you're laughing at them and you don't want to upset them.'

One afternoon, the Principal called an unexpected assembly. Miss Jenny met me in the playground and we stood with our class, shepherding them into lines. As the Principal took up the microphone and the heat of the playground shimmered beneath our feet, Miss Jenny and I modelled good listening and made tiny gestures of quiet to children who were showing signs of disinterest.

After a while, a few black crows descended on the bitumen. They were scavenging, seeking the very food scraps that the Principal was currently admonishing the students for leaving on the ground.

'Arrrk!' cried one crow, hopping forward to take a crust.

'Arrrk!' It was louder this time and the Principal had raised her voice to try to cover the sound.

'ARRRK!'

'Hey, Miss Jenny?' It was a whisper from a child nearby.

'Yes, love.' Miss Jenny crouched down.

'It sounds like that crow's saying *fuck*.'

Miss Jenny turned her head, just the slightest way in my direction, her expression comically shocked. I had to look away.

As we debriefed about the farking crow after school, I laughed so hard that tears ran down my cheeks.

'My stomach hurts,' I wheezed.

'Well, just don't wet your pants,' Miss Jenny said. 'That's happened to me before.'

And we collapsed onto the tiny classroom chairs and laughed some more.

A sound system was used at that school to convey messages from the office to every room. Each morning, the Principal's voice would float into our classroom saying: *Good morning,*

boys and girls and good morning, teachers. This is Mrs Suchberry and here are your messages. The class would listen with rapt attention as we heard about soccer games for Year Five at lunchtime and the student council selling icy poles at recess and reminders about correct school uniforms and using your manners at the tuckshop. Occasionally throughout the day random messages would be issued: *Sorry for the interruption, teachers and students. Just to let you know Mr Harris has been doing some work on the southern playground, so that area is out of bounds until Thursday.*

One day, after lunch, we had the students engaged in a craft task that required glue and crepe paper and googly eyes. There was folding and sticking and a small amount of cutting, which meant that Miss Jenny and I were working the room trying to get around to every child.

Suddenly, the sound system gave a crackle. We paused, waiting for the gentle tones of Mrs Suchberry. But instead there was an audible breath and a wet kind of sound—a mouth too close to the microphone.

'This is Luke Chakalovick from Miss Jenny's class.'

We froze, Miss Jenny locking eyes with me before quickly doing a head count.

'Good afternoon, boys and girls and good afternoon, teachers,' Luke continued.

Miss Jenny was out the door and down the hall. Our class was silent, all of us staring at the speaker above the blackboard.

'Well,' Luke's voice said through the sound system, 'it's my birthday tomorrow and I'm going to be eight.' There was a pause and another wet, mouthy breath. And then urgent whispering and Miss Jenny's voice saying, 'Come with me now.'

'That is all, boys and girls. Have a good day of learning.' Luke's words came out in a rush, fading at the end.

We continued to stare at the speaker for a moment before a child said, 'That really sounded like Luke.'

'It *was* Luke,' said another child.

'It can't be Luke,' argued the first. 'Luke's just a kid. Kids can't do the messages, can they?' He looked up at me, one hand holding a paintbrush dripping with craft glue.

'Umm.' I frowned and adjusted his paintbrush so glue would drip onto his project and not over his shorts.

At that moment, Miss Jenny rushed in, towing Luke behind her.

'Pop back to your activity, love,' she said, directing him to his desk.

She stepped into the storeroom and motioned that I should go in with her.

'What happened?' I was breathless, the tidal wave of laughter welling inside me. 'How did he get into the office to do that?'

'He told them I had asked him to put a message over the PA,' Miss Jenny was whispering, her hand over her mouth. 'But listen to this, Gab.' She squeezed my arm. 'It's not even his birthday tomorrow. He won't be eight until next year!'

We roared laughing then, both of us doubled over and filling the tiny storeroom with the absolute hilarity of the past five minutes.

'It's a great job,' Miss Jenny wiped at her tears. 'Who else gets to laugh like this, every day?'

In my final weeks of uni I had been given a scholarship for excellence in pre-service teaching. The award was three thousand dollars, just enough to consider going overseas for my first year of teaching. Towards the end of my prac with Miss Jenny, I had a phone interview with the Head Teacher from a school in the East End of London. Days later, the job was mine. I would start in the first week of January.

'Miss Jenny, guess what?' I bounced into the classroom. 'I got the job!'

'Oh, love, I knew you would!' She left the tiny desk where she was cutting out teddy bear templates and enveloped me in a hug. 'Oh, Gab, I'm so pleased for you. You'll be brilliant. What class? Do you know?'

'Grade Six,' I told her. 'They say "Grade" over there, but it's the same as our Year Six. Eleven-year-olds.'

'Oh, they're going to love you!' She hugged me again and we sat down together at the desk. I took up a pair of scissors and started cutting.

'And what does Matthew think about you going away?' Miss Jenny had met him a few weeks earlier when he'd arrived at school to pick me up.

I shrugged. 'He's sad, but he says he'll come and visit.'

'Well, it is an amazing opportunity, too good to pass up. It's the start of your career,' Miss Jenny said. 'And I'm here to see it happen. I could cry I'm so happy for you.' She dabbed at her eye. 'Who knows where your journey will take you . . . you could be a school Principal one day.'

'I don't think so,' I said, curving my scissors around the bear's ear. 'Did you ever want to be in management?' I asked. 'Like an Assistant Principal or a Principal?'

'Oh no, love,' Miss Jenny said. She picked up another bear and slid the scissors into place. 'I did my fair share of that when I had to—filled in for people on leave and what not. But I always just wanted to be a teacher, you know? A classroom teacher.'

'Yep,' I said, placing my freshly cut bear onto the pile. 'Me too.'

'Just enjoy your teaching, love,' Miss Jenny said. 'Find joy in it. Every day.'

Landscapes

'Where was I when you were teaching in England?' Sophie looks up at me from her colouring book.

'You weren't even born yet,' I tell her.

'Where was Olivia?'

'She wasn't born either.'

'Was Daddy born?'

I laugh. 'Yes! But he wasn't with me. He just came over for a visit. In England, it was just me and I wasn't a wife or a mummy. I was just a teacher.'

'How old were you?' Olivia chimes in from behind her book.

'Twenty-one.' So young, I realise. Brave.

'Did you meet the Queen?' Sophie pauses in her colouring.

'No, I didn't meet the Queen! But I went to Buckingham Palace—that's where she lives. And to Windsor Castle, where she goes for holidays.'

'Cool!' Sophie's crayon races across the page. 'What's for lunch, Mum?'

I serve them sausage rolls and Sophie squirts out too much sauce but I don't say anything. My mind is back in time, traversing my memories, remembering myself.

The Boeing 747 lowered me through layers of sky and light and sunshine until we came to clouds that were dark and thick. Down, down, down. Burrowing into a new life with all the optimism and exuberance I'd brought from my bright Australian landscape.

It was 1999. I was a grown-up on my first real adventure. In England! The East End of London! Houses were joined together. Prices were in pounds. The Royal Warrant was badged onto shopfronts. For a time, even the sky delighted me with its British gloom.

I was to live with Elaine, a teacher from my school who welcomed me with a calm and reassuring steadiness. She had once lived and worked in Australia and knew what it was to be jet-lagged and homesick and excited all at once.

We walked to school together, traversing streets still dark at eight in the morning. Our breath shone before us and I hugged my coat around myself, watching my step on icy pavements.

'Alrigh', Miss?' asked a student as we entered the gates. I looked to Elaine and she nodded and said, 'Yes, thank you, Isaac.'

'Alrigh', Miss?' I heard again as we crossed the school yard. I could hear now that it was a question.

'Alrigh', Miss?' Another student. I looked at Elaine and thought about all our letters and phone calls before I arrived. Had she been sick? All these students asking if she was alright. Then a teacher was introduced to me. Nathan. He shook my hand.

'Alright?' he asked, releasing his grip.

'I'm not sure,' I said and he laughed.

'It's a London thing,' Elaine said. '*Alright?* It's like saying, *How ya going?*'

'A bit like how you Aussies say good day,' said Nathan.

It's nothing like g'day, I thought.

'Just say, *Yes, thanks,*' said Elaine. 'Or you can say *alright* back to them.'

'So . . .' I paused. 'You say alright? And I say alright?'

'Yeah, that's it,' Nathan said. 'Now, come wiv me and I'll show you round.'

He led me to a classroom that was neat and clean and well resourced.

'You mighta heard some stuff about the East End,' Nathan said. 'But it's not like that here.'

I felt the cinch of panic in my throat and glanced at Elaine.

'Nothing to worry about,' she said. 'It's a lovely community.'

'Yeah, it's not like Harlow, up the road there.' Nathan inclined his head to show the direction. 'I heard a teacher at the secondary school there had his car stolen by the students *while* he was teaching a lesson.'

'Oh, surely that's not right,' Elaine said, and Nathan shrugged. 'It's different here,' Elaine continued. 'All the parents have steady work and the students are well behaved. You won't have trouble here.'

Through the window I could see parents dropping off their children. Many of them were arriving in BMWs and Mercedes Benz. I let out a breath.

'But don't be fooled,' Elaine said, following my gaze. 'Those cars are on hire. It's very much working class here, although some of them would like us to think otherwise.'

Finally, in front of my very own class, I was overcome with a chronic case of Miss Jenny's N.I. I had no idea what to say, no idea what to do, no idea how to start, no ideas at all—despite the over-prepared and almost scripted lesson plans laid out on my desk. I studied the students before me: eleven-year-olds in blue collared shirts, striped ties and blazers cloaked over the back of their chairs. They looked at me intently. I wondered how long the silence could go on. Could we fill the entire morning just staring at one another? Eventually, a girl spoke.

'Could you jus' talk to us, Miss? We wanna 'ear your accent.'

'Okay!' I swallowed. 'Maybe you might like to ask me some questions about Australia?'

'Oh gawd—I love the way she says 'Straylia like that. Could you say it again, Miss?'

I laughed and said *Australia*. And their hands shot up with questions about sharks and kangaroos and *Neighbours*. I could feel myself lighting up, their interest igniting my enthusiasm.

'Do you get *EastEnders* over there?' someone asked.

'No,' I said. 'And I don't get it over here.' They laughed.

'You got a boyfriend, Miss?' It came from a boy with a ratty nose and freckles all over his face.

'I'm not answering that.' I could feel a blush glowing on my cheeks. It had been an emotional farewell to Matthew at the airport.

'That's alrigh',' said the boy, giving me a wink. 'I get it.' A few other boys laughed and I felt the ground, so solid beneath me just moments earlier, somehow now slippery and dangerous. *Don't lose control of this class*, my inner voice fumed. *Don't lose it on the first day.*

'How old are you, Miss?' the winking boy asked.

'Twenty-one,' I told him. 'And what's your name?'

'That's Benny, Miss,' said one of the girls. 'You mostly just wanna ignore 'im. My sister's twenty-one. You 'ave a par'e?'

'Sorry?' I glanced at the name on her pencil case. 'What do you mean, Ally?'

'A par'e? You know, wiv cake and wine and that?'

'Uh, yeah,' I said. 'A little one.' It was a lie. My twenty-first had been huge, but I was suddenly so aware that I wasn't all that much older than these students. Only ten years. And they could sense it, too. My youth.

'Last question,' I said firmly, nodding to a boy sitting up the back. He was still wearing his blazer.

'My name's Kyran,' he said.

'Hello, Kyran.' Elaine had told me about him. Gifted. Exceptionally clever. 'What's your question?' *Please God, let it be something I can answer.*

'How long have you been teaching, Miss?'

I glanced at my watch. 'About twenty minutes now,' and a nervous laugh escaped.

'Thought so,' he said.

It was a Friday night and I was trying to stay awake so I could ring Matthew. We were still figuring out the best time for phone calls. I had a feeling Friday nights weren't going to work for me.

I had recovered from the jet lag but now I was battling a new fatigue. After a few weeks of teaching, a weariness had settled into me that I had never known on prac when I'd shared the load with a mentor. It was a cumulative tiredness that seemed to layer heavily on top of itself, no matter how much sleep I got each evening. By the time 3.30 p.m. on a Friday rolled around I would shuffle into the staffroom feeling spent, as though I'd been running a marathon all week long. I was half-expecting an Olympic podium with a crowd of dignitaries waiting to present me with a gold medal. Instead there was a pile of newspapers on the table and a pint of milk going sour on the sink.

Most evenings, I couldn't do anything more than lie on the lounge. Every part of me was exhausted, including my voice. I struggled to concentrate on TV. I didn't want to go out. Even the thought of leaving the flat to walk down the road for a takeaway feed of fish and chips felt impossible. This was a unique fatigue that permeated my body and mind and often consumed my whole weekend. It was teacher-tiredness.

Something was diminished within me. A part of me given away day after day.

I picked up the phone and pressed in the numbers from my phone card along with the international codes and Matthew's number. There was a pause as the string of digits were processed and then the familiar Australian ring tone.

'Hello?' Matthew's voice was suddenly in my ear.

'Hey, Matty,' I said. 'How are you?' There was a hush as my words were delayed, travelling through technology to find him in Australia.

'Yeah, good,' he said. 'What time is it there?'

'Eleven-thirty, Friday night.' I consulted my watch. 'Eleven-forty actually.'

'Sounds right. It's 10.40 Saturday morning here. It's going to be a hot day. Forecast is thirty-seven. I'm playing golf after this. I'll probably melt. What's it like there?' As he spoke, I heard the wolf whistle of a currawong from his garden. A feeling of homesickness swelled within me.

'It's so dark,' I said, my voice low so I didn't wake Elaine. 'It's dark when I get to school at eight and it's getting dark when the kids leave. The days are really short! It's been about five degrees every day.' I heard the currawong sing again and had to dab at my eyes. 'I miss you.'

'Yeah, me too. It's going to be a long year.' He yawned, audibly.

'Hey,' I laughed. 'You don't get to yawn. I'm the one struggling to stay awake! Why are you so tired? Did you go out last night?'

'Nah, the tennis. Stayed up late. Philippoussis is out.'

'Oh, bummer. I've hardly seen any news over here. I'm always at school or getting stuff ready for school or marking.

There's so much marking, especially with Grade Six.' I glanced at the tub of exercise books I had carried home, felt my biceps twinge with the memory.

We talked on for a while.

'Hey, guess what?' I said. 'I'm getting a car soon. The Head Teacher's son is going to sell me his for the year—really cheap—kind of like a lease and then I give it back to him at the end. I might be able to go exploring on weekends.' Already I was doubtful I'd have enough energy to drive to the shops let alone Cambridge or Southend.

'That's great,' Matty said. 'What kind of car?'

'Hmm,' I giggled. 'I think he said it was blue.'

He laughed. 'Well, find out and let me know. So did you get paid? You right for money?' There had been a delay in my pay, I'd been teaching for weeks and living off my savings.

'Yes! Finally!' I rummaged in my handbag and found the payslip. 'It works out about three hundred and fifty pounds per week, that's after tax and all of that.'

Matthew whistled, low and impressed. 'That's great. That's about . . .' he paused, calculated the exchange, 'nine hundred Australian dollars. That's more than I make.'

The hush came again, but this time it stretched between us. I didn't know what to say. Three hundred and fifty pounds seemed like it might not be enough, given the intensity of the work and the hours I was putting in. London's cost of living wasn't cheap either; I'd already started budgeting for fuel and car insurance.

Just as the silence was bordering on awkward, we both tried to speak at once. I laughed and told Matthew to go ahead.

'Nah, I should let you go,' he said. 'It must be after midnight now. What were you going to say?'

'Oh, I was just going to say, it would be interesting to work out a teacher's pay based on an hourly rate. You know— adding up all the time spent planning and preparing and marking.'

'Yeah,' Matty was noncommittal. 'I still reckon it'd be better than mine.'

We said our goodbyes and I found my way into bed. I thought about Matty and how he'd be driving out to the golf course, eighteen holes and a few hours on the nineteenth would be the sum of his Saturday. My own Saturday, when I finally slept into it, would be full of marking and planning and preparing. I wondered, for a vague sleepy moment, what a teacher's time was really worth.

I quickly discovered that the landscape of the staffroom was treacherous. There were cliques and alliances and factions; boats that should never be rocked. I was quickly put into my place as the new, young, foreign and inexperienced woman.

The staff were led by the Head Teacher, whom I feared and admired in equal measure. She was a formidable woman with a commanding presence. On my first day, I watched as she entered the gymnasium for assembly and four hundred students fell silent as she walked along the aisle. By the time she reached the podium at the front I realised I was holding my breath and I had a sense that everyone else was too.

She was generous, often giving the teachers twenty quid on a Thursday when we barrelled out the door for drinks at the pub. *No, I won't come,* she would say, grinning wryly and waving away our invitations. *I've got wine at home and nobody wants to drink with the boss.*

Generosity aside, she seemed almost unapproachable and I would often have to work up the courage to ask her the most basic of questions. Many of the students in my class had told me they were terrified of her. I couldn't imagine that she'd ever been a classroom teacher. But Elaine assured me that she had taught for many years before moving into school leadership.

One morning, the Head swaggered into my classroom, her hand poised in imitation of a gun, ready to shoot.

'*Bang, bang, bang,*' she said gravely, shooting at students. 'You're all dead. Why isn't that classroom door locked?'

'I'm sorry.' I could feel a blush flooding my cheeks. I had been instructed to lock the classroom door at all times, even when we were inside during lessons. There had been a school massacre at Dunblane in Scotland three years earlier. A gunman had walked into the school hall and opened fire. Consequently, this school now had a stringent security policy.

'Dunblane,' she said and dropped a pile of notes on my desk. 'Lock the door.'

I followed after her as she left, locking the door behind her with a shaky breath. From then on I locked it all the time, but probably not for the right reasons.

University does not prepare you for life in the staffroom. I listened and watched the other teachers carefully, trying to discern the unwritten laws of the land. I spent my time in the staffroom stepping around conflict, deflecting judgements and trying to remain neutral. Even so, I still fell into traps.

There was a teacher Elaine had warned me about. *Be careful around Lilith*, she had told me. *I don't trust her.* Initially, though, Lilith had been welcoming, adopting me as her new Australian friend and inviting me around to her home. For a while I doubted Elaine's judgement, but as the term wore on I saw Lilith behave in ways that were no better than some of the children in the playground. She held court in the staffroom, excluding some teachers while drawing others close. She steered the staff meetings with pointed questions and sly allegations. She manipulated parents, planting seeds of doubt and sprigs of gossip. Lilith was playing us off like cards in a game and, whenever the Head Teacher came into view, she turned up the charm until she was dazzling.

As the year wore on, she took to toying with me whenever we were alone. I had no recourse for the tiny arrows that were shot my way—comments about a ribbon in my hair, my 'accent' or my students' behaviour at assembly.

'Oh, you're still here,' she said as I entered the staffroom on the first day of Term Two. 'I was hoping you'd been deported back to Australia.'

Supposedly, she was joking but her words punctured my homesick heart. I started avoiding the staffroom, wary of Lilith, and found refuge in the school kitchen, where I was befriended by Dawn.

Dawn was a dinner lady employed to cook and serve a hot lunch for students each day. Afterwards, like the other dinner ladies, she donned a high-vis vest and went out on playground duty. Dawn was the opposite of Lilith: warm, genuine and kind.

She was always up for a chat, curious about Australia and the most recent events on Ramsay Street.

'That Kylie Minogue's done quite well for 'erself, ain't she?' Dawn said. 'I loved her as Charlene. My son reckons he saw her one day, jus' walkin' along in Trafalgar Square. You bin ta Trafalgar Square, yet?' she asked.

I shook my head.

'Blimey, love—it's April!' Dawn said. 'You gotta get inta the city. I'll take ya in on Sunday.' She was wiping down the benches as she spoke. 'What do ya wanna see first, love? Big Ben?' She took off her apron and pulled on her fluoro vest. 'Aw, it's gonna be lovely.'

And it was lovely. A crisp, blue sky kind of day. Buckingham Palace. Big Ben. Westminster Abbey.

'You should see ya face, love,' Dawn said, snapping pictures of me. 'Ya eyes might fall out, ya got 'em open so wide.'

The next day, waiting for staff meeting to begin, I found myself alone in the staffroom with Lilith. She asked after my weekend and her interest caught me off guard. I told her about my day in London with Dawn.

'Dawn Laurence?' she asked.

'Yes,' I said. 'I bought this, too.' I held up a mug, emblazoned with the Union Jack. Just last week, Lilith had reminded me to use the visitors' mugs rather than the ones hooked over the sink. *They belong to the staff*, she had told me.

After staff meeting, the Head called me into her office. She peered at me over her spectacles as she asked after my weekend.

'It does sound like a lovely trip to London,' she said. 'But I can't understand why you went with Dawn.'

'Well, I go most places on my own.' Trying not to let my voice waver. 'But I didn't feel confident doing the city. The other teachers said they'd take me one day, but they never set a date, and so when Dawn asked me . . .'

'She's a dinner lady.' The Head's tone was flat. 'Teachers don't socialise with dinner ladies.'

'Yes, Miss,' I said. 'I'm sorry.'

As I left her office, Lilith just happened to be walking by.

'Alright?' she asked with a grin.

'No,' I said and brushed past her.

'Is this the biggest wine glass we've got?' I held up a goblet that could easily house a goldfish. Elaine nodded.

I had rushed home after the dressing down in the Head's office. Elaine had listened as I sobbed my way through the story of Lilith's set-up and the Head's reprimand.

'We need wine,' Elaine announced.

'And probably chocolate eclairs,' I said.

We bought supplies, threw on our pyjamas and settled in for the evening.

'Lilith's nasty,' Elaine said as she filled my glass. 'But you just have to ignore her. She won't change.'

I gulped at my wine and was rewarded with the sensation of choking. I coughed and snorted before regaining composure. 'I can't believe there are teachers out there that behave like she does!' I fumed. 'I can't believe she works with children.'

'Oh, there's plenty of them,' Elaine handed me an eclair. 'Lilith's a great teacher from what I've seen and heard. I think she just feels threatened by other teachers.'

I shook my head. 'It doesn't make sense. I'm no threat to her.' I bit into my eclair and watched with satisfaction as cream oozed onto my finger.

'You're young,' Elaine said. 'You're new, you're from Australia . . .' Her voice trailed.

'Yeah,' I said, 'so what?'

'Well, for Lilith, that makes you a threat. You're *younger*, you're *newer*.' She emphasised each word.

I grunted. 'Still makes no sense and I don't understand how she's allowed to behave that way. Why hasn't someone called *her* into the Head's office? And,' I picked up my wine glass, took another slug, 'and why can't we go out with dinner ladies?'

Elaine shrugged. 'I think it's just the way of schools. I've worked at loads of schools and it's always the same. Some are better than others. This one's actually not too bad. But there's always a Lilith, there are always factions and groups—people who want change and people who don't like change. There are always unspoken rules and codes of conduct. Schools can be very political places.' She leaned forward and topped up her glass of wine. 'I try not to get too involved in all that.'

It sounded like good advice and I would certainly be avoiding and ignoring Lilith with renewed determination. But something about Elaine's comment caused an itch within my teacher psyche: *Try not to get too involved.* What did that really mean? And how would you do it?

On staff, a teacher named Maria was leading the campaign for better quality toilet paper.

'I'm serious,' she said at staff meeting. 'I'm in the cubicle and it's life and death. The stuff we've got just isn't absorbent—it's like Teflon. Surely we can afford something a bit better!'

A few teachers laughed.

'I could arrange a fundraiser,' she went on. 'Have a raffle, you know? I could make the tickets from the toilet paper we've got now.'

Maria's classroom was next to mine and she often held doors open for me as I lugged boxes of books out to my car.

'Whatchya doin' with all that, Koala?' she asked as I inched through the door and out to the car park.

'Marking.' I hefted the box onto the roof of my car and hunted for the keys. 'I'll mark them this weekend.'

'Will ya?' she frowned at me.

'Yeah,' I said, still fossicking.

'Really? Koala, look at me. Will you really mark all of them?' She pointed to the box.

I found my keys and looked at her.

'Probably not,' I admitted. I had taken the same books home the previous weekend and only marked fifteen before falling asleep. When I did wake up I had felt too overwhelmed to finish the job. I'd spent a guilty weekend on the lounge watching Prince Edward Earl of Wessex marry Sophie Rhys-Jones.

'Don't you take marking home?' I asked. She looked light and carefree, her little handbag swinging off her arm.

'Course I do.' She held up two exercise books. 'I'll mark this lot and do them really well—take my time and read their work and write good comments. I take four home on the weekdays, but just one or two on the weekends. If I do it that way, I mark everything within a fortnight. Here, let me help you with that.' She held the door for me while I lifted the box into the back seat.

'Have a good weekend, Koala. Come over and have a drink if you get finished marking.'

'Yeah okay, I will, even if I *don't* get the marking finished!' I smiled at her and felt some of the stress I was carrying slip away. With people like Lilith lurking around corners, it was nice to have Maria as my friend.

'You've got my number.' She walked away, the two green books held loosely in her hand. *No wonder she's so happy on a Monday morning,* I thought.

I developed a habit of 'popping in' to Maria's classroom most afternoons to debrief, ask questions and borrow resources.

'Alright, Koala?' Maria was at her desk marking worksheets at speed, her handbag and keys already poised for departure.

'Yeah, I'm good,' I said and she laughed.

'You should say "I'm well". That's better English.' She stopped marking and swivelled her chair. 'Hey! Listen to my Australian accent.' She took a breath and then said, '*A dingo took my baby.*' She smiled. 'What do you think?'

'Well,' I replied, giving my best imitation of the Queen. 'I want to say it's good, but I'm not sure if it's proper English.'

We laughed and Maria ran through a few more lines: *Put another shrimp on the barbie! That's not a knife, this is a knife!* And then another phrase that she'd adopted of her own:

How'd ya like me real Australian opal? She pointed to the keyring I'd given her—a koala shape embedded with white opals.

'Now your turn,' she said.

'Bollocks!' I grimaced. 'It just sounds so ridiculous!' I shook my head. 'Surely you've got better swear words than that?'

'Course we do,' she said. 'We've got the same as you Down Under, but *bollocks* is a very British word. You've got to say it like you mean it.'

We practised swearing for a few minutes.

'Anyway,' I said, 'I didn't come in here to swear with you. I came in here to talk about a student. Leonard.'

'Okay.' She returned to her marking, eyes darting from the papers to me. 'Tell me what's going on.'

'I was working on reports over the weekend,' I said. 'And as I wrote Leonard's report I realised that he is really far behind. I mean, he is at a really, really low level in everything. He even struggles with Science and Art.'

'Okay.' Maria stopped marking. 'So, what are you going to do?'

'I don't know.' I slumped against one of the desks and picked absently at a piece of sticky tape stuck to the surface. 'He is so far behind, Maria. I knew he was low in his reading and that's why he goes out each day with Mrs Carol, but his Maths and his writing and just his basic understanding of stuff . . .' I sighed. 'It's like he needs to be back in Grade Three or Four.'

'So, you're modifying his work, aren't you?'

I nodded.

'And his parents are aware of the situation?'

'Yeah. I looked up his file and it's documented on his past school reports and at parents' evening. He's got quite a lot in his file. He's been behind ever since he started, but he hasn't been diagnosed with anything.' I picked again at the tape, drawing it off the desk to reveal an ugly gummy patch. 'Oh, and there's stuff in his file that shows his vision and hearing have been checked more than once, too.'

'Wait a minute.' Maria frowned. 'Are you talking about little Leo? Short guy? Dark hair? Really quiet?'

I nodded.

'And he plays football out here with Benny and Kyran and those other lads?' She pointed in the direction of their playing field.

'Yeah,' I said. 'Leonard Thornleigh.'

'I know Leo,' Maria said. 'I taught him ages ago.'

'So, what did *you* do with him?' I sat up straighter hoping to be offered a magic spell.

'Well, when he was with me, he was always making progress, so I didn't worry. Is he making progress?'

'Umm . . .' I considered her question. Leonard was trying hard consistently. He was always engaged, always listening and paying attention. His work was improving, slowly and slightly. I had recently gone over speech marks with him and he had tried to include them in his story. They weren't all correct, but they were there. Plus, he was now using the Maths trick I had shown him for the nine times table. He was slow at getting the questions done, but he was now completing more of them and getting more correct.

'Yes,' I answered. 'He is making progress. It's slow but I have seen improvement.'

'Well, then, we shouldn't worry,' Maria said, capping her pen and reaching for her keys.

'But he's so far behind,' I said again.

'Behind what?' Maria said, watching as I frowned. 'If a student is making steady progress then they're learning. It just depends on where we put the benchmark as to how quickly and how well they're learning.' She used her fingers to wave quotation marks around *well*. 'Learning takes time,' she added.

I thought about what she was saying and saw myself almost physically adjusting my expectations for this kid, like the lowering of a high jump bar. I had always thought the syllabus and curriculum to be like the Bible—*Thou shalt not deviate from these standards of achievement*. But Maria's words made so much sense and not just in regard to Leonard Thornleigh; there were many of my students who needed the bar adjusted—a little lower here and a little higher there. Perhaps the curriculum standards weren't the correct measure. The thought flashed like something illicit.

'Anyway,' Maria was saying, bundling up the worksheets. 'Leonard Thornleigh's going to be a dustman.'

'A what?'

'You know.' She shrugged and reached for her handbag. 'A rubbish collector.'

'Maria!' I refused to laugh. 'You can't say that. You can't even joke about that.'

She looked at me—a rare moment of seriousness. 'I'm not joking. That boy will grow up to be a dustman or something similar. And I take that seriously.' Ready to leave, Maria crossed the room and flicked off the lights.

'Well, I don't think that's right,' I said, hurrying to follow her into the car park. Four-thirty and it was dark. 'I think that as teachers we have a responsibility to help our students lift their lives so they can aspire to anything.'

'Absolutely,' Maria said, weaving through the few remaining cars before stopping next to her new white Micra. 'But what you also think, Koala, is that being a dustman isn't a good job; isn't a good enough thing for a person to want to be.' She was using her keys to point at me. 'But what I think . . .' Here, she clutched the keys to her chest. 'What I think is that being a dustman is an important occupation. Almost noble. We need good dustmen. I hate to imagine our world without them. I believe that it's my job to help a student like Leonard Thornleigh become the best dustman he can be.'

She slipped into her bubble of a car and wound down the window. 'I've decided I'm going to start bringing in my own toilet paper,' she said. 'You want me to bring some in for you?'

I watched as she zipped out of the car park and paused to give way at the road. 'HOW'D YA LIKE ME REAL AUSTRALIAN OPAL?' she shouted at me, her arm waving madly through the window.

'BOLLOCKS!' I shouted back, grinning and waving. It suddenly occurred to me that I was standing outside the Head's office. 'Bollocks,' I said again, with a great deal of feeling and a very quiet voice.

Things have gotta be standard

Each week in England, I met with my colleagues to plan lessons. At our first meeting, I was told that Art and PE and a few other subjects would have to wait until the SATs were over.

'What are SATs?' I asked.

'Standardised assessment tasks,' Nathan told me. 'National tests, you know? The school's results get published in a league table in the papers. Don't you have SATs in Australia?'

'We have the Basic Skills Test,' I said. 'That's in New South Wales. Other states have other things. But—' I paused, considering. 'We don't publish BST results in the newspaper and we don't have national testing.'

'Oh.' The other teachers looked at one another and nodded. Then they picked up their pens and prepared to fill out the columns of the weekly program, slashing lines through History, Geography, Music, Dance, Drama, Visual Arts and PE.

'Don't you think they're a bit young,' I asked, 'to be sitting a major exam? Some of the kids in my class have told me they're really worried about it.' Just that morning Benny had said to me, 'Blimey, Miss. It's only a few weeks 'til SATs. I'm gutted.'

'Oh, they're alright,' said Nathan. 'They survive.'

'Why do they only test Maths and English?' I asked and I thought I heard someone give an impatient sigh.

'Because SATs are just English and Maths,' Nathan said. 'And Science.'

I watched them leaf through the curriculum document, marking pages with folded down corners.

'But ...' I hesitated, knowing it was getting late and everyone wanted to get home. 'I don't understand why? Why not test *all* the subjects? And why not use classroom assessments that the teacher collects over the year?'

This time the sigh was audible.

'Things have gotta be standard,' Nathan explained. 'This is just the way they do it. We've been doing it like this for ages now. And it's important, yeah? The results we get from our cohort affects how our school sits in the league tables.'

A new pile of questions arrived in my head: *Would there be allowances for students like Leonard? He was still spelling said as 'sed'? What about the lad in my class with Asperger's? Would Kyran be tested on a more difficult paper—he was already doing algebra? And what would we do with the results? By the time they were published these students would be on their way to high school.* But I let the questions fall away because it was five o'clock and already dark outside.

Over the following weeks, I learned about the SATs and the implications these exams had for students, teachers and the school. I watched as students became tired and disinterested during lessons where we covered endless dry content and wrote texts that were almost clinically manufactured. Students presenting as 'borderline' on practice tests (achieving high results on Level 3 and showing potential for 4) were taken out of class for intensive programs that would supposedly boost their results.

I started giving my class sneaky 'interlude' lessons where we would sit on the mat and recklessly indulge in a singalong or abandon the afternoon of Maths revision to draw and paint. I let them out earlier at break time and watched as they raced onto the playing fields like captives set free. I even discovered an outdoor area where we couldn't be seen from other classrooms. I would take them out there when the sun was shining and play class games of handball and tips.

'You're a good teacher, Miss,' said Benny, the winker, as we snuck back into class after a particularly competitive game of English football.

'Yeah,' added Ally. 'I love you.' She patted my shoulder. 'What results do you expect I might get on me SATs, Miss?'

'I really don't know,' I admitted.

'Oh, well,' she said, flicking her hair up into a ponytail. 'I bet it's not like this in 'Straylia, is it?'

'No,' I said ruefully, unable to imagine this happening back home.

'We should all go live in 'Straylia, then,' said Benny. 'I reckon I'd fit right in.' And he raised an eyebrow and winked at me again.

I couldn't buy into the feeling of pressure even as the SATs drew closer. Perhaps it was because I knew my time in England was limited, perhaps because I was ignorant or inexperienced, or perhaps because I knew, even then, that standardised tests revealed very little about student learning. The idea of these major exams for such young students just seemed ridiculous. I found it hard to take it seriously, even though the daily papers blasted headlines that implied I should feel threatened, if not terrified.

My housemate Elaine read the papers though, every evening on the lounge in her flat while I drank red wine and ate chocolate eclairs from Tesco.

'Look at this,' she said one night, pointing to a headline that declared *Teachers at Fault*. There was a downward graph embedded in the article.

'Does it worry you?' I asked, leaning over to read the fine print. *Teachers have lost confidence . . . Lowered results . . . Scaremongering . . . Leaving the profession . . .*

'Yes, it does.' Elaine reached for the bottle of wine. 'Performance-based pay worries me right now.' She sighed and flopped back into the cushions.

I flipped the newspaper page only to find another article on education: *How Shame Can Raise Standards*. I set my wineglass over the words and slumped beside her.

'Let's watch *EastEnders*,' I suggested, reaching for the remote.

As we watched TV I felt Elaine relaxing by degrees, her face softening, her limbs becoming loose. Those articles were putting pressure on her teaching, lurking like sinister shadows over her future career. I was lucky, I realised, to be returning to a country where I wouldn't have to worry about SATs and performance requirements and shame and standards. In Australia, there wouldn't be someone looking over my shoulder, checking I'd done my job, forcing me to prepare students for exams they weren't ready for. I wouldn't face newspapers with threats from politicians and depressing downward graphs. I wouldn't have someone testing my students as a means of testing me. As I let my mind be carried away to the dramas of *EastEnders*, I truly couldn't imagine a time when Australian education would ever look anything like it did in England.

As I finished my year in England, I felt older and infinitely wiser. I had survived my first year of teaching and my rose-coloured glasses weren't damaged, only clouded. The reality of teaching—the workload, the fatigue and the emotional demands had been acknowledged. I would go into my next job aware of these things. But my enthusiasm was still brimming— the cup was still half-full, and as far as I was concerned it was top-shelf champagne and there was enough for everybody. Who wouldn't want to be a teacher?

I finished my stint abroad with a month of travel. Matty came over and we toured Europe together. France. Italy. Germany. Austria. Switzerland. The Netherlands. I fell in love with the sights, the flavours and the people. As the tour guides brought each place to life with anecdotes and facts, I filled my notebooks, trying to capture a brief history of Europe, as well as documenting my own adventures. My notes were random and hasty, recording things that caught my eye and piqued my interest: *Gargoyles on Notre Dame* look like they're rotting. *Eiffel Tower completed 1889. Charle-magne promoted literacy. Leaning Tower of Pisa smaller than I thought. Vienna is classy. Today I saw a glacier! Holland—a province of the Netherlands.*

I became a student of the world during that trip and I wanted to bring that world to the students I would teach. During the plane ride home, I wrote a kind of manifesto reflecting on the kind of teacher I wanted to be.

I think about the type of teacher I want to be and the type of person I want to be . . .

I want to be an organised teacher who is bubbly and happy like Maria.

I want to be thoughtful like Miss Jenny.

I want to wear bright colours to brighten my students' day.

I want to be knowledgeable and prepared.

I want to read with the children each morning and finish the week with board games on Friday afternoon.

I want to bring the newspaper into the classroom each day and make the world accessible.

I want to celebrate a new country each week and show it labelled on a world map.

I'll let them do their spelling test on a Thursday and then again on Friday if they need another go at it.

I won't go back on my word.

I want to show my students that I'm a learner too.

I want to make children feel fantastic about themselves.

Paradise

Returning to Australia, I landed a job in a small town called Paradise on the far south coast of New South Wales. As a child, I had holidayed near Paradise and knew it to be a beautiful fishing town. My parents had recently bought a holiday home nearby and it was only a few hours' drive if I ever felt like a trip back to the farm.

Matthew had proposed and I had a solitaire diamond on my finger. We were renting a place half an hour out of Paradise and Matty had found work at a joinery. Already we were thinking about buying in the area. The beaches were gorgeous, the temperatures mild and the people were friendly. After the gloom of my year in England, everything here seemed brighter, lighter and just more *sunshiny*.

The school was located on a cliff, where burgundy sandstone dropped away like the land had been sliced through.

The inky Pacific Ocean yawned and roared below, and I couldn't imagine how I would concentrate on playground duty with such a stunning view distracting me.

'This is an interesting place,' explained Peter, the teacher commissioned to show me around the school. 'You've got very wealthy people living side-by-side with the poorest of the poor.'

Peter was a big man with a booming voice and I trailed behind him as he narrated local history, funny anecdotes and thoughtful advice. He told me he'd been teaching for thirty-five years.

'Do you like teaching here?'

'It's challenging,' he said and ushered me through a doorway. 'Staffroom. Toilet.' He unlocked a door, walked me through a foyer. 'And now you can meet Bro.' He opened another door, revealing a classroom with a lone teacher working at his desk. 'Bro teaches the other Year Five and Six class,' Peter said. 'You two will be the Stage Three team.'

'Welcome to Paradise,' Bro said. He stretched his arm out, a gesture that encompassed his room. There was a diction-ary propping up the leg of his desk and a squadron of empty drink bottles on the window ledge behind him. A sprawl of coloured paper was spewing out of a desk and leaking onto the floor like a fractured rainbow. The carpet was littered with crumpled Christmas wrap, shags of tinsel and empty chip packets. Two of the windows were cracked, lightning bolt lines jagging down the pane. Thick grey gaffer tape held the fractured pieces together.

At that moment, as if startled by Bro's gesture, a faded rugby league poster slipped from the wall, wafting to the ground like an enormous leaf. I looked at Bro and he winked.

Another winker. He looked older than me. Maybe thirty. *Old enough to know you don't wink at your colleagues.* I tried not to be irritated.

'I'll leave you guys to it,' Peter said, juggling the collection of keys in his hand. 'Good to have you on board.' His smile was wide and sincere.

This'll be alright, I thought, warmed by his friendliness.

Bro tore two strips of sticky tape from a dispenser. He picked up the poster and stuck it onto the wall. Then he stood back to survey his work. A faded Des Hasler was locked in a tackle with Laurie Daley, their faces distorted and ugly.

'It's funny how it's still rugby league country here,' Bro said. 'We're so close to the Victorian border, but AFL's just never taken off.'

'Hmm,' I nodded. His blackboard still had last year's final day scrawled all over it in colourful bubble writing: *Thanks Bro, You Rock Bro* and *Class of '99 are the Best.* In the bottom-right corner there was an enormous penis drawn in yellow.

'You're just out of uni?' Bro was back at his desk and the sun was shining through the window behind him.

'Second year out. I just got back from teaching in England for a year.'

'Oh, yeah.' He leaned back in his seat. 'How was that?'

'Um . . .' I couldn't stop noticing things. A hole in the wall. A crooked ceiling fan. A blind that was drawn well past the window like an overgrown tongue. I remembered my classroom in London: neat, ordered and clean. 'Um, good,' I said, bringing my eyes back to his sunlit glow. 'Do the students call you Bro?'

'Yeah,' he said. 'Or Mr Brotherton.'

I raised my eyebrows, nodded, trying to be cool with that.

'Listen,' he said and he leaned forward, elbows thumping onto his desk. He was out of the sun now, no longer glowing. I could see his face, earnest in the plain light of the classroom. 'I know you're recently out of uni and you've taught a bit, but I'm going to tell you something and it's something I've had to learn myself and I think they should tell you this at uni and maybe they do now, but I never got it . . .' He paused and I waited. 'Teaching is all about relationships, okay? That's what matters. Your relationship with the kids and with the parents and with the staff.'

'Yep.' I nodded. 'I agree.'

'No,' he said. 'I really mean it. If you're going to survive here, you need to understand this. It's all about relationships.'

'Okay,' I said carefully.

He scrunched up the paper he was working on and threw it vaguely towards the bin.

'I think I'm gonna call you Gabsie,' he said. 'C'mon, I'll show you your classroom.'

It was a shed. The only thing that made it different to the dark, cavernous sports' shed adjoining it was that it had ceiling fans, carpet and windows. It would be a freezer in winter and today, mid-summer, it was an oven. It was dusty and grimy, with spider webs hanging like decorations and dead flies rotting on every surface.

I loved it.

In England, I had known that the teacher who I was replacing would return and so I hadn't done anything much to the classroom. But this—this dirty, filthy shed—was all mine and I couldn't wait to make it a space where my students could bounce into each morning, ready to learn and discover.

The room would need a team of people to work on it, but before I roped my parents in to help, I took all the desks and chairs outside, scrubbing them for ages with hot, soapy water and a scouring brush to remove all the scribbles and swearwords. I didn't want my folks to see the things that were written on those desks and I shushed the voice inside me that asked, *What kind of child writes that on a desk?*

For days on end during that hot January my parents and I scrubbed walls and vacuumed floors and washed windows. My mum sewed new curtains while I sorted out the storeroom, throwing away paints and glues that had dried like bricks in a bottle. I bought a second-hand sofa, along with cushions and beanbags, to create a cosy reading corner. I discarded books that were riddled with silverfish and crinkled with the sadness of being unread and I restocked the bookshelves with books of my own: John Marsden and Morris Gleitzman, Paul Jennings and Jackie French. I set up a computer corner, put fresh coloured paper over the display boards, repainted the blackboard and set up a quiet work area where I planned to have ongoing investigations that the students could work on whenever they wanted. I cleaned the teacher's desk until it sparkled and arranged my talismans on it—gifts from Benny and Ally and other students I had taught in England. With exhausted satisfaction, I surveyed the room from a wobbly swivel chair.

The scene was set. All I needed were my students.

'What's all this shit, then?' It was the first student to walk in. I scanned my class roll: only twelve students; surely I could work it out.

'Ryan?' I asked, and the slight, blond-haired boy who was flicking on the computer looked up at me.

'Nuh.' He continued to start up the computer while I hovered nearby. I didn't want him using the computer. The bell hadn't even rung yet. I glanced at my watch.

'Are you normally allowed to come into the classroom before school starts?' I straightened things on my desk, tried to sound casual.

He shrugged.

'Hey, Ryan!' There was a kid at the window, almost hidden in the long grass that was out of bounds. 'Come and check this out.' He held up a crushed beer can. 'Some still in it.'

Ryan abandoned the computer and raced out of the room, toppling a chair as he went.

I took a slow breath and crossed the room to straighten the chair. *I should go out and find those boys and take the can from them*, I thought.

But then the bell went and I was seized by relief. Children's voices began to swell outside my classroom door: *Shove over, dickhead.*

I closed my eyes for a moment and reminded myself that I was a teacher.

Only bad behaviour

They didn't sit where I had planned.

They came into the room like wild cats, darting and lurking and diving and looking. Ryan went back to the computer and another boy dragged a chair over to sit beside him. One girl set up camp at my investigation area, shoving my equipment aside to make way for an oversized pencil case.

'Can I sit here?' A boy hovered near my desk, a pencil tucked behind each ear.

'No, I . . .' I fumbled for words. 'That's mine. That's the teacher's desk.' I sounded feeble.

Three kids were squashed on the sofa; one threw his legs out to rest on the table I'd placed nearby.

'The room looks nice.' It was a girl, tall, with auburn hair. She was sitting neatly at one of the student desks. She smiled at me.

'You reckon?' It was Ryan, eyes stuck on the computer screen. 'Where are all the games?' he asked, flicking the mouse around. 'Where's all our stuff from last year?'

'I took those games off,' I said. 'Now, let's get started.' I tried to herd them into the area where their desks were located, but Ryan was going ballistic—like a fire cracker had been let off in the corner.

'Well, that's fucked!' He stood up and flicked his chair behind him so that it crashed against the wall. 'You're a shit teacher!' he shouted, pointing. 'I'm not doing any work you give us!' He picked up a piece of chalk and threw it hard against the back wall. It splintered into pieces and left a white mark like bird shit.

'Ryan!' My voice didn't fail me. It was firm and loud, even though my heart was thundering, my hands shaking.

'What?' He stood in front of me. He was no more than thirty kilos, no more than four feet tall, no more than a boy.

'Let's sit down and get started.' My voice had only the slightest tremor.

'Alright.' He marched down the classroom, pulled a table and chair from its ordered place and turned it round so it faced the wrong way. He sat there, his back to me, staring at the wall.

'Thanks, Ryan,' I said and he raised his arm in the air and gave me the bird.

By eleven I had all the students, except Ryan, sitting in their seats. I had gone through the roll and established everyone's name, although two of the boys were playing funny buggers and I couldn't be certain who was really whom. They had completed the first 'getting to know you' game I had prepared, but it had only taken five of the twenty minutes I'd allocated. I hadn't considered the fact that these kids had already been together for four or five years. They had a shared history and they knew each other's personal history, too.

The literacy activities I tried with them were way too hard. They struggled to give full sentence answers to basic comprehension questions and they couldn't make inferences from a passage of text—even when it was read out loud for them. I realised with a sinking feeling that most of my program would need to be rewritten. I had spent two weeks of the holidays preparing that program—saying no to Matty when he suggested the beach, no to family BBQs, no to coffee with potential new friends. Hours and hours in front of a computer with syllabus documents bookmarked in a stack beside me. All that time and typing and formatting and decision-making. I had almost filled a lever arch folder once I printed it out. All of that wasted.

The bell rang for recess and they raced out, Ryan leading the charge. I followed them to the bag racks, watching as they grabbed tennis balls and biscuits and leaped over steps and slid down handrails until they were in the playground eating area.

'It's been a nice morning,' one girl said to me, plunging her hand into her bag to bring up a handful of cream-filled chocolate biscuits. Nearby, a boy was foraging in his own bag, his arm buried almost up to his shoulder.

'Well, thank you,' I said to the girl. 'Your name's Kilarney, isn't it?'

'Yep.' She smiled and waved clumsily, dropping a biscuit as she did. 'Oops!' She shifted, made to pick up the biscuit but then stepped on it, squashing it like a pancake. 'Oh, well,' she laughed, and ran off.

I turned, ready to find a broom, but as I moved away the foraging boy darted forward. He grabbed the squashed biscuit and shoved it into his mouth. I saw him wipe at his face and look around like a fox before racing away. I swept up the crumbs, positioning myself so that I could peek into his bag. It was empty.

Down in the staffroom, the other teachers asked how my morning had been. They looked calm and unaffected as they filled their mugs with coffee and reached for newspapers. I told them it had been good.

'How's Leyton?' Peter asked me, glancing up from the *Telegraph*.

'Leyton?' I frowned, wondering why no one was asking about Ryan, wondering why no one had warned me about him. I shrugged. 'I'm not sure who that is?'

'Lovely kid, dark-blond hair, plays soccer.'

I shrugged again.

'You'll know him soon enough. His dad's unwell with cancer,' Peter said.

'Gotten worse, then, Pete?' It was Bro, looking up from the local paper.

Peter nodded. 'He's not going to get through the year. Terrible.'

I made my tea and listened as they talked about this man I didn't know: father to four, local business owner, musician and all-round great guy. *How was his son coping?* I needed to work out who this kid was.

I was due out on playground duty and I burned my tongue on my tea rushing to finish the cup. I adjusted my hat as I walked out to the yard, seeking the teacher I was meant to relieve.

'Good luck,' she said as I approached. 'I see Ryan's out of his tree.'

I glanced across the playground to see Ryan swinging on the soccer goals like they were monkey bars. The other kids were shouting at him to get down and move so they could play their game.

'What do you normally . . . ?' My voice trailed off. The teacher was gone.

I set off towards the soccer game, scanning the players to determine who Leyton might be and thinking about how I might coax Ryan away. As I crossed the quadrangle, a tiny Kindergarten student ran past, throwing his food wrapper onto the ground.

'Hey,' I said, but the child kept running.

'BURT!' It was another kid—bigger, maybe in Year Three.

The boy stopped in his tracks and shouted, '*WHAT?*'

The bigger kid, an Aboriginal girl, pointed at me as I walked towards him.

'Is your name Burt?' I asked, squatting down to meet him. He nodded.

'You dropped your rubbish there, Burt,' I said, pointing to the chip packet, now ghosting its way across the yard. 'You go put it in the bin.'

'Fuck off,' he said and ran away.

I stood up and waited for a moment, feeling the slap of his words.

'That's Burt Mater,' said the girl, folding a peanut butter sandwich into her mouth. 'He's new.'

'Thanks,' I told her.

'You're new, too,' she said, falling into step beside me.

'I am!' I smiled.

'How do you like our school?' Her eyes met mine before darting away.

'It's . . .' I was still bruised from punches the morning had thrown at me. 'It's *different*,' I said, happy with my answer. I hadn't lied.

'I like you,' she said, and she slipped her peanut buttery hand into mine. 'We should go and tell Ryan to pull his head in.'

'Is Ryan always like this?' I asked.

She shrugged. 'He's okay. His sister's in my class.'

'He's got a sister?'

'Two of 'em,' she said. 'He sits with 'em at recess and lunch. Gives 'em food and stuff. I'm not scared of him.'

After recess, my class had Library and I felt my body flood with relief as I handed them over to the librarian who had been teaching at the school for years.

'Hat off, Ryan,' she called as they filed in. 'And you can forget about telling me to eff off. Just take your hat off and sit down.'

I went to the Principal's office and knocked on his door. He welcomed me in and I was overwhelmed by the smell of cologne. There was another scent too, something I couldn't place. He apologised for not checking in with me earlier, then sat his heavy-set frame behind a big glossy desk.

'Now, what can I do for you?'

Initially I had planned to tell him about Ryan and all he had thrown at me that morning. But Brydie, the Aboriginal girl, had made me reconsider. I had a feeling there was a bigger picture that I wasn't seeing yet. Ryan was part of the long game—I would give him a bit more time.

It was more the little kid who had bothered me—a five-year-old telling me to fuck off. Surely if we got him to change his behaviour now we'd avoid another Ryan five years down the track. I looked at the Principal, noticed his name inscribed on his pen.

I took a breath. 'On playground duty just then,' I laughed nervously, 'there was a Kindergarten boy, Burt Mater, and he . . . uh.' I smiled. 'He told me to eff off.'

'I see.' He kept his face unchanged. It was a calm face with the start of a smile. 'And what did you do?'

'Well, that's the thing. He ran off.'

'I see.' He nodded. 'And *then* what did you do?'

'Well . . . I . . . uh . . .' I could feel myself fumbling again, looking for words and explanations. I took a breath. 'I had asked him to put rubbish in the bin so *I* put the rubbish in the bin and uh . . .' I swallowed. 'I mean, he ran off; he was across the playground.' I gestured, limply.

'Well, you should have chased him.'

'Chased him?'

'Yes,' he said, nodding. 'He needs to know that kind of language is not acceptable.'

'Is that . . .' I paused, looked around the office, saw a set of syllabus documents lined up on the shelf. Their spines had never been cracked. 'Is that school policy?'

'Our policy is no swearing,' he said, and his eyebrows might have moved a millimetre.

I thought of Ryan and his comment: *You're a shit teacher.*

'Okay,' I said, rising from my seat. It was a heavy chair, wooden with a plush kind of cushioning. 'I get it.' *Cigarettes,* I thought, *that's what I can smell.*

I went back to my room and sat at my desk. Two of my talismans were missing.

After lunch, I introduced the class to the topic we would be studying that term. It was an integrated unit that included Art, Music, History and Geography. I had spent a long time planning it, thinking about the local community and the demographic. I wanted something that would challenge the students, but I wanted them to also feel a sense of owner-ship and intrinsic motivation.

'This term,' I told them, 'I thought we'd do a unit of study on Aboriginal culture.' I gestured to the bookshelf where I had a selection of thoughtfully chosen books borrowed from the Library. 'I thought we could consider the question: What can we learn from Australia's Indigenous cultures?'

'Not much,' mumbled Ryan. He was still sitting at the back of the room, facing the wall. When they had left for lunch

I noticed he had been etching his name into the desk with a blade he had dismantled from a sharpener. It had kept him quiet, so I hadn't tried to stop him.

'This is going to be great!' exclaimed the biscuit-dropper Kilarney. 'I love Oprah.'

'Sorry?' I tried not to stare.

'I love Oprah!' she chirped again. 'She's an Aboriginal.'

'*Ahhh*.' I felt my jaw slacken. Kilarney was sitting next to a quiet girl named Teisha. Earlier, she had told me they were best friends. Teisha was Koori—a local kid from the Yuin Nation. I'd done my homework and asked Peter a few questions. He told me there were almost twenty Koori students at the school, which was almost twenty per cent of the entire student population. He also told me about Teisha's grand-father, a well-respected elder, and he showed me the photo of him in the school's foyer raising the Aboriginal flag.

'You idiot.' It was another kid, a boy named Adrian. 'Oprah's African–American. She's talking about Aboriginal Australians. You know, the people that were here first.'

'Yeah,' added the tall girl with auburn hair. Natalie. 'You know, like Eric and Sal down in Bro's class? They're Aboriginal.'

'Are they?' Kilarney frowned.

'Yes!' Natalie went on. 'And Jerry.' She pointed to a boy across the room.

'But his skin's white,' said Kilarney.

'And Teisha,' Natalie added. 'Teisha's Aboriginal.'

'Are you?' Kilarney screwed up her face and studied her friend. 'I never knew that.' She shifted her pencil case away from Teisha's arm.

'Okay,' I said, trying not to release the sigh that was welling in my throat. 'Let's have a look at this map of the Indigenous nations throughout Australia.'

'Aww, this is gonna suck.'

'C'mon, Ryan,' I said, almost pleading. 'Eyes to the front.'

When the bell rang at 3.15 p.m. I wanted to run, just like the kids did, out of the classroom and out of the school grounds. I wanted to get home and put on my pyjamas and crawl into bed.

Instead, I had bus duty. I stood with the kids and shepherded them as best I could onto buses that would take them to farming areas just out of town. Two little girls, maybe from Year One or Two, loitered at the gate.

'What are you girls doing?' I asked.

'Waitin' for Ryan,' one of them said.

'Dunno where he is,' said the other.

'Who's Ryan?' I asked, hoping they might be waiting for another nicer Ryan.

The first girl laughed. 'You know Ryan. He's in ya class.'

'Ryan Morris,' said the other one.

'Why are you waiting for him?' They didn't look anything like Ryan; they couldn't be his sisters.

'Sometimes, if he's in a good mood, he meets up wiv us and we go into the bush.' The first one swung her bag off one shoulder and onto the other.

'And we're making a cubby,' said the other one, her face lit up with excitement. 'It's really cool and Ryan helps us with it.

And then we play in it: we play, like, cops and robbers and mothers and fathers and stuff.'

The first one jabbed the second one hard with her elbow. '*Shhh,*' she said firmly. 'Ryan doesn't want other kids to know he plays wiv us b'cos the big kids will tease him for playing with little kids. Look, here he comes.'

There was Ryan, slogging his way up the hill with his bag almost larger than his torso weighing down on his back. He looked so small against the vast expanse of playground.

'Fuck off,' he said to the girls as he walked through the gate.

'Please, Ryan?' they called. 'Please?'

He waited until he was well across the car park before finally shouting back to them. 'Hurry up, then. But I'm not carrying ya bags!'

The girls raced after him. I watched them for a while, noticing the sag of Ryan's shoulders and the way those girls knew to keep a few steps behind.

It wasn't until I was home and nestled next to Matty on the lounge that I realised I'd felt sort of unsafe all day. A knot was twisting in my guts and I was already dreading tomorrow.

'Some of those kids are rough,' I confessed to Matty. 'They scare me a bit. One boy pegged a piece of chalk across the room within the first five minutes.'

'I'll peg some chalk at him,' Matty said. 'Did you tell the Principal?'

'No, not about the chalk. But I did tell him about the Kindergarten kid who told me to eff off.'

'*What?*' Matty's face was so disbelieving it made me laugh.

'Yeah,' I said. 'This boy told me to fuck off and then he ran away. When I talked to the Principal about it, he told me I should have chased after him.'

'Chased after him?'

'Yeah,' I shrugged.

'Then what?' Matty pressed. 'You chase him, you catch him, then what?'

I shook my head. 'I don't know.'

'What did they do about stuff like this in England?' Matty yawned, picked up the remote. I watched him and realised that my reality couldn't truly be felt by him. He couldn't know the fear I felt when that chalk went crack against the wall.

'This stuff didn't happen at my school in England.'

'Well, think back to uni,' he suggested. 'What did you learn about teaching bad kids?'

I smirked, remembering the tutorial in the hall that had felt so fun and so *significant*. 'There's no such thing as bad kids,' I said. 'There's only bad behaviour.'

'Do you believe that?' Matty was flicking through channels.

'Yeah,' I said gently, thinking it through. 'I do believe it.'

'Will we watch this?' Matty gestured to the screen and I nodded, ready to forget the day. But the knot of dread had settled firmly in my stomach and I didn't sleep well that night.

Empty vessels

The next morning, as I drove into Paradise, I tried to dredge up enough courage and stamina to last the day. There are no bad kids, I reminded myself primly. There's just bad behaviour. *But what does that mean?* my thoughts raged back. *What does that mean when a kid throws something at you? Swears at you? What do you do about it?* And suddenly a memory came to me.

I was at uni, in a tute, passing notes with friends because we were immature and texting still wasn't a thing, Facebook not even invented.

Our tutor, one of the inaccessible academics, wheeled a TV out from the storeroom and started plugging in the cords. He was one of those lecturers who made abstract comments on your assignments; made you wonder if he was drunk when he wrote them. *How so?* he would write. *Interesting! But also interesting?* I doubted he'd be able to manage a class of even ten primary school kids. The only reason he was managing us was because he held the power to fail us.

'Can everybody see?' He slotted a video into the player.

'Gab!' shouted a voice from behind me. It was Davo. Big guy. Big mouth. 'Can you shove over? Ya hair's so big I can't see. Ya hair's like pubes. Anyone ever told you that?'

I turned to glare, but we were all laughing.

The video started. It was footage of a group of children aged about ten. A woman, presumably a teacher, was working with them. She was dressed in a particularly fetching beige twin piece, circa 1970s. My friend Cath giggled.

'I might wear that for prac next week,' she whispered.

We watched as the children worked through their activity. It looked like reading groups, with books and worksheets and a cassette player with headphones. Suddenly, one of the boys picked up the tape player.

'This fucking tape player doesn't work!' he shouted, lifting the player over his head like he was going to throw it.

Our lecturer pressed pause. The boy was suspended onscreen, tape player overhead. In the background, I could see the teacher, a blurry, beige blob, stage right.

'What a little shit,' I heard Davo say.

'Now,' said the lecturer, rubbing his hands together, 'I want you to write down how you would respond. What would you do?'

'It wouldn't happen in my classroom,' Cath whispered. 'The kids in my class would know you weren't allowed to swear.'

I filled a page describing how I would sensitively and calmly remove the student from the room. I wrote about how I'd use '*I Messages*' to let the boy know that I found his language offensive: *I don't like to hear swearwords. I feel uncomfortable when people swear in the classroom. I'd like you to choose other words.* I detailed how I would direct him to our classroom rules, which had been carefully negotiated with the group at the start of the school year, and I would point to the rule that read: *We use positive words.* If the student had accrued any house points or sticker rewards, they would immediately be stripped of them. This would be done in front of the other students, sending a clear message that I didn't tolerate bad language. I concluded by suggesting an age-appropriate consequence, aligned with school policy, probably a time-out and a letter home to parents.

After a while, the lecturer asked us to share our responses. There was a range: some stricter than others, but all of them in line with the sort of stuff I had written. We would be positive but proactive, fair but firm—each of us politically correct and demonstrating our burgeoning understanding of how this thing called teaching was to be done.

The lecturer nodded, smiling in a way that was both gleeful and patronising. He pressed play on the video and we watched as the scene returned to life. The beige teacher walked to the boy and lowered the tape player.

'What's happening here?' she asked, inspecting the tape player.

'It's not fucking working,' the boy said.

'Let's see if we can figure it out.' The teacher's voice was warm with a disconcerting calmness that matched her earlier dialogue.

The lecturer stopped the video again and turned to face us. He rubbed his hands together again. Raised his eyebrows.

'Well, that's fucked!' Davo threw his pen on the desk, leaned back in his chair and looked like a Year Six kid I had been observing on prac just a week before. 'How's that kid gonna learn not to swear?'

The lecturer raised his eyebrows even further. 'That's right,' he said. 'I agree with you.'

'I'm not making a statement,' Davo insisted. 'I'm asking a question.'

I folded my arms and waited. I was with Davo on this one.

'Perhaps a better question might be . . .' The lecturer paused. 'Perhaps a better question might be: How did that child learn to swear?'

'From the playground,' someone said.

'From TV,' said someone else.

'Music.'

'Movies.'

'The internet.'

'Yes,' the lecturer said. 'And maybe he learned it at home.' He said the words carefully, slowly. *Maybe he learned it at home.* 'Maybe,' he continued, 'that child has a father who tells him every day that he's fucking useless. Maybe that child has a mother who asks him to pass the fucking vodka. Maybe that child didn't have breakfast that morning because the fucking car's broken down and they don't have enough fucking money to fix it. Maybe there's not much lunch in his fucking lunch box. Maybe the lunch he *has* got he's given to his little sister. Maybe that kid spends as much time as he can at Grandma's house because he knows she's always got a tin of tomato soup in the cupboard and he prefers the smell of cigarettes that's embedded in Grandma's carpet to the smell of drunken vomit

113

in his own house. Maybe it's just great that this kid turned up at school today. And maybe he was right. Maybe the fucking tape player didn't work.'

As his words filled the room, I felt a sudden expansion of my mind and my heart and a twisting in my gut. Tears came to my eyes.

Not every kid has had my childhood. Not every kid has a childhood.

'They're not empty vessels,' the lecturer said.

At the time it had made such perfect sense. They were not empty vessels waiting for the teacher to fill them up. They were children with lives beyond school and experiences beyond the classroom. I had left that tutorial feeling empowered. I vowed I'd be as calm as the beige lady when a student swore at me.

But I hadn't felt calm, I realised as I steered my car towards Paradise school. All day I'd been on edge, on high alert, ready for something bad to happen. And as I pulled up outside the school, I felt my heart rate kick up a notch.

'You know what?' I said out loud. 'Teachers aren't empty vessels either.'

'We need to talk about Burt Mater.'

It was Peter, his confident voice taking command of the staff meeting.

'Why?' It was the Principal, his face set in that familiar passive expression.

Bro laughed. 'Because we're sick of being told to fuck off by a five-year-old, that's *why*.'

'Well,' said the Principal, 'that five-year-old keeps our census numbers up, which affects our staff allocation and our resources. Without him we could lose Verna.' We all glanced at the door to the school's administration office, expecting Verna the office lady to still be sitting there, but it was almost five o'clock. She was long gone.

'I'm not saying we should expel him,' said Peter. 'I don't want to see the little fella go, but we need to have some boundaries, something consistent for every time he swears at us.'

'We need something consistent for *all* the students, Peter.' It was Rose, the Kindergarten teacher—the one who had to deal with Burt Mater every day. I had never seen Rose ruffled or stressed, even though I suspected her class was one of the hardest in the school. Burt Mater wasn't an aberration. Rose's class was littered with swearers and biters, fighters and liars. 'Burt should be given a consequence for his swearing, certainly,' Rose went on, her curly grey hair moving emphatically as she spoke, 'but so should Ryan, and Evan and Montana and that boy in your class.' She pointed to the Year Two teacher. 'Little guy with red hair? Came last year?'

'Mikey,' we all said, and Rose nodded.

'They all need the same consequence. I've been thinking about this,' Rose went on. 'I think we should have a three-strike policy. Three warnings, and on the fourth you're suspended. We need to be fair but firm, and we need to show these kids that we're not joking around.'

'We can't do that,' the Principal said.

'Why not?' Rose was insistent. 'We have to do something.'

'If we suspend children then it's very inconvenient for their parents,' the Principal said.

'Is it?' Rose pushed. 'I've worked it out. Only two out of my eighteen students have parents that work. These kids can have a day at home for swearing.'

'Yeah,' said Peter. 'But there's another aspect to it, Rose. You ever notice how our kids are never away? I mean, sometimes you just wish they'd stay home for the day, but they always turn up.' He shrugged. 'Even when they're sick. Even when they don't have a clean uniform.'

'Even when they don't *have* a uniform,' Bro added.

'For most of them, they come here because it's better than being at home,' Peter said.

I thought about all the times that Ryan and other kids had exploded like landmines in my classroom, ricocheting off walls with anger and fury at some small injustice. Occasionally, they stormed out of the classroom, but they never went far. I would find them later, huddled behind the sports shed, tucked up in a tree or hunched beneath the classroom window, still listening to our lesson. They could easily have left the place, the fence was low and the gates were loose, but they never did. Peter was right—they were rarely absent, even when they were coughing like pack-a-day smokers (which some of them already claimed to be).

'Okay,' Rose said. 'What if we did in-school suspensions? After their third warning, they spend a day out of their class. Perhaps they're in with you for the day?' She gestured to the Principal, who was already shaking his head.

'No,' he said. 'We can't have that. Parents will be outraged. They'll go above us and complain. They'll take their kids out of the school. Send them down the road. We'll lose numbers.' He glanced at his watch, suddenly keen to wrap up the meeting that normally dragged on until six. 'Let's all think about it and we can discuss it again next week.'

'We need to be firmer,' Rose said before anyone could leave their seats. 'These kids need it. We need to make our decisions out of love, not fear.' She gathered her diary and papers together. 'Love,' she repeated, 'not fear.' And she left the room.

'Well, Gabsie,' Bro said after a moment, 'I reckon this meeting's over. Come and have a drink?' He nodded in the direction of the pub. 'You look like you need one.'

I'm sure I must have protested, but by 6.30 p.m. I was on to my third glass of wine and holding up the bar at the Paradise Grand.

'Can you remember what I told you on the first day, Gabsie?' Bro asked. He put his schooner down, right next to the coaster.

I sighed. 'Something about relationships,' I said. The wine was sinking to my knees and tiredness was seeping through me. *How would I get home?*

'That's right,' Bro said. 'And in this town, relationships are built here.'

'At the pub?' I made a face.

'Unless you want to play football?' he said. 'That's the other place relationships are made.'

I laughed. 'No thanks.'

'I didn't think so.' He finished his drink. 'Anothery?' He reached for his wallet. 'Ah, look, here's Kilarney's dad.'

During the next hour, eight of the twelve parents from my class came through the pub. Some were just there to pick up their takeaway from the restaurant out the back. But others came and sat with me and Bro, asking how their kid was doing and talking about the football—local and national—even though the season was months from starting.

'Hope my fella's not givin' ya any trouble,' one bloke said to me. 'If he is, you just tell me and I'll give him a clip over the ear, love.' I watched as he sculled down his middie. *This is a strange parent–teacher interview,* I thought as I accepted a fresh glass of wine.

By nine o'clock everything was messy.

'We need some chips.' Bro put in an order over the counter. I didn't see any money change hands. 'The place'll clear out soon,' he said, resuming his seat.

'Why? What?' I was slurring one syllable words.

'Boats leave,' he said. 'Fishermen.' He jabbed a thumb in the direction of the wharves. 'Not a lot of dads at home in this town.'

'What's with Ryan?' I asked when the chips arrived. My words were closing together.

'Ah, that kid,' Bro said and his voice lowered, softened. 'He was abused by his stepdad. Sexual, you know? And when he spoke up about it, his mum told him to get out. Disowned him. Been in foster care since the start of Term Three last year. Poor little guy.'

I felt an awful sobriety wrap around me.

'Hard to get them in foster care round here, too,' Bro went on. 'Specially with a damaged kid like him. He's been in three different homes that I know of.'

A sense of misery began fermenting in my guts.

'Worst thing is that his little sisters are still with the mum and the stepdad. Pretty shit situation. It stresses Ryan out.'

I made my way to the bathroom; I could feel vomit surging up my throat. But, when I found a cubicle and locked myself in, the sensation had gone. I waited a moment, waited for the sickness to return and engulf me, but it didn't.

When I stepped out of the cubicle I became aware that I was in the men's. There was a bloke standing at the urinal. He glanced at me and I apologised, edging past him as quickly as I could.

'Hey,' he said as I opened the door, 'don't you teach my kid?'

The next day I nursed a hangover and struggled through my lessons.

At recess, I bunkered down in the staffroom.

'Gabsie!' Bro chortled. 'How ya feelin'?'

'I hate you,' I said and he laughed.

'It was a good night, but.'

I glared at him.

'Let me make you a coffee,' he said and busied himself at the urn. 'Here ya go. I put two sugars in.'

'Thank you.' The coffee was hot and sweet. I sipped it slowly, watching the clock as it ticked towards my duty time. 'Bro?' I said, using my most serious voice.

'Yeah, Gabsie?' He was flipping the *Telegraph* to read the sports section.

'I will give you one million dollars—cash—if you will do my playground duty for me right now.' I let myself look as pathetic and miserable as I felt.

'Ya that bad, Gabsie?'

I nodded.

'Aww, just this once,' he said. 'But don't tell Pete, okay? I still owe him about ten duties from last year.'

'Thank you,' I said, closing my eyes with relief.

The staffroom was quiet for a beat and then the change-over from first recess occurred. Rose came in, peeling off her sunhat and ruffling her hair back into shape.

'Hello, Gab,' she said, sitting down beside me. 'Phew! It was hot out there. How are you going?'

'Bit seedy today if I'm being honest. Bro took me out for a drink last night.'

'Say no more,' she said. 'I've been there and done that.' She hopped up and poured two glasses of water before resuming her place. 'This'll help you.' She sat one glass beside my coffee mug. 'I've got Panadol in my bag too, if you need it?'

'No,' I laughed. 'I'm not that bad. Tired more than anything. Thanks for this.' I picked up the glass. I glanced at the staffroom door and did a quick visual inventory. The Principal was nowhere to be seen. 'Hey, Rose?'

'Yes?'

'Do you think this school's *normal*? I mean, like, is it normal to let this kind of culture fester? Swearing at teachers and letting troubled kids just be . . . well . . . troubled?'

'I knew you were a smart girl,' Rose said. She turned her body so her knee touched mine and our space became a closed bubble. She lowered her voice just a tiny bit. 'I've taught in many schools around the world, my girl, and I've never seen anything like this. There are difficult kids here, but you can find them anywhere. But difficult kids don't have to be this difficult!'

She spoke earnestly. 'What's lacking here is *management*. This Principal is too scared to make the hard decisions. Plus, he's been out of the classroom too long. He's forgotten what it's like to be a teacher.'

'And what about kids like Ryan?' I pressed. 'Bro told me some stuff about him last night. It was stuff I should have known.' I shook my head, felt the sick feeling inside me that had nothing to do with alcohol and everything to do with Bro's disclosure.

Rose put her hand on mine. 'Those kids break your heart, my girl. There's very little we can do for them. Everything that can be done is being done.'

'But why didn't anyone tell me?' I insisted.

'Confidentiality?' Rose shrugged. 'They forgot? Someone decided it wasn't relevant for you? Who knows?'

'It just would have been nice to be told before I started teaching him, so I could be prepared, you know?'

Rose gave me a tiny grin. 'Do you think there's anything you could've done that would've prepared you for Ryan Morris?'

'Nope,' I laughed as the bell rang.

'I didn't think so!' Rose crossed her eyes and put on a goofy face. 'Come on, kid. Let's go teach them something.'

Ed

The boy who ate the squashed biscuit on my first day was Ed, one of my Year Six boys. He had the brightest smile of any kid I'd ever taught. He was curious and attentive, ready to learn about the world, about books, about Music, about Art. He was the lone AFL supporter in a school dominated by rugby league. Sometimes I worried that I wouldn't be able to keep the content flowing quickly enough for Ed, but he was self-motivated and enthusiastic. He created his own tasks when mine had petered out. He loved to draw and his artwork was detailed and intricate. I had started giving him old art supplies from the storeroom to save him the indignity of looting from the classroom rubbish bin. I even bought him chalks and pencils, telling him I'd found them at the back of the cupboard.

There was something about Ed I hadn't seen in other kids, a gritty determination and indomitable spirit. It was like he understood that school could offer him something that he wouldn't get anywhere else. And he was going to take everything on offer.

In the first few weeks of school when we were trawling through the long grass on Clean Up Australia Day, the kids started talking about their fathers and the things they did for work. Those that had a dad were telling stories about the boats they worked on. Kilarney explained that her dad was special because even though he worked on a boat he was an abalone diver and that was very different to being a fisherman.

Ed and Jerry were the two loners in my pack and they straggled behind the group, snatching up beer cans and cigarette butts with their gloved hands.

'What does your dad do?' I heard Ed ask Jerry.

'Don't have one,' Jerry said, swiping his hand down for a faded old fruit box. 'What about yours?'

I watched as Ed moved closer.

'He sells drugs,' he said quietly.

'Really?' Jerry's voice was a hush.

'Yeah.' Ed kept his eyes ahead. 'But don't tell those guys.' He nodded towards the rest of the class.

That afternoon, I asked Bro about Ed's father.

'Yep,' he confirmed. 'He works on the boats too, but he's also a dealer.' He shrugged. 'I'm amazed at what a great kid Ed is, considering his dad. He's a real rough fella, you know? Scary. Beats up his missus.' Bro shook his head. 'She tries to leave and takes the kids and they spend a fair bit of time in the women's refuge.'

'We should be able to do something,' I said.

'You know what, Gabsie? Best thing we can do for that kid is to keep him safe here at school. And make his mum feel welcome, too.'

'But what about a counsellor?'

Bro laughed. 'What's that?'

'It's just so frustrating,' I raged at Matty. 'I mean these kids need help. They need support. They need proper food to eat and clean clothes to wear. Ryan needs a secure foster home and Ed needs to know he's going to be safe when he goes home each night.'

'It's tough,' Matty agreed. 'Do you want me to cook this garlic bread?'

'Yeah, I guess.' There was aggravation in my voice, my mind a million miles from garlic bread. *How could you make someone understand what it was like to be a teacher?*

'What do you think I should do?' I asked as we sat down to eat.

Matty loaded up his fork and swallowed a mouthful. 'I dunno, babe. But I don't think you should worry so much about it.'

'Great support,' I said with sarcasm.

'No,' he said, and he put down his fork and touched my arm. 'What I mean is that it shouldn't be your problem. You shouldn't have to worry about these things. Your job is teaching. But caring for Ryan and Ed? That should be the Principal's job.'

I nodded and gave him a smile. I didn't want to fight. Matty wasn't the problem.

'I don't think it works like that though, Matty.' I tugged a piece of bread from the loaf. 'I don't think the Principal's at home right now worried about what Ed's eating for dinner and thinking up ways to better support his school experience.'

'Well, if he's not worried about it, then you shouldn't be either.'

I took a breath and discovered I was too tired to build my case against his point.

'Guess what happened to me yesterday?'

Ed always bounded into my classroom somewhere between 8.00 and 8.30 a.m.

'What happened?' I was rearranging artwork, tactfully trying to hide the penis Ryan had drawn on the display board with permanent marker.

'When I was walking home I found two dollars.'

'Did you?' I pressed a thumbtack into the corner of a painting and stepped back to ensure the scrotum was hidden.

'Yep,' he said happily. 'Just outside the post office. So, I went in to check if anybody owned it.'

I stopped pinning and smiled at him. 'That's a very honest thing to do, Ed,' I told him. 'Most people would have just kept it.'

'Well, I did get to keep it. The man at the post office said I could have it.'

'Good for you.' I nodded. 'That's because you were so honest. What'd you buy with it?'

'I went straight across the road to the supermarket and I got my mum a packet of jam fancies.' He grinned at me, his face nearly split in two with the width of his smile. 'You know the biscuits? They're her favourite.'

'That's lovely,' I said, the words coming out of me in a breathless exhale. 'Go outside and play now, mate.'

I stepped into the storeroom and felt the tears come. Jam fancies. For his mum.

On most weekends I went in to school. Sometimes I'd bring in Shirley, my golden retriever, for company. After the depressing slog of school work was finished I would walk her along the beach.

One afternoon I ran into Ed ranging along the sand with his own dog and his little brothers and baby sister. Ed was moving them along the beach slowly, stopping when his brother noticed a shell, waiting for his sister who trailed behind.

'G'day, Ed,' I said. 'Who have you got here?'

He introduced me to his siblings, dusting sand off the front of his brothers' shirts and stroking his sister's fringe aside. He hoisted the baby girl onto his hip and she smiled at me, her face lighting up just like Ed's.

'It's a nice afternoon for a walk,' I said, laughing as our dogs started playing and their leads became tangled. 'I've been up at school doing work.' I made a face.

'We walk a fair bit,' Ed said. 'It's good to get out of the house.'

We walked together, the children never complaining as the afternoon stretched. We built castles and drew in the sand

and raced the waves up and down. Ed told me stories about all the coves and caves he had discovered along the beach.

'They sound beautiful,' I said. 'I need to do some exploring.'

'I like to explore,' he said. 'When I can get out without these guys, I like to take a pencil and draw the things I see.' He grinned. 'Drawing and exploring are just two of my many hobbies.'

On Monday, he brought in some sketches, revealing them from a folder that he handled with care. The images were stunning: black-and-white scenes of the coastline, feathers on sand, seashells and waves. His work was sophisticated and delicate, beyond anything I'd ever seen a child produce.

Howdy, Gab. Thought you might like to see my latest designs.

It's an email from Ed—we've kept in touch. He's a graphic designer now and has a business in London. I click open the link and catch my breath. It's a drawing—inks, perhaps—of the ocean roiling beneath a tall ship. Clouds loom at the corners, their round, puffy shapes forming faces, wind immortalised, blowing the ship along. The picture appears technically perfect, the proportions and lines make sense, but there's character in the image, too, in the way the shapes are made to taper, and how the waves appear like mountains. I study it with awe, privileged to know this artist.

Amazing, Ed! I type my reply. You are so talented and I am so proud of you.

He replies with an email longer than anything we've ever exchanged before:

Hey Gab,

I just wanted to say I'm so glad I was taught by you. My little sister is battling through her last year of high school. She needs a teacher like you right now. You were a guide, a teacher and a friend. I remember all the things you did for me (thanks for covering my books, by the way). My childhood was such a tumultuous time. But school was my great escape and it felt more like home than anywhere else. So, thank you.

Cheers, Ed.

I reply a few days later; his message stirred feelings that I am reluctant to dwell on. I have worried about Ed over the years, berated myself for not doing more when I taught him. I send an email of thanks and promise him that I will always hold memories of him like treasure.

I close the email by asking Ed if he knows the whereabouts now of Ryan Morris. He's another one I have worried about over the years. I often wonder what became of him.

The next day Ed replies:

I'm not sure about Ryan. Last I heard he was in jail.

I close my laptop, shut down the thoughts before feelings can come, and I remind myself: *You cannot save them all.*

When you get the button

That year in Paradise felt long. The days dragged. The terms seemed to move in slow motion.

Everything felt like a battle and in hindsight I can see that I was learning more at that school than I would at any other in my teaching career. Battles reveal things about yourself, battles teach you about others, and battles help you to discover the person you want to become.

During that long year, my student Leyton was facing battles of his own. His dad was dying of cancer. In the staffroom, Peter would give us updates, but whenever I asked Leyton how his dad was going he would shrug and say, *Pretty good*. As the months went by, Leyton's behaviour changed. He would punch his mates, just joking around, but they would frown and rub their arm, saying, *Take it easy*. One day, as I dropped the class off for Library I reminded him to take his hat off.

'Stupid bitch,' he whispered.

I was set to ignore it, but Kilarney gasped and dobbed.

'Stay here with me, Leyton,' I instructed. Once the entire class had gone in, I opened my arms and he stepped into them, sobbing and sobbing and saying, *I'm sorry*. He didn't go to Library that day; he returned with me to our classroom where he kicked a soccer ball against a brick wall while I worked at my desk inside.

It was hard for me to watch Leyton's pain. I could see he was standing on the edge of an abyss, destined to fall. I had been there myself, so I knew.

Each year, at Christmas, my mum would make a traditional pudding complete with some old sixpence and a button. It was my job to wrap the coins in foil, but the button was dropped into the mix just as it was—round and brown and ugly.

'I don't want to get the button,' I confessed to Mum. 'I don't want to be an old maid.'

'You won't get the button,' Mum said.

'I want a coin,' I told her boldly. I was five or six and coins in cakes seemed magical and special.

'We'll see. Now you give it a stir for everyone in the family.'

I pushed the wooden spoon through the heavy mixture, naming each person.

'One for Mummy. One for Daddy. One for Granny.' Push. Push. Push. 'One for Anni and one for Cheryl and one for Jacqui.' Push. Push. Push. 'I'm doing two for Phil,' I told Mum. 'Cos he's my favourite.' Push. Push. 'And one for me.'

I watched as the fruit and batter moved thickly around the old bowl. I saw the glimmer of a silver coin and poked it under the mix when Mum wasn't watching.

On Christmas day, after lunch, Mum announced it was time for pudding. She sliced it in the kitchen, adding brandy butter and cream and custard. Jacqui delivered the bowls, haphazardly following Mum's instructions.

'That's your father's. And that one's for Granny.'

As each bowl was delivered, I peered over, watching for slivers of silver. A coin in your pudding would bring wealth and good luck in the year to come.

Jacqui plonked my dish in front of me. It was more custard than pudding—just the way I liked it. I picked through it, seeking treasure but finding none. All around me, my sisters were pulling coins from their mouths, unwrapping foil to reveal their bounty.

Despairing, I put the last of the pudding in my mouth. I could feel tears welling, but I pushed them down and tried to be a big girl.

And then I felt it! The roundness and the hardness. I grinned and felt my tears subside. Triumphant, I pulled it from mouth and was horrified to see the ugly brown button.

'You got the button!' Jacqui shouted.

'That's not right,' Mum frowned and inspected my bowl. 'That was meant to be for Granny.'

'You're going to be an old maid,' Jacqui told me. 'No one's going to marry you.'

'Yes, they are,' Mum said, reaching across and grabbing the button from my hand. She pressed it firmly into Granny's pudding.

'Old maid,' Jacqui whispered and I started to sob.

'Come here.' It was Phil. He pushed his chair back from the table and pulled me onto his lap. I cuddled into him, felt the strength of his chest and the security of his arms. He held me for a while until the hiccupping had stopped.

'I don't want to be an old maid,' I told him mournfully.

'You won't be an old maid,' he said. 'I will marry you.'

It was a hard, cruel shock when Phil killed himself.

I was in Year Eight and two weeks away from turning thirteen. He had been missing for a day and Mum had stayed awake all night, sitting by the phone while Dad had been out searching.

I had been called out of my class and asked to wait in the Assistant Principal's office. She smiled at me thinly and I tried to smile back.

Where's my brother? I wanted to ask.

My sister Cheryl came and collected me. We sat in her car together.

'He shot himself,' she told me and I asked, 'Is he dead?'

'Yeah,' she said. 'He's dead.'

And it felt like I had died too. I became a different person right there in the car with my sister moaning beside me.

'Gab, you're wanted on the phone.'

Dad's face had changed. Everything had changed. Everything was stained and wrinkled and browned with grief. He handed me the phone.

'Hello, Gabrielle.' It was Mrs Dee, my English teacher. The fleck of little girl still left inside me felt a jolt of shock. *My teacher's on the phone.* 'I wanted you to know that I'm thinking of you and your family.' She paused. 'And I also wanted to say something especially to you, Gabrielle.' She paused again. 'There is only one way you're going to get through this.'

I pressed the phone hard against my ear. *Tell me,* I thought. *Tell me what I'm meant to do.*

'You have to write,' she said. 'You're a writer and so you have to write. You need to get a book and write down what you're feeling and what's happening. You have to write through it. Do you have a book?'

'Yes,' I told her.

'Good. Write through it.'

She hung up without wanting to speak to my parents. She had rung just for me.

I found a notebook. Hardcover. Blue. With outlines of clouds.

And I wrote.

When I returned to school, two weeks later, I felt nervous and anxious and sick in my guts. I was ready for questions and for rumours. I was ready for curious interest in me and my brother and my family. And, although I was dreading it, I was craving it too—I needed my worlds to align: this family world that was all broken and changed needed to be reconciled with my school world that was so safe and secure and predictable.

But there was nothing.

I stood at assembly, body clenched, waiting for my brother to be named as we prayed for those who had died. But there was nothing.

All day I waited for a call from the office. Surely I would be called up so the teachers could say something to me. My world had changed and my teachers would want to talk to me about that. This was my school. My school. I loved school.

But there was nothing.

I went home on the bus that afternoon, still paralysed by grief and now confounded with delusion. It was the first time I had felt let down by school, disappointed by the place that usually gave me such hope. *You have to say something,* I thought. *When something like this happens, you have to say something.* I wondered if my teachers hadn't *seen* me. Couldn't they see that I had died as well? Couldn't they see that I knew things now that some people never know?

Days later I was treading water in a double period of Art. Grief had broken something in me and I felt I was reading from a script at school: saying my lines and playing along and taking my cues from my friends. But inside I kept thinking things over and over, circular thoughts that were endless and unproductive.

He's dead. None of this matters.

Over and over. The same thoughts.

Bad things happen. People you love die.

Over and over.

It doesn't matter how much you love someone. People leave.

My teacher, Mrs Payton, came over to me. She leaned down close. 'I have something for you,' she whispered. 'It's in my office.' She gestured with a nod to the back of the Art room and a tiny childish part of me thought, *Phil? Are you hiding Phil back there?*

But then she went on to say, 'It's bright and colourful and it's wrapped in yellow with a purple bow.'

My heart, which had fluttered with little-girl hope, sat unmoving in the cavity of my chest. *It couldn't be Phil.* I made myself walk to the back of the Art room and through a door I had never entered before. On a desk that was covered with papers and artworks and folders and boxes of charcoals, there was an enormous bunch of flowers. Bright and colourful and wrapped in yellow with a purple bow.

'They're just for you,' Mrs Payton said quietly. 'From me. I wanted to do something.'

I have often thought of those flowers in my life and in my teaching. The way Mrs Payton made me feel has stayed with me. I knew that she had *seen* me and my pain and her response was to show me something of herself.

Suicide's a tricky, tricky thing—I understand that better than most. My adult self, my teacher self, can see how Phil's death presented an impossible ambiguity for my Catholic high school in that little country town in the year 1990. But Mrs Dee and Mrs Payton got it right, and I'm forever grateful for that.

As the year crawled along in Paradise, Leyton started hanging around the classroom after school.

'Mum said I can hang out here,' he said one day, 'and help you.'

'Okay,' I said. 'I just have to do something at the office. Can you please sort these out for me?'

I rang his mum. She apologised, said she never told him he could stay at school, said she was worried when he hadn't arrived home. I suggested that we might go up the street to have a milkshake. Then I'd run him home. She agreed, her voice thin and laced with sadness.

'Just don't wanna go home,' he confessed at the cafe. I nodded and told him that my brother had died just a week before my thirteenth birthday.

'Whoa,' he said. 'That sucks.'

'Yeah,' I nodded.

'It's weird at home,' he said.

'I know. I can remember one day, after Phil died, when Mum forgot to collect me from the bus stop. It was only a kilometre walk, but I was pretty angry, you know?'

Leyton nodded.

'But then I got inside the house and all I could smell was vanilla. Mum had made all these patty cakes and they were all over the bench, falling onto the floor. Hundreds of them, Leyton. She'd iced them in pink and dusted them with coconut. And she was sitting there in the middle of the mess, crying. *I made his favourite*, she kept saying. *I made him patty cakes.*' I stopped talking as I felt the choke of tears.

Leyton nodded and then said, 'I think my whole family's gone mad.'

We sat there for a moment, a comfortable pause holding our thoughts of sadness, of home. Then we talked about music and soccer and funny things that had happened at school. We blew bubbles in our milkshakes and watched them overflow.

The next morning, Leyton came into the classroom before the bell. 'I've got this for you,' he said, presenting me with a cupcake, small and neatly iced just like the patty cakes my mum had made. 'My sister was making them when I got home last night and I thought of you.'

'Thanks, mate,' I said and I set my jaw, determined.

And then, a few nights later, he rang me at home.

'He died,' Leyton said, a voice full of defeat. 'He died a few hours ago.'

I told him I was sorry and I would pray for him and that his dad's suffering had finished now. I think I told him that I loved him.

'Everyone's making phone calls,' he said. 'I wanted to ring you.'

Leyton came to school the next day. I wasn't expecting him, but his mum dropped him off and said, 'He wanted to come, to be here with his mates, and he wanted to see you.' I hugged her, while Leyton's classmates gathered round him, kicking at the grass and saying, *Heard about ya dad* and *It's pretty shit*.

I could see that Leyton's face had changed. There was a weariness on his temple and a tension in his jaw. His eyes told me that he knew something now, an adult thing, that children shouldn't have to know.

I bailed up Bro in the staffroom just minutes before the bell. 'We have to do something,' I told him. 'We can't . . .' I started to cry. 'We can't do *nothing*.'

'That's really bad grammar, Gabsie,' Bro said, putting his arm around me. 'I'll take your class and mine for an hour. You get something ready.'

When Bro brought the classes into my room, they found it darkened, lit with candles and quiet music playing. The desks had been shoved aside and we sat in a circle on the floor.

'We all knew Leyton's dad,' I said, 'so we all feel sad, Leyton especially.' I glanced at Leyton who was sitting across from me. He was flanked by his best mates. He kept his head down as I spoke. 'I thought we might do a picture for Leyton, or write him a letter. Yes?'

The students nodded.

We shared out paper and coloured pencils and a box of tissues. The kids sprawled out on the carpet and worked on their pages for the longest time. Eventually, as they finished, they began to share their gifts with Leyton, reading aloud what they had written, or giving him their picture and sharing their memories, offering their sorrow.

I was last and I crawled across the space to Leyton, dragging my picture with me. I had drawn a bunch of flowers. Bright and colourful, wrapped with yellow and tied with a purple bow.

I sat in front of Leyton and said, 'When my brother died, one of my teachers gave me a bunch of flowers just like this. When he died I thought it was the worst thing that could ever happen. But I've realised that good things come from bad and because he died I've been able to . . . um . . .'

I never got to finish that sentence because Leyton leaned forward, rested his forehead against mine and together we cried.

Whenever I go to Paradise now, taking my own kids there for fish and chips, or to watch the whales, or for a swim at the beach, I find that I remember the place with a fierce and loyal affection. I tell my girls about the men who work on those fishing boats and the time they spend away from their families. I tell them about the local Aboriginal people I know and their achievements in footy and the arts. I tell them about the whales I rushed to see from the viewing platform right near the school. I tell them about the students I taught, the parents I met, the teachers I worked with; the bonds that I made.

That year in Paradise, that long year, was also the year I got married. I walked down the aisle grinning like a Cheshire cat while Matty waited nervously at the altar. I planned the whole wedding and honeymoon to fall neatly within the Term One holidays. I was ready for Term Two without even missing a beat.

That was also the year we bought our first house. It was a little three-bedder with views of the beach in a town near Paradise. The place needed work and when I wasn't at school I was with Matty, painting walls and installing a kitchen and pruning a garden that was well overgrown. We were settling into domestic life. We made plans and cooked meals and walked Shirley together.

All these things were happening in my personal life, a life that seemed to run parallel to my teaching life. And when I think back on that year, that long year in Paradise, I know that it was teaching that took the better part of me.

Building a school

I'm traversing the Woolies carpark with Olivia and Sophie chattering endlessly around me. My mind is on dinner, maybe gnocchi or sausages.

'Mum!' Livvy says. 'Mum?'

'What darlin'?'

'That man's waving at you.' She points to a guy, late twenties, who's sitting in a Commodore.

'Mrs Stroud!' he calls and stretches a tattooed arm out the window as though drawing me closer. 'You wouldn't remember me.' He's wearing a cap and I don't recognise him until he gives a tiny smile.

'Anthony! How are you?' I pull my kids along. They're quiet now, unsure.

'Yeah, not bad.' He shrugs, produces a cigarette and lights it.

'What've you been doing with yourself?' I study his face. I had taught him more than fifteen years ago. He'd been a very quiet student, almost an elective mute.

'Not much,' he gives a half-hearted laugh. 'But I am working, Mrs Stroud. I'm doing something.'

'Good on you, Ant. I'm so happy to hear that. I'm proud of you.'

He beams. 'Do you still teach at St Peter's?'

'No,' I shake my head with a smile. I want to tell him more, give him a picture of where I am in my life, but it suddenly feels so hard. Ant seems to understand, though. He drags on his cigarette and nods slowly, as if I've given him a much longer answer.

We say our goodbyes and I move my girls along, tugging at Sophie who is hopping instead of walking.

'How do you know that guy?' Olivia asks.

'I taught him, ages ago, at St Peter's.'

'He didn't think you'd remember him,' Liv squeezes my hand. 'But you did!'

'Yep.'

'He smokes,' Sophie announces. 'You should have taught him not to smoke, Mum.'

I agree with her and we walk into the supermarket.

As we trawl through mundane aisles, I can feel my heart glowing. It's the same feeling every time a student I've taught stops me to say hello. I feel like a candle that's just been lit.

A new school was opening, St Peter's, a Catholic secondary school in a town north of Paradise and closer to where I lived.

'I think I'm going to apply,' I told Bro one afternoon as we studied the advertisement in the local paper.

'Good for you, Gabsie,' he said. 'They'd be lucky to have you. But we'll miss you here.'

I read the advertisement again and tried not to hold my breath. The thought of another year in Paradise was debilitating. I couldn't fathom another twelve months of constant worry and frustration, while dysfunction and poverty festered around me. I needed to get out.

A week later I rushed into Bro's classroom. 'I've got an interview,' I said. 'At the end of next week.'

'That's great, Gabsie, but we're on camp next week.' Bro shook his head. 'How will that work?'

'I told them about camp when they rang. They said I can do my interview late Friday when I get back.'

'So, straight off the bus and into a job interview?'

'Yep!' I could feel myself shining with hopefulness.

I arrived in a tracksuit with dirty hair. The panel, almost glossy in their appearance, assured me that they understood. Their questions were typical: *What can you bring to the position? Tell us about your experience. In the cycle of teaching, what is the most important element?* I rambled through my answers, delirious with fatigue and the smell of carsick still clinging to me; I had held the bag for three vomiters.

'And what do you teach?' It was a question from Paul—the man who would be Principal of this brand-new school.

'Um . . .' I wondered if it was a trick question. 'Children?'

142

The panel laughed.

'No, no,' Paul said. 'What subjects do you teach?'

'I'm primary trained, so I know all the syllabuses,' I said. 'I suppose I'd like English the most. It was my understanding the school would begin with just Year Seven. I'd have to do more study if I were to stay on and teach, you know, Years Eleven and Twelve in the years to come.'

The panel smiled and dismissed me.

Paul rang me later that evening. 'How does English sound?' he asked. 'And Human Society and Its Environment? I was also thinking Maths and Religion and Music?'

'It sounds great,' I said with a voice so calm he would never have detected I was dancing in my pyjamas. Paradise was behind me now. The fighting and the swearing and the emotional workload. I was about to be a foundation staff member. I was going to build a school.

'Again, I'd like to thank you for coming in to school before your contracts have commenced.' Paul's voice bounced around the space that would become the Art room. 'I know this is unpaid time. But we have so much to get through, and our school and our students will benefit from the work we do this week.' He sat down in a camping chair—the furniture still hadn't arrived. 'Let's begin by introducing ourselves.'

The guy sitting in the deck chair opposite me stood up. 'I'm Mick and I'm English and History.'

'I'm Rachael and I'm PE.'

'I'm Gerry and I'm IT and a bit of Food Tech, just for this year.'

I told them I was Gabbie and that I'd been teaching at Paradise, down the road.

'Bit different clientele there, I reckon?' said Mick.

I smiled at him and shrugged. My students weren't clients.

'What subjects?' Rachael asked.

I recited my list: 'English, Maths, Religion, HSIE and Music.'

'Holy shit!' Rachael said. 'You Superwoman?'

'No,' I said quickly. 'I'm a primary teacher.'

'Oh,' they all said, and I couldn't miss their tone. Like I'd just made a hole in the rowboat we were sharing.

'Thanks, everybody,' Paul said when the circle of introductions was complete. 'And, now, if I can get you to come over here.' He moved to a trestle table and hauled onto it a cylinder of butcher's paper, rolling it out like a long, narrow tablecloth. 'Everybody take a marker and I want you to start writing down all the dreams you have for our school and our students.'

I glanced at Rachael whose eyebrows had nearly jumped off her face. I watched as she reached for a texta and yanked off the lid.

'Dreams?' she said, her tone dubious.

'Yes!' Paul said. 'What do you hope to achieve here? What do we believe about teaching? And what do we believe about learning?'

I took a texta and tried to think of something I might contribute. At uni I had been so good at these activities, but my few years of teaching seemed to have shoved me into no-man's-land. I had lost confidence in things I thought I knew and I had questions around things I had once blindly accepted. *What did*

I believe about teaching and learning? And, more importantly, *why did it matter what I thought?*

We stood impotently around the paper, each of us looking at the grainy blank canvas rolled out before us.

'I'll start.' Paul scrawled a few words in the centre of the page. His handwriting was illegible.

'What's it say?' Rachael asked, squinting and frowning and turning her head to one side.

'We don't give up on kids. That's important to me. I want every student who walks in this door to know that we're invested in them.'

Rachael raised her eyebrows again and nodded. 'Okay,' she said. 'So, you don't want us to tell you pedagogical theories and teaching approaches and stuff?'

'No.' Paul capped the marker. 'I want to know what's in *here*.' He tapped his heart. 'What do you know about teaching and learners and learning and teachers? That's what I'm interested in.'

Rachael leaned over the page and in perfect printed script she wrote: *We create lifelong learners.*

'I love it!' Paul said. 'What else?'

'Well, I think respect—respect can underpin everything,' Mick said. 'Self-respect, respect for others, respect for rules, respect for property.'

'Great! Write it down,' Paul said.

'*Ohhhh*,' Mick said in a kind of drawl that would soon become familiar. 'I think Rachael can write for me. My handwriting's worse than yours, Paul.'

We all laughed then and Rachael began to write.

'What about you, Gab?' Paul prompted. 'You haven't said much.'

I knew what I wanted to say, but it was so simple I didn't want to sound trite. I could imagine Bro winking at me as I thought of it. *Just say it*, I berated myself.

'It's all about relationships,' I said, then hastily tried to dress it up. 'Effective teaching relies on healthy relationships—'

'Stop there!' Paul said. '*It's all about relationships*. That's all that needs to be said. Write that down, Rachael.'

Told ya. Bro's voice sounded in my head.

'Okay.' Paul surveyed the broadsheet, now brimming with our ideas and feelings and sentiments about teaching. 'Do you see what we have here now?' He held the sheet up, and it trembled and folded with his touch.

'A whole heap of ideas?' Gerry suggested.

'A brainstorm?' Mick said.

'Evidence of a touchy-feely activity?' Rachael's sceptical tone made me grin.

'More than that,' Paul said. 'Now we have the vision. We can see here what we believe. This activity has answered all our questions. It becomes our map and our guide. When something comes up for us—and things will come up—we can go back to this and remember what we believe. We have already decided on these fundamental things. *We don't give up on kids, we value respect, we create lifelong learners, we foster relationships.* It's all here.' He shook the paper and it sounded dangerously fragile, like it could rip down the middle at any moment.

'It's a map?' Mick said, folding his arms. 'Just as well we got Rachael to scribe. It's very neat.'

'If he makes us write one more thing on a sheet of butcher's paper, I'm going to pin him down and draw glasses on his face with his stupid permanent markers.' Rachael wrangled her deck chair into submission and slumped into it, opening her laptop moments later. 'I just want to get my programs written,' she said. 'All this warm fuzzy stuff is great, but if we don't have programs then what the hell are we teaching?'

'Yeah,' I agreed, perching on a wobbly stool. I wished I had a laptop I could tap away at with teacherly efficiency.

'I'm more worried about the furniture,' Mick said, joining our group. 'It'd be nice to know we had desks and chairs. Be good to have our rooms set up.'

'They'll be here,' Paul assured us as he walked in. 'Now, today I thought we'd really spend some time getting to know each other.'

'Oh, excellent,' I heard Rachael mutter.

Paul gave each of us a Post-it note and placed a pile of coloured pencils on the table.

'I want you to tell us where you are with teaching right now,' he said. 'How you came to be here. And on the Post-it, I want you to draw a symbol that represents your story.'

Beside me, Rachael gave a sigh that was really a thinly disguised groan.

'Okay,' I said, when it was my turn to stand out the front and tell my story. 'I've tried to draw a seed cracking open to become a seedling. I've only been teaching for two years so that's why I'm just like a seedling. But, also, I've found the past two years really . . . challenging. I suppose, if I'm honest, I'm hoping that this year will be easier, and I might be able to really develop myself as a teacher—sort of grow, you know?'

I added my image to the wall where others had already posted theirs.

'Mine's blank,' Rachael announced. 'I've been typing up my program while you guys were drawing. I like to be organised.' She pressed her note against the wall. 'And that's my story, too. I like to get things done.'

'Thanks, Rachael,' Paul said. 'Mick?'

Mick stood and held his note up so we could see. He had drawn two concentric circles.

'A funny thing happened to me the other day,' he said. 'I took my boys to ride their bikes at the old racecourse down the road. That's it here.' He pointed to the circles. 'Anyway, we were halfway round, and my youngest son, he just stopped. It was getting kind of dark and the temperature was cooling and there's very long grass there; you can't see too far ahead. It had an eerie sort of feel. And my son says to me, "Dad, I don't want to go on." And I said to him, "But mate, we're halfway. There's no point turning around."' Mick cleared his throat and touched a finger to his glasses, pressing them into the bridge of his nose. 'And that's my story.'

'That's quite profound,' Paul said.

'Is it?' Mick laughed.

I watched as he pressed the sticky note into place beside my picture of the seedling. I would soon learn that Mick's stories often had no point but for me, on that day, the story of his son feeling stuck on a racetrack resonated within me. I knew exactly what his kid was feeling: that sense of being scared to go on yet unable to go back. It was exactly how I felt about teaching. I wondered if Mick felt the same way.

Beautiful, beautiful arseholes

The students arrived. Seventy Year Seven kids who seemed to always be looking around the vast campus, wondering when everyone else would arrive.

'You are paving the way,' Paul told them at assembly. 'You are leaders, building a school alongside your teachers.' They looked at him with adolescent nonchalance. *If you say so*, their slumped shoulders seemed to say.

It felt strange to me, teaching different clusters of students at different times of the day. It was not like primary school where you seemed to be suspended in conversation with the same students day after day. The timing was a shock as well—I had to learn to watch the clock, ready to dismiss them after fifty-two minutes or face the wrath of Rachael when her PE class arrived late.

There was one group of students I saw frequently: my

home group. I taught them for at least three periods every day. As their home-room teacher it was my job to check in on their welfare and well-being. I called them 'my team' and we shared jokes on a Friday and riddles on a Monday. I nagged them about assignments and wearing hats and using manners. They asked me where I'd bought my shoes and if we could play music while they worked.

Within that group was a girl called Billie, completely unexceptional except for the disfigurement of her face. Before St Peter's opened, her parents had met with me, sharing their hopes for a fresh start and happier days for their daughter.

'I don't think she's really even got a friend,' Billie's mum said while her husband rubbed her shoulders. 'We just want her to feel happy and safe.'

Billie had been bullied relentlessly in her last school. Her face was stained red—a capillary malformation that blotched across her skin from her lower left jaw up to her right eyebrow. It was a strange, leaky shape, like red wine had been splashed over her face. It looked almost painful.

Billie had come from a local primary school, the same one many of the Year Seven students had attended. Despite the new school, new uniforms and new teachers, the same teasing, taunts and torments had found their way to St Peter's. Paul delivered endless Teacher Speeches about starting something new and being like Christ and overlooking difference. But Billie still sat alone to eat, still walked with me when I was on yard duty, still spent most of her free time in the Library.

I tried to tackle the problem in class. I had the students work cooperatively. I mixed their table seatings around. I did lessons on valuing diversity and gave them projects where they had to interview another student and report back to the group. I allocated Billie's interview to a student name Clara.

Clara was, as Rachael described her, one of the Beautiful Girls. 'Every school has them,' Rachael explained. 'It's easy to think of them as the popular kids, but what it's really about is their beauty. Notice how Clara has started wearing makeup?'

'No!' I shook my head.

'Yeah, bit of foundation, bit of mascara,' Rachael went on. 'And notice how they get the bright, sunny seat on the edge of the playing field?'

'But that's just a place where they sit,' I said.

'You can see the whole playground from there. Prime real estate. You can watch the boys play soccer, see who goes into the Library, you walk past that seat to get to the toilets. It's a mission control location.'

'That's a warped way of looking at it.'

'I've got no evidence to back it up,' Rachael admitted. 'It's definitely a personal theory, but I'm just saying Clara's a beautiful girl and as such she's powerful.'

'Well, I think Clara *is* a beautiful girl,' I said. 'But only beautiful in the real sense of the word. And I have doubts about your theory, although I do think it's funny.'

Rachael shrugged. 'Like I said, there's no science behind it.'

'Well, I've paired Billie and Clara up for the Getting to Know You Project. Maybe, once Clara gets to know Billie, she'll invite Billie to join them at mission control.'

'That's a bad idea,' Rachael said. 'Switch Billie to a different partner.' Rachael scooted her chair over to my desk and tried to look at the list of students I had paired.

'No,' I said, shaking my head. 'I'm not changing it.'

'Mrs Stroud?' It was Clara, timidly knocking at my office door.

'Come in, Clara,' I said. 'Sit down.'

Clara sat and then pointed to a picture I had pinned above my desk.

'Is that your dog, Shirley?' she asked with a grin. 'You should totally bring her in one day. The whole class would love to meet her. She could be our class mascot. Our team mascot!'

'I think I will,' I said. 'Maybe I'll get my husband to drop her off at lunchtime and she can just have the afternoon with us.'

At her desk nearby, Rachael gave a sigh. Then she stood and yanked open the filing cabinet. There was a scraping sound, metal on metal, as she sorted pages into their folders.

'Is everything okay, Clara?' I leaned forward, trying to be warm and approachable.

'Yeah, I just wanted to talk to you about the Getting to Know You Project . . .'

'Mmm.' I leaned back. Earlier that day I had issued the task and assigned the partners.

'You put me with Billie. And, don't take this the wrong way, I think Billie's a great girl—I've known her since preschool—but, the thing is, I know her really well and . . .' Clara looked at me and suddenly I could see it, clear as anything, a tideline of foundation around her chin. 'The thing is I have tried to get along with Billie. I have tried to like her and be her friend. But'— Clara looked down at her hands, as though she had something difficult to say—'we just don't get along. And before you say anything, Mrs Stroud, this has nothing to do with her face.'

Rachael slammed the filing cabinet drawer shut. She stood behind Clara and glared at me—her expression clear. *I told you so.*

'Right,' I said, carefully. 'I'm not sure what you really want from me, Clara. The assignment asks you to interview someone and get to know them. It doesn't require you to make friends with them.'

'But I already *know* her,' Clara said.

'So try to find out something new,' I said. 'That's what a good journalist would do.'

'You won't swap my partner?' Clara's tone had changed. I was being challenged.

'No,' I said firmly. 'And I'm disappointed that you've even asked.'

Clara smirked at me then and I felt something rise up inside me that was ugly and childish. As she left the room, Rachael held the door open for her.

'Remove that makeup,' Rachael said to her. 'Don't wear it again.' When she shut the door she looked at me. 'I was never one of the Beautiful Girls.'

The Getting to Know You Project went on seemingly without incident for three lessons. And then, on Friday, I left the staffroom at the end of lunch to find Billie being escorted into the office by Mick. She was crying and her uniform was splattered with mud, like she'd done a few rounds of paintball. Her face was smeared with dirt and I could see a little chunk of soil clinging to her fringe. I reached out my hand to dust it away and Billie flinched.

'What happened?' I asked, but Mick shook his head. He ushered Billie into the sick bay where admin staff took over. Stepping outside, he closed the door and talked to me quietly.

'I was on duty and one of the kids kicked a ball and it hit another boy in the face and his nose started bleeding. By the time I got him down to the office and dealt with the kid who did the kicking, there was a funny feeling in the main yard. Sounds crazy, but I've experienced it before. This kind of tribal thing. I could see almost all the kids grouped together down there on the bottom corner. They didn't seem to be doing anything. Then I saw Billie and she was trying to cross the yard, but every time she moved, these kids were throwing dirt at her— you know the soil that was dug up last week for the new garden beds? They were just grabbing it and pegging it at her. She was bailed up like a bloody dog against the fence.' He shook his head, pulled off his glasses and pinched at the space between his eyes. 'Arseholes.'

I could feel my heart accelerating, rage snapping at my jaw and tugging at my fists.

'Where was Clara?' I asked, already walking away.

'Oh, she wasn't part of it,' Mick said. 'She was just sitting there, watching.'

I slammed the classroom door so hard that a row of textbooks fell off the shelf.

'Sit down,' I growled at the student who attempted to dash forward and collect them.

I stood at the front of the room, folded my arms. 'Who saw what went on at lunchtime?'

Hands shot into the air.

'It was awful,' one kid started to say, but I cut her off.

'Don't talk,' I snapped. I took a breath, tried to control the smoke and the steam and the fire. 'Put your hand up if you threw dirt at Billie?' I glared, staring each one down until many had raised their hands and lowered their gazes. I counted twelve, and I felt control slip away.

'Twelve arseholes!' I announced. But I didn't stop. 'Now raise your hand if you saw it happening, if you sat there while Billie had dirt and mud thrown at her while she tried to cross the playground?'

More hands were raised.

'You're arseholes, too,' I said. 'Because if you see it and you don't stop it, you're just as bad.' I was going to cry, I could feel it, so I moved to my desk and sat down.

'I wouldn't treat my dog like that. Now we're just going to sit here and think about what you've done.'

I swiped at a tear, furious that it had escaped. Then I felt anger subside and reality returned.

What did I just say?

I stayed in my office until 5.30 p.m., waiting for Paul to call me down to his office and tell me that I was fired. No call came. Eventually I gathered my courage and my marking and made to leave the building. Paul was waiting for me at the front door.

'Mrs Stroud,' he said in the singsong way he reserved for our after-hours banter.

He doesn't know, I thought.

'Hey, Paul,' I said. *Just tell him, just say it and be done with it.*

'I've just had a phone call,' he said.

Here it comes: the end of my brilliant teaching career.

'Yep,' I said, my voice a yelp.

'At St Peter's,' he said gently, 'we don't call our students arseholes, no matter how bad their behaviour has been.'

'I'm sorry.' I sniffed, my eyes brimming. 'But what they did to Billie made me so mad. I lost control of what I was saying. Will I lose my job?' I swallowed hard, holding tight to the sobs.

'No.' He reached out and put his arm around me. 'I won't let that happen. Anyway,' he said, glancing at his watch, 'it's nearly six. And I've only had one call. Sometimes things like this don't get the reaction we anticipate. Sometimes kids cop it on the chin—especially when they know they did the wrong thing.'

'Which parent called?'

'Clara's mother,' he said, and I rolled my eyes. 'But she said Clara begged her not to ring. I could hear Clara crying in the background.'

'I'm sorry, Paul,' I said again.

'What for?' he asked. 'For being human? For having compassion? For wanting your students to stand up and be all they can be?'

'How's Billie?'

'Hard to know for sure. I'll call round to her house when I leave. You go home now,' Paul said. 'Try not to worry about it. You did the right thing, you just used the wrong word.'

'What word should I have used?'

Paul smiled. 'I'm not sure.'

The next day, I received letters. Not letters of complaint from the parents. They were letters of apology from the students.

'I'm sorry,' each said as they handed it over.

When they had all taken a seat in front of me, I bundled the notes together and thanked them.

'But you know,' I said softly, 'it's not me you should be apologising to.'

A few nodded and one child held up an envelope and said, 'I've written something to Billie as well.'

'Okay,' I said, smoothing my hands down my shirt. 'I want to say I'm sorry, too. I should never have called you . . . *that* name.' The words came out stilted and I realised that deep inside I probably wasn't as sorry as I should have been. 'The Principal wants to meet with everyone at recess today. There needs to be consequences.'

Again, there was nodding, combined with nervous glances.

'It was pretty bad, wasn't it?' one kid said.

'Yes, team, it was,' I said.

Clara raised her hand. 'I've never seen a teacher cry before,' she said. 'I felt really bad. I hope you know I'm really sorry.'

Her mascara was smeary; perhaps she'd shed a tear as well.

'The thing is, Clara,' I said, 'you don't just say sorry, you have to show you're sorry. Otherwise it's just words.'

That year, the act of teaching felt almost incidental. A brand-new school meant brand-new work. We had to create policies that would form the school's foundation. Discipline. Assessment. Safety. Uniform. Pastoral Care. Enrolment. Shelves in the Library were filled with folders, each carefully labelled. Policies. Procedures. Mission. Vision. Enrolments. Excursions.

I would arrive at seven most mornings to chip away at a document until the students started flooding through the doors.

'Ever done this before?' Mick asked me early one day as we sipped coffee and pillaged other schools' documents for truths that could become our own.

'Nope,' I said. 'It's a lot of work.'

We looked at each other with the same expression: *Why the hell did we agree to this?*

'Hey, Mick?'

'Yeah.'

'Do you remember that story you shared in the first week we were here? The one about your son on his bike? On the racetrack?'

Mick shrugged. 'Nah, not really. I tell a lot of stories, Gab.'

We laughed.

'Nah, it was a good story, Mick,' I said. 'It was exactly how I feel about teaching. I'm too far invested to turn around and study something different. But I can't seem to feel excited about the future. It's just so much work.'

'Yep,' Mick took a slug of coffee. 'And it seems to me that the workload never ends.'

We resumed our typing, squinting at screens that were flooded by sunlight. The blinds still hadn't been installed.

'It's 8.40,' I said eventually. 'We should stop.'

Mick gathered up his paperwork. 'You're right, you know? Teaching is like being stuck on that racetrack. That's a good metaphor, Gab.'

'I think it was your metaphor, Mick.' I grinned at him.

'Was it?' He scratched at his head. 'Like I said, I tell a lot of stories.'

Our staff meetings ran late and we watched the darkness come and the stars appear while we planned the swimming carnival and parent–teacher interviews and open day and the first annual fundraiser. We attended the inaugural every-thing—board meeting, parish meeting, parents and friends meeting. Sometimes it felt like we weren't a group of teachers but a representative sports team, training and touring like we might one day make it to the grand final.

As the inaugural Year Seven group of St Peter's morphed into Year Eight students, their innocence and eagerness became tainted with hormones. I didn't know if I had the tenacity to do battle with their angst every day. I also knew that if I was to stay in secondary teaching I would have to do further study. It would be arrogant to presume I could go on to teach at higher levels without adequate training. Plus, there was still so much 'new school' work to be done. Existing policies would need to be extended and new policies developed. Excursions would need to be planned. Elective subjects considered. The reporting template required consolidation. A website should be created. I could see a future ahead of me where I drowned in study and 'administrivia'.

'Let's travel,' I suggested to Matty. There had been a teacher exchange leaflet kicking around the staffroom. I had brought it home and we looked at it together.

'Let's go to Canada,' I said. The idea filled me with excitement, but it wasn't the prospect of travelling that had thrilled me. It was the idea of getting away, escaping the workload that was heavy and relentless.

We did our homework, saved our dollars and filled in the application. Towards the end of the year, I had secured a twelve-month position in Toronto. We would fly into Pearson International Airport on Boxing Day.

Paul was disappointed. We were sitting in his office, a packet of chocolate biscuits stretched open between us. I knew that I would miss Paul. We had established a close, collegial relationship. I understood his vision for this school he was building and I had great respect for him as a Principal, even though we were very much just like friends.

'I need to go back to primary,' I said. 'And I love travelling.'

He frowned as he leaned back in his chair. 'It's like you're seeking something,' he said. 'You're searching.'

I shrugged, too exhausted to psychoanalyse myself. I just wanted to hand over my letter of resignation. I wanted red wine and a big bowl of spaghetti bolognaise.

'Maybe I am searching,' I said eventually. 'I don't think so, though.'

'Sometimes when you're searching for something you need to stay in the same place,' he said.

'You reckon?' I took a biscuit and slid my resignation letter along the desk. 'Maybe I'll find it in Canada.'

He gave a wry smile. 'You're being flippant, Mrs Stroud.'

'I'm sorry, Paul. But I just feel the need to move on.'

'Will you come back to us? Back to St Peter's?'

'No,' I told him. 'I want to go back to primary school. I hope you understand.'

He nodded slowly then steepled his fingers under his chin. '*I teach children.*' He waited. 'Do you remember telling me that?'

I shook my head.

'Your job interview, for this position. I asked you what you taught and you said, *I teach children.*'

I laughed, feeling myself blush.

'It was the best answer,' he said. 'I've interviewed a lot of teachers over the years. And that's the best answer I've ever been given. Never lose sight of that. We teach children, our students. We don't teach subjects.' He took a biscuit. 'Thank you for teaching me that.'

As I drove home, Paul's question looped in my head. *Am I searching for something?* No, I realised suddenly, Mick's story returning to my mind. I thought of his son not wanting to go on and Mick's sage advice: *There's no point turning around.*

It was obscure but precisely how I felt. I wasn't searching. I was just trying to survive.

Clara gave me a card on the morning of our last day together.

I want to say thank you, she wrote. *I have had lots of good teachers, but you're the first teacher who made me think about how I acted. You're the first teacher who ever made me change my behaviour. Those kids in Canada are really lucky.*

I am a washroom

'*I* love these dolls,' *Sophie says, playing at my dressing table.
'What are they again?'*

*She nests them, planting one doll inside the other, matching
heads with bellies, tops with bottoms.*

*'Babushkas,' I tell her. 'Please be gentle with them. Don't lose
the little one. They're special.'*

*'I know.' Sophie tips up the biggest doll to find the inscription
underneath.*

To Mrs Stroud, Love from Corin.

*'Where are they from, again?' she asks. 'Are they Canadian
dolls?'*

*'Russian. Well, these are Armenian,' I say. 'But they were
given to me in Canada. A little girl I taught made them for me.'*

*Sophie plucks them from their nest again and lines them up
in a straight, ascending row.*

My Year Two Canadian classroom had a neat line of twenty-eight pairs of shoes waiting at the door.

'They change into these when they arrive,' explained Dave, the Principal. 'I don't suppose it gets cold enough in Australia for your students to wear snow boots?'

'No,' I said, delighted at the way he said *Awe-stralia*, delighted further by the shoes. 'So, the children learn French here? And Italian as well?'

'That's right,' he explained, walking me through the gymnasium. 'Canada's a bilingual nation—English *and* French—so learning French is mandatory in every school. But this particular school is what we call a heritage school. It was established a long time ago by immigrants to this area. They were mostly Italian, and so as an ongoing legacy the students learn Italian as well.'

'That's wonderful,' I gushed. 'Do the kids pick it up fairly quickly?'

'Some do.' He was non-committal. 'Some are just learning English so . . .' He shrugged.

'Right,' I said and felt the pinch of a frown tug at my eyebrows. *Here we go again,* I thought. *Nothing is ever straightforward.*

'This area remains a popular suburb for immigrants. But they're not usually Italian now.'

'What nationalities can I expect?'

'Every kind. Mainly Filipino, but also Korean, Russian, Armenian, Iraqi, Mexican. Let's rug up, I'll show you the playground.'

'Do they all get along?' I was stomping through thirty centimetres of snow, trying to identify the playing fields that Dave was pointing out.

'Yeah, mostly,' he said. 'Oh, look, there's a squirrel. Do you have those in *Awestralia*?'

So much time was spent helping my kids get dressed. When I arrived in Canada it was minus 5 degrees Celsius—even colder sometimes—with a wind chill that made it feel more like minus 20. I would layer each child with parkas and snowpants tugged on over their casual clothes (no school uniforms here). Then there would be boots, mittens, scarves and beanies. I became an expert at shifting zippers snagged on waterproof fabric. I could tie shoelaces with fingers still numb from the cold. My class would be lined up before me, unrecognisable and incapacitated, like a row of scarecrows ready for a ski trip.

After play time, the students peeled off their outer layers, hanging their snowsuits on hooks above their snow boots. But there was one student, Ali Mourad, who was always so keen to get into class that he'd be yanking off clothing as he came into the room. Ali didn't have time for hooks and hanging clothes.

'Ali! Your beanie shouldn't be on my desk!'

'Sorry, Mrs Stroud,' he would say, his hybrid accent sounding rich and gravelly. 'But you know we call it a *touque* in Canada? We don't say beanie.'

'A touque or a beanie—it doesn't belong on my desk! And is that your scarf draped over the doorknob, Ali?'

'Oh, yes,' he would say, grinning. 'I was looking for that.'

'Now, whose mittens are these?' I would hold them aloft and the students would strain to look up, their eyebrows burdened by hats and headbands and balaclavas.

'Ali's!' Their voices were united.

'Ali!' I admonished. 'You need to keep your clothes on your hook. It looks like you're having a garage sale here with your stuff all over the room.'

'*Yard sale*, Mrs Stroud,' he corrected me. 'In Canada, we call it a yard sale.'

Ali was a clever boy, and had stumped me with a question on my very first day.

'I have a query,' he announced.

I took in his black eyes, his olive skin. I was expecting something simple, something typical, like all the other kids had asked. *Do you have a pet kangaroo? Have you stood on Uluru? What is your koala's name?*

'Go ahead, Ali,' I said.

'I have always wanted to know,' he said, words well formed and carefully pronounced, 'is the platypus a marsupial?'

'Oh, it's . . .' I was confident, then faltered. It *was* a marsupial, wasn't it? No—it was something else, not a mammal. 'You know what, Ali?' I said. 'That's the best question anyone has asked me since I came to Canada.'

He beamed.

'And I'm not sure of the answer. I *think* they're a monotreme. But I'm going to need to look it up. Will we find out together?'

'Yes,' he said. 'I like to find things out. Right now, at home with my grandfather, I am investigating rocks and crystals. Do you know the difference, Mrs Stroud, between a rock and a crystal?'

I shook my head, still smiling. 'I have a lot of learning to do, I'm so glad you're in my class. We can learn together.'

Ali had stolen my heart. His mother came to see me early in the first month. She told me that he was so happy at school and was loving his new Australian teacher. She told me that Ali's grandfather had come from Nazareth, traversing Israel and living like a gypsy, to bring his family to a safer country. She had hugged me and put her hands on my face. 'I want you to feel welcome,' she said.

It was a strange new experience for me, teaching a class that was made up of students who knew English only as a second language. Parents would come to the door and their child would act as interpreter, summarising what their parents had spent many moments saying in their native tongue.

'Mum says she hopes you like Canada,' one boy told me, his voice low. 'She said she hopes you will come around for dinner one night.' He glanced up at me. 'But you don't have to, Mrs Stroud. No one at home can speak English, so . . .' He shrugged. 'She says she will make you *bulgogi.*' He shifted, his parka making a scratching sound as it buffered the doorway.

'Well,' I said, 'tell your mum I would love to try her *bulgogi.*' I watched his head drop. 'But,' I added, 'I'd love for her to send it in with you for my lunch one day. Tell her it's hard for me to drive on these snowy roads at night.'

He grinned at me, nodding. Then he relayed the message to his mother and I marvelled at his fluency, his expertise with his own language.

'Mum says very good,' he said. 'Next week she will bring. And she does make very good *bulgogi*. You'll love it.'

Two Russian students arrived new to my class. Arthur and Kristina. They knew almost no English and formed an immediate alliance with Corin, an Armenian girl, who they relied on for translation. Corin, who struggled with her reading and writing, was buoyed by the responsibility. She would bounce up to me, her blue eyes shining beneath her mop of dark hair.

'Arthur wants to go to the washroom,' she would tell me.

'To have a wash?' I would say and Corin would laugh.

'In Canada we say washroom, Mrs Stroud,' her voice thick with accent, a laugh at the corner of her words. 'We don't say toilet like you do in Oztraylior.' We would giggle together, but then Arthur would tap Corin's shoulder with urgency.

'Yes! Yes!' she would say to him. 'Ayo, ayo!' And Arthur would run from the room, his fingers already moving against the button of his jeans.

There was no money for programs to help these students with their English, and Corin couldn't be charged with the task of teaching them. So twice a day, during French and Italian lessons, I took Arthur and Kristina out for a crash course.

'I am Arthur,' I would say.

'I am Artur,' they would mimic.

'No, no.' I laughed. 'Not you, Kristina.'

'Not you, Kristina,' she said, a perfect imitation.

I laughed again. 'I am Kristina,' I said, pointing at her.

'I am Kristina,' they said, pointing at me.

'Gymnasium,' I said, walking them around the school. 'Office. Hallway. Car park.'

Slowly, their words came together and they became competitive with one another, rattling through colours and numbers and letters faster than I could flip the cards I had made. Kristina was bolder, more confident than Arthur, and I had to remind her more than once to let Arthur have his turn.

One day, in the classroom, a squabble erupted between Corin and Arthur. Kristina moved to the corner where they were arguing and there was a lot of very fast Russian going on. Corin was shaking her head and saying something to Arthur, who was blushing.

'No,' I heard Corin insist, folding her arms across her chest. She marched to her seat and continued with her work.

'You can,' I heard Kristina say. 'You can, Artur.' She nudged him in the back and he stepped forward slowly. 'You can,' she said again, her eyes bright. She glanced at Corin, who was pretending not to watch.

Arthur made his way up to my desk and put his hand gently on mine.

'I . . .' he began

'Yes?' I said, hoping for the right mix of encouragement and tenderness. 'You tell me, Arthur.'

'I . . . I . . .'

I nodded.

'I am . . .' He glanced back at the girls, who were huddled together now. Corin flapped her hands at him.

'I. Am. A washroom?' Arthur said and touched his belt by way of explanation.

'Yes!' I told him, my smile triumphant. 'You can go to the washroom.' I went on to say how clever he was, but he was already out the door.

'I am a washroom!' Corin was laughing with Kristina.

'Girls!' I said, my tone warning. 'We should feel proud of Arthur.'

'I am,' said Corin. 'But it is a little bit funny. I will help him get it right next time.'

Despite being a melting pot of multicultural identities, there was a Canadian-ness to these kids. They would proudly tell me about their unique cultural backgrounds, bring me endless traditional dishes and show me dances and costumes from their home nations. But alongside that was a desire to be part of something homogenous that would bring them into alignment with this country they were living in. Each day they sang the national anthem with pride, their little hands pressed on their hearts as their voices proclaimed, *Oh Canada! Our home and native land*. They were all mad-keen ice-hockey supporters and it was as though the blue maple leaf symbol— insignia for the Toronto ice-hockey team—was their unofficial school uniform.

Like every school, there were also unique traditions and expressions and inside jokes. During a writing lesson one afternoon, one of the Filipino boys returned from the bathroom. As he took his seat, I saw him lean over and whisper something to the child next to him. Within minutes that child came to me, asking if he could use the washroom.

'Quickly,' I told him. 'We've got important work to do here.'

Of course, when he returned, he stopped off at another boy's desk before taking up his own seat. On and on it went, a strange game of Chinese whispers that kept leading the boys to the toilets.

I left the student I was working with and positioned myself at the classroom door. In the hall, I saw that an unusual number of boys were scurrying from their classrooms to the toilets. They were like ants at a picnic.

'Alright,' I said, bailing up two boys from the class next door. 'What's going on?'

Their cheeks were flushed and their eyes glittery. One of them giggled and nudged the other one. He shook his head.

'Boys?' It was the deep baritone of Albert, the school janitor. 'I'm seein' a lotta you little guys goin' in and outta that toilet. There somethin' I should know about?'

Three more boys scampered past just as five burst out from the bathroom doors.

'BOYS!' Albert shouted. 'What's goin' on down there?'

'The moose is loose, Mr Baylon,' one boy shouted and broke into a run. The other boys followed his lead, charging to their classrooms, shouting, *The Moose is Loose, The Moose is Loose.*

'Oh, man,' Albert said, his shoulders slum ped.

'What does it mean?' I asked, wondering what emergency could warrant this rush of attention.

'It's nothin',' Albert said, leaning down close to my ear. He lowered his voice. 'It's just somethin' these kids say. It means someone's shit didn't make it into the toilet bowl. I better go get my clean-up kit.' He sighed.

I tried very, *very* hard not to laugh.

While we were in Canada, Matty had taken up casual work with a construction company. Like my school, his work crew was a broad mix of cultures. They quickly named him 'Aussie' and he was sent from site to site doing everything from high-end carpentry in inner-city apartments to building and installing fireplace mantles in family homes. At times, the work lapsed and on some of those days he would come into my school to help out.

The first day he came in, he was taken with the miniature desks, the size of the shoes lined up at the door and my careful printing on the blackboard. But as the students arrived I could feel a growing sense of frustration emanating from him. He sat at the back of the classroom and observed. I tried hard to ignore him and redirected the students every time they attempted to use him as a distraction.

On that particular day, I was rostered on for recess duty so it wasn't until one o'clock that I finally got a break.

'How ya travelling?' I asked him. 'It's lunch now so we can grab something to eat and go to the toilet—the washroom!' I chuckled.

'Is this what it's always like?' Matty's face was a picture of horror.

'What do you mean?'

'Well, you don't get a break. You can't leave the kids for a minute—not even for the loo. And they just don't listen, do they? I was watching one kid back here when you were talking and he was pulling a thread off his jumper. That girl over there has been whispering to her friend and the boy across from her, what's his name? Is it Ali? He did all of his Maths work in green pencil. I watched him. It's mayhem.'

I laughed. 'Welcome to teaching.'

'You can have it,' he shook his head. 'No wonder you're exhausted.' He looked at me with a tenderness not normally shown by him. 'Where's the staffroom? I want to make you a cuppa.'

As I made plans to leave Canada, I started looking for jobs back in Australia. There was a position going in Belmora, yet another town 'further up the road' from our house. It was a place much like Paradise, although it was bigger—a regional centre, of sorts. The same kind of honesty and grit lingered about the people who walked the streets, but there was also a sense of certainty there. Paradise had been a town in transition, its timber and fishing industries affected by a growing awareness of their environmental impacts. In Belmora, families were surer of their financial future, however tight it might be. They were farmers and factory workers in a town that wasn't changing much. *Salt of the earth,* my parents would say. *Good country people.*

I had the interview over the phone and was offered the position just hours later.

'I'm thinking about putting you down in the juniors,' the Principal said and I heard the gentle hush of the telephone line as I paused.

'Okay,' I said. 'Year Two over here has been wonderful. I've really enjoyed them.'

'The thing is, we've got this new kid . . .' He cleared his throat. 'Warren. He's got a sad story, but his behaviour's terrible.

I think you might be the one to sort him out. I just wanted to run it by you before I finalised the classes.'

'Can I call you back? I just need to think about it.'

I considered what the Principal had said—a challenging kid, probably around seven years old. I thought of Ryan, his stubborn face flitting through my memory. I considered the workload a student like that can create, the emotional toll it can take. *But there's no easy workload,* I rationalised. *Look at every school you've been to. There's always something extra, some kind of challenge. There's always a Lilith or a Ryan, ready to suck the life out of you. Or there's a need that's not being met—an Arthur that needs English or a Billie that needs a friend. And there's always gonna be paperwork. Teaching is really hard.*

But I was getting better, I realised with surprise. I'd gained experience. I knew what to do when a student tried to hijack my lesson. I knew how to keep parent–teacher interviews on time. I knew the steps I should take when I saw a student falling behind. I knew that one hand raised to say '*I don't get it*' represented many more that weren't brave enough to admit it. I knew that teaching was as much about explaining the same thing in several different ways as it was about disseminating information. I knew that a facial expression could reveal so much more than what my students were telling me. I knew that what students were learning socially at school mattered just as much as the content I was presenting them with each day.

I sat on the bed and considered the proposition again. It was a permanent job offer at a school I had heard great things about. And there was one badly behaved kid. One unknown quantity.

Outside, heavy snowflakes were beginning to fall, and a dusting of snow had already settled on the ground. Inside, the floor around me was a wasteland of international travel: passports, luggage locks, thank-you cards. When the phone had rung, I had been deliberating about where I could pack the beautiful, hand-painted dolls Corin and her mother had made for me.

I glanced at the clock before calling the school in Belmora. 'Yeah,' I told my new Principal. 'I can do it. Put him in my class.'

We hung up and I rolled the babushkas into layers of clothes, tucked them deep in the chest of the suitcase. They would be alright. They were nestled inside each other.

Warren

'*I* have something for you,' says Soph, fossicking in her school-bag. '*I just gotta find it.*' Wariness creeps in: the last time she did this she presented me with a worm.

My daughter burrows further into the bag. She looks war-torn after a day at Big School. Her hair has been pulled loose from the amateurish braid I attempted earlier that morning. Woodchips cling to her trackpants. There is a yoghurt stain down her front and a smudge of black paint on her jaw.

'It's a note!' She presents it with a triumphant flourish. 'I'm getting a new teacher on some days.'

'Oh, that's exciting,' I say. The note is clammy and frail having been made soggy from her drink bottle. 'And what's Mrs Mac doing while this new teacher teaches you?' I glance at the note.

Sophie shrugs. 'I dunno,' she says, snatching at a pencil she *has spied at the bottom of her bag. 'Probably lying down and having a rest. Dimitri is a lot of work.'*

'Hmm.' I feel a tug of anxiety in my guts. I know the boy she is talking about. I've seen him at school assemblies, rolling on the floor when all the others are listening, throwing things at the children, being escorted through the gardens by a teacher. I have taught that child. Every teacher knows that child.

I settled into Belmora school and braced myself for Warren. But he didn't arrive on the first day of school. He wasn't there on the second day either, or the third. I wondered if he'd been enrolled somewhere else.

'It would be a good thing if he was,' said Joan. 'He's hard work, Gab.' She had taught Warren last year. 'He is the most difficult child I've ever come across. He was just so violent with the other kids. I find that behaviour very hard to tolerate.'

'So, what's his story?' I asked.

'I wasn't told much. It's all pretty hush-hush. Clearly his mum is a drug addict. You'll meet her and you just know straight away. He's got a brother, a little brother. He talks about some older siblings sometimes. Parents aren't together. Dad lives out in the sticks somewhere. I don't think he sees his dad much. I heard that he was in prison, but that's just gossip so I can't be sure.'

'Why isn't he with community services? Surely a foster home would be better?' My voice was wary. I was thinking of Ryan as I said it, remembering his circulation through home after home.

'He's in and out of foster care already,' Joan said. She lowered her voice. 'The mum uses it like a babysitting service. She told me she rings them when she can't cope or when she's got to go to Sydney to "pick stuff up".' Joan made inverted commas with her fingers.

'She *sells* drugs?' This was becoming a horror story. 'How old is this kid?'

'We think he's seven,' Joan said. 'His paperwork's not complete. No birth certificate. No date of birth recorded.'

After the first teaching week, I spent my weekend finalising my program, allocating my students to reading groups and creating Maths resources. By 10 a.m. on Monday, there was still no sign of Warren.

And then, at 10.05 a.m., he arrived.

'So fuckin sorry,' said his mother. 'I thought school started today but they just told me down at the office youse have bin back a week.'

I guarded the classroom door, wanting to welcome her in but sensing a need to protect my students: she had the smell of bourbon and cigarettes. She was small with white-blonde hair, and wore a Megadeth singlet. Her arms were thin and rangy, the sinews stretching taut around her neck and shoulders. Her eyes darted over me and into the room.

'You got computers in here,' she said. 'Hey, Warren! Come here, mate, and look at the computers ya got!' Her voice was loud but scratchy-thin. A baby boy came over to her, he was sucking on a dummy with a thick line of mucus seeping from his nose.

'This is Errol,' she said, hefting him onto her hip. 'He's a shit of a kid.' She stepped back from the doorway and looked around the playground. 'WARREN, YA LITTLE FUCKER!' she shouted. 'GET OVER HERE.' She turned back to me. 'Sorry about me langwich, they just don't listen to me otherwise.'

Her face was layered with makeup, a sheen of foundation so thick it made me think of the paint I scraped off the paint trays last Friday. But there were wrinkles and lines around her eyes and her mouth. *You're quite old,* I suddenly thought.

'I've got six kids,' she said then, and I realised I needed a poker face. 'These are me babies,' she went on. 'But I've got a twenty and a twenty-two.' She paused and put the baby down, scratched at her arm. 'And Jonno's got to be about twenty-four and Linda—she's the little bitch that won't speak to me—she's twenty-six.'

'Me too,' I said and I felt myself blush. *What a stupid thing to say.* 'And how old's Warren?' I could see a boy coming towards us. He was solid and rounded; too big to be in my class. He looked like he should be in Year Four.

'I think he's seven,' she said and she turned away from me. 'Warren, how old are ya?'

The boy clumped up the concrete steps, his body too heavy for the task.

'I dunno,' he said. 'And you don't know either, ya pisshead.' He roared laughing then, pointing at his mother.

'Be good, mate,' his mum said and she scratched her arm again, produced sunglasses and threw them on. 'I'll see ya.' She trotted off down the steps, lighting a cigarette as she went. Baby Errol stood and watched.

'Go with her,' Warren said and he pushed his little brother towards the steps. 'Follow her. Run.' The baby fumbled his way down, across the playground and out the gate.

I watched him, wondering if he had caught up to her, wondering what he would do if he lost sight of her.

'What are you staring at?' It was Warren. 'Aren't you meant to teach me something?' He walked into the classroom and shouted, 'Hey there, Motherfuckers!'

'I'm going to need more aide time.' I was back in the Principal's office. I'd been there every afternoon since Warren's return to school. Apparently, there was nothing more we could do to help Warren. No money. No programs. No support system. The staff at Belmora were incredibly supportive and there was a behaviour management policy that was in place and adhered to. But for a student like Warren, letters home and 'time-outs' were ineffective token gestures.

'Just keep him safe,' the Principal said. 'That's your key role for this child. His basic needs aren't being met so we can't expect that he's going to learn. At least when he's here at school we know he's safe.'

'Well, that's great,' I replied, sarcasm oozing. 'What about the other twenty-something kids in my class. What about *their* safety?' That morning when I had raised my voice at him, Warren had thrown a chair at me. It landed on Lydia's desk, the legs stopping just centimetres short of her face. The day before he had pressed his finger against one nostril and blown a perfect blob of yellow snot onto Terence's hand. When I had asked why he did it, Warren told me it was about line-up. He had wanted to be the leader.

'If I could have more aide time . . . Having another adult in the room helps so much.' I could feel myself wheedling, the tone of my voice only notes away from begging. 'Bonnie's great with him, too,' I added. 'He really enjoys the one-on-one time with her.'

'Bonnie's time is accounted for.' The Principal pointed to the timetables tacked against his pinboard. 'You know how it works—aide time goes to the kids who are funded and to our Aboriginal students.'

'Could I get two more Aboriginal students put in my class then?' I was defeated. Reduced to thinking of ways I could game the stupid system.

'I know he's hard work,' the Principal said gently, 'but you're doing a great job.'

'Morning Gab!' It was Jule, a teacher who had been at Belmora since dinosaurs roamed the earth. 'How are things going with Warren?' she asked. He had been at school for four days and already I was sick of the question.

'Why don't you ask me about Terence?' I snapped. 'Or Saphron?'

Jule held her ground. 'You sound a bit frazzled.'

'I'm sorry,' I said, feeling my anger dissipate. 'I just feel like I'm parenting Warren while my class misses out on their teacher. I'm not getting through my preparation, my lessons are ordinary and I haven't even started on the individual reading assessments.'

'Come and sit down,' she said and directed me to a seat in the staffroom. 'You're doing a great job. A child like Warren is a massive task, I've taught plenty like him over the years. Could I make a suggestion? I think it'll help you.'

I gave her a withering look. 'You can only suggest something that makes my life easier.'

'I think you should start a logbook, create a document on your computer and just type up a few lines about how the day went. I've done it many times and it helps me process what's gone on throughout the day. Sometimes I've noticed patterns in the child's behaviour, recognised that Tuesdays are great and Thursdays are terrible and then I've been able to dig deeper and find out why. You like to write, don't you, Gab? I'm sure you mentioned that at our staff development day. This'll be good for you.'

'It'll be time consuming,' I moaned.

'Just a few lines,' she insisted. 'I think you'll be surprised. You'll probably see progress too. And it's a great thing to have a record of everything if you're ever called in to court.'

'Court?' I was alarmed.

'Highly unlikely, but always a possibility. Especially with kids like Warren.'

'Oh God,' I moaned again.

'Try it,' Jule urged. 'Just try it.'

There's no such thing as bad kids—just bad behaviour.

All behaviour serves a purpose.

Don't engage in arguments.

He's just a little boy.
Redirect to appropriate tasks.
Always remember: you're the adult.
Praise as much as you can.
I don't give up on kids.

The drive to school became a half-hour pep talk where I tried to summon motivation, energy and a sense of hope.

Please, God, let him be away, I would pray as I pulled into the car park. For two reckless minutes I would abandon all sense of professional responsibility and compassion and ask the higher realms for a cosmic intervention. *Just for one day, God, please. I need a break.*

But he was never away—always late, but never away. Sometimes he was dropped off by different people. There were men that he called Punk and Cuz and Dude and then there were others—Mary and Denise and Murray, foster carers who would make sure his lunch had been packed and his clothes were clean. Sometimes he arrived without a bag, without food, or wearing the exact same clothes since Monday. Once he came with odd shoes: one a perfect fit, the other two sizes too big, and both for a left foot.

'Whose shoes are these?' I asked as I bent to tie the laces.

'I dunno.' He swiped his hand at a fly.

'Do they belong to that guy that dropped you off yesterday?' A teenage kid, maybe fifteen, but already tattooed. Warren had called him Rooter.

'Nuh. I think they belong to the brother where I'm staying. You know, the big guy at that house where I'm staying?'

'No, I don't,' I said sadly.

The Principal took him down to Target at recess and bought him new shoes. They were the right size, a matching pair and proper leather lace-ups. Warren even said thank you. But his mum picked him up that afternoon and I never saw him wear those shoes again.

I started packing lunch for him each day. It was easier than foraging around in the tuckshop that was only open on Mondays. Other teachers discovered what I was doing and together we created a stash of grocery staples in the staffroom cupboard that I could draw on each day.

'Does he have breakfast?' Jule asked. She often talked with me about Warren, made suggestions and tried to help.

'I don't know,' I shrugged.

'Offer it to him,' she said. 'It might help settle him down each morning.'

A routine gradually emerged. I'd get to school and make Warren's lunch. When Warren arrived, Bonnie would take him to the staffroom for breakfast. He'd smash through four Weet-bix while she read him a story. When his clothes were dirty we changed him into gear from the lost property box and took his clothes home for a wash.

He never said thank you and for some reason that irritated me. I felt constantly torn between my compassionate desire to nurture him and an infuriating rage that he was causing me to neglect my teaching.

Warren had a case worker, an older lady named Dorothy who looked like the world had never kept a secret from her.

'How's he going?' she asked at one of our endless Warren meetings.

'Pretty well, I guess, considering the cops were at his house last night.' I sipped my tea, one eye on the time: I was due out on playground duty. 'They came at 2 a.m. First he told me his mum called them because someone was breaking into their house. But then, after recess, he said Mum's boyfriend broke the window and *then* they rang the cops. I don't know what goes on half the time.' I gathered up my keys and the first-aid kit, and tried to throw down the last of my tea. 'I have to go out on duty.'

Dorothy followed me out. 'You're really making progress,' she said. 'He obviously trusts you.'

I adjusted my sunhat and said hello to the kids playing in the sandpit.

'Gabbie,' she insisted. 'His trust in you is significant. I need you to start documenting everything he tells you.'

I sighed, tried not to sound rude. 'Dorothy, I've been documenting Warren every day since he arrived. I spend an hour most afternoons just writing down the Warren Story—who he spat on, what he threw, who he punched, what he ate, what he wore and the horrors he told me about the night before.' I lifted my sunnies and pressed my hands against my eyes, trying to keep the tears at bay. 'I don't think I can possibly do anything more.'

Weeks later I was back in the Principal's office. Dorothy and some other people were there. They wanted to see my documentation.

I sat there while they read it, watched as they made copies and dragged highlighters all over my sentences.

Logbook

Jule had been right. I did find it somewhat therapeutic to spend time each day writing and reflecting on my experiences with Warren. Dorothy and her team certainly valued it. More than once they came in to read it and make copies.

I didn't realise what a fraught and frightening life Warren was leading until I tried to make sense of it with words of my own.

12 February

Warren was unsettled this morning. Walking down to fitness he proudly showed me the 'smiley' he had burned onto his arm last night with a lighter. Later in the day, I asked to see the burn again. I asked if it hurt when he did it and he said no. I asked who he was with when he did it—was he with his mum? Or his friends? He replied, 'I don't have many friends. I have one and his name's Jacker, but he's older.'

I have felt sad all day. Warren's home life is so far removed from my own experiences and the experiences of the other children in the class.

1 March

Warren's mum saw me on Thursday morning. She explained that she is trying hard to get her life back on track. She said she and Warren had gone through a lot together, and now she was studying at TAFE. 'I get a bit nervous talking to you,' she admitted, and I said, 'I'm here for Warren and I'm here for you so that you can help him.' She took my hands and said, 'Thank you so much!' It's easy for me to judge her but I need to remember that I can't ever know her story.

15 March

Just before lunch, Warren came and said, 'I can read now.' I asked him how he knew how to read? (His literacy is low; he can read his name, but that's pretty much all. I'm working on getting him to write it, but he's reluctant.) He said he is learning to read from the computer at home, but when it gets too hard he just quits that level and starts over. I was surprised: it's the first time I've heard him say he can do something. He seemed proud.

2 April

Warren was chasing a kid around the playground this morning with scissors. I talked to him about it and he didn't see what the problem was?! He said he wasn't going to hurt anyone.

He doesn't seem to be aware of the possible consequences of his actions.

I had a chat with Bonnie about Warren today. I was saying how he has no idea on how to behave and she said, 'You've got to remember: he doesn't know what normal looks like, Gab, but he's got a sense of it and he knows it's better than what he's got right now.' She is so brilliant with him, but she's only with me for forty-five minutes each morning.

18 April

It's been raining for a week. Warren got himself soaking wet by standing under the overburdened drains. I rang his mum and asked her to bring dry clothes. She explained that she didn't have any way of getting to the school and asked if I could find lost property stuff for him instead. I assured her I would find him some dry, clean clothes (I do it for him at least once a week), but I was frustrated. I feel like I'm always acting as Warren's parent and it's so demanding.

5 May

Warren's mum dropped him off early today. She seemed to be in a great mood, very chatty. She told me all about her new boyfriend and how they had just gone de-facto the day before—'down at the court house and everything'. She told me she had quit TAFE, too, and was going to learn something on the job because she can't settle down and learn in a classroom. She's getting her car and licence back today; the government was going to pay for it. She asked me if I liked Warren's hair that she gelled into a spike. I told her that this term we really need to get the homework started and a good routine happening with his reading and writing. She promised me she would make time for homework every afternoon.

8 May

Warren was dropped off by a foster carer this morning. He told me there was a burglary at his house and police came in the night and took him to a new family for a while. At lunch, I rang Dorothy. She told me Warren's mum rang *her* in the middle of the night and said she didn't want the kids anymore and someone had to take them: 'I'm not a fucking fit mother for the fucking kids. Just take them away from me.' Dorothy went around and picked them up. She said Warren's baby brother Errol was kicking and screaming.

15 May

This has been a tough week. Warren has been like a pendulum: violent and aggressive to silent and withdrawn. He has stayed with four different families this week. I have to practically drag him down to the buses after school. Yesterday when we got to the bus lines he wouldn't sit down. He said he had to keep his eyes on Courtney (she's another girl in my class) so that he'd know which bus to catch. He asked me who would pick him up and for the fifth time this week I had to say I didn't know. Then he asked where he would be sleeping that night and again I had to say I didn't know.

I told Warren he was so brave and he must be feeling scared. I told him I would be here at school waiting for him tomorrow. I said I was so glad he was in my class. He asked why? I said because he is such a special boy and is going to grow up to be a fine young man.

Putting him on the bus is always hard. He looks to me and nearly hugs me goodbye. He always asks me how many sleeps until he sees his mum. When I say I don't know I feel like I am letting him down.

My heart has started to ache. Last night I came home and cried on and off all evening. I just kept thinking, *Even my dog knows where it's going to sleep at night.*

18 May

Today Warren and I had a chat at recess. He expressed worry about his mum and when he would see her again. I told him to wait another week before we started to worry.

Today, for news, he wanted to talk about his recent experiences. He said to the class, 'What's it called when your mum goes away for a bit?' And the students suggested *holiday, trip, vacation.* 'Nah,' said Warren. 'When she says, "Get lost, kids, I don't want ya"?' It was heartbreaking to hear, but we had a chat as a class about divorced families and parents needing time out. Then he proceeded to tell us about the family he stayed with last night. They had horses and he got to feed them. He demonstrated how to feed a horse with a calm, flat hand. And then he said, 'And they had two dogs and I loved those dogs.'

At 2.10 p.m. I got a call from the office to say that Dorothy had rung. Warren's mum has said she wants to turn the kids over to the department for long-term foster care. I was told that I should tell Warren that this was happening—that he wouldn't be seeing his mum for a while.

My class was in Library for the afternoon and I asked Warren to come outside. I told him as much as I could, explaining that his mum just needs a break and wants him to stay with a foster family for a while longer. He seemed almost resigned, as though he knew it was coming. He said he hoped he'd go to the horse family. He said he hoped it wasn't the other family, the family in town here, because Errol just gets smacked there. 'Smack, smack, smack, smack, smack,' he said.

23 May—Excursion to Wetlands

Warren was great on the bus and continued to be great, right up until the activities. We had a long walk to begin with and he wasn't happy about it. He swore and threw sticks, but then I think he realised he had very few options, so he eventually trailed along. All the students had picked up walking sticks, but Warren picked up a log that must have weighed close to five kilograms. He carried it for the duration of the walk (a good two hours) and often fell over, but he wouldn't give up the stick. He was destructive to the habitats we saw, which surprised me, and he wasn't interested in the talk.

After lunch, we were meant to go on another hike, but Warren cracked the sads because he wasn't chosen to be a group leader. He refused to join in the activity and I was left with him. After twenty minutes Warren finally said he would like to do the walk, but by this stage the rest of the group were well on their way. I used the walkie-talkie and the guide advised me to follow an alternative marked track. He said that we would intersect with the larger group.

Warren seemed excited to be on an adventure together. I told him I was angry because the other kids were missing out on having their teacher with them and that he was missing out on being with them. He smiled and said, 'It's worked out good, hasn't it?' I caved in, laughed and said, 'I've worked you out, Warren. You secretly like me and you want me all to yourself.' He said, 'Yes. It's quieter and better without all them others.' He chatted on amicably while we went bush-bashing.

He talked a lot about his mum and I asked him if he loved his mum and he said, 'Of course.' I asked if his mum loved him and he said, 'Yes, because sometimes when she tells me she cries.'

He was still dragging the five-kilo stick. I suggested it might be easier if he put it down, but he refused. After a while he said, 'Did you know I dream about you most nights?'

'What happens in those dreams?' I asked, and he said, 'You're with me and my dad and Errol's there and we go camping.'

We eventually found the rest of the group. Warren barged his way to the front so he could see what the guide was demonstrating. Then he picked up his stick and cracked two kids against their shins.

I'm so exhausted I can barely contemplate driving home.

25 May

Yet another foster family for Warren. He's become quite violent. The rest of the class are so generous and patient with him; they will happily swap things with him, let him go first, let him have a longer turn . . . They forgive so easily. I could learn a lot from these children.

30 May

There's been a change in arrangements. Errol, Warren's little brother, has been taken out of foster care. He gets to stay with his dad while Warren is left in care. Warren is NOT HAPPY.

2 June

Warren spits, punches, throws things, threatens, trips the other children, scares them and just makes everyone feel miserable.

Today I pulled him out of Library for a chat. I asked if he was angry and he said no. Then I said, 'If I were you I'd be angry at Mum for making me go to a foster family, and I'd be angry at Dad because Errol gets to stay with him. I'd be angry that I have to catch different buses and go to different houses and different families.'

He said he was a bit angry about all that. I told him that was okay, but reminded him he can't take that anger out on me or the other kids. I told him he was safe at school— I am here for him and I want him to have a happy day, but nobody's happy when he behaves with violence.

I told him that from now on whenever he was violent I would send him to the Principal's office, which he doesn't want to do. He told me he could behave.

Then I asked him something I've never asked before. I asked if I could have a hug. He said he'd probably squeeze my guts out. I said, 'Go on, then, let's try.'

And he nearly did squeeze my guts out, so I squeezed back too!

5 June

This has been so hard. Every time Warren's violent I have been sending him to the office. He hates it. I just feel like everything is unravelling. And the other kids in my class probably haven't learned a thing all year; right now I'm just trying to keep everyone safe.

Today he toppled a table over when he didn't win a spelling game with the other kids. I ordered him to the office, but he refused. I said, 'You can either walk or I'll carry you.'

He sat down hard in his chair so I moved behind him and put my arms under his arms and lifted him up. Then he really cracked it. He kicked and threw his arms around and I copped a beauty in the face. He was shouting and growling. The kids scattered, and I carried Warren outside still shouting and kicking and thrashing about.

The moment we were out of the classroom he gave up the fight and went limp in my arms and cried. I have never seen Warren cry—not when his mum first sent him to foster care, not when he didn't know where he was sleeping, not when I've shouted at him. It's a big moment.

13 June

Met with Dorothy today. Warren's mum had a visit with him on Sunday. She told him he would be back with her by Friday. Warren has been good. I'm trying to get school reports written. Haven't left school earlier than 7 p.m. all this week.

16 June

Warren's been counting the sleeps to see his mum. Yester-day Dorothy said she had arranged for his mum to have both boys just for the weekend. At lunchtime today Dorothy rang and said Warren's mum has changed her mind about the weekend. I arranged for another teacher to have my class for a while so I could tell Warren he wouldn't be going home to Mum tonight.

'Nah,' he told me. 'You're wrong. I'm catching my usual bus and going home tonight. I'm not going to catch that other dickhead bus.'

I told him that Dorothy had rung and told me that plans had changed, but he wouldn't believe me. When the end-of-the-day bell rang, he didn't want to go. He was clinging to my hand. We had to rush to the 'dickhead bus'. He hopped on and gave me a wave as it drove by. My heart has broken so many times for this kid. Sometimes I can completely understand why he's such an angry little boy.

19 June

I was having a fine morning out on playground duty when Warren started a fight with another kid. I went to check it out. As I approached, Warren made a leap for the flying fox and missed. He fell to the ground. We all heard the crack. His eyes went wide and he looked straight at me and said, 'I've broken my arm.' I scooped him up and he just kept whimpering, 'Mummy.' He must've asked me fifty times if I could get his mummy for him.

It was an ambulance trip and a day at casualty. We called Dorothy and she located his mum (at the pub) and brought her in. She didn't know his weight or correct birth date. I had brought along his dodgy enrolment form and filled in a few of the blanks—not sure they were correct, though. His mum said he had no allergies, so they administered morphine.

His reaction was immediate and massive. He was convulsing and his veins rose up, throbbing blue like he had scribbled on himself. A red rash raced along his skin.

Then his mum says, 'Aw, hang on, if that's morphine he can't have that. He's allergic to that.' The doctor gave him pethidine without any reaction.

He had broken both bones in his right arm and for a while they thought he may require surgery. But the orthopaedic surgeon set it without needing to operate. It was a long day.

I was so frustrated by his mum, who had been standoffish towards this boy who was just longing for his mummy. All she wanted to do was talk about her new boyfriend.

Before Warren was moved to the wards I took his mum home to get her coat and have something to eat. I returned to school to gather up my own gear. When I went back and picked Warren's mum up, I noticed she was empty-handed. I suggested she bring some PJs or clothes for Warren, but she said the hospital would take care of that. She said she wouldn't stay the night with him.

20 June

Before school, I checked in with Warren at hospital. He was roaming the ward and getting roared at by the nurses. He wasn't that pleased to see me; just asked where his mum was. He was wandering around in his boxers and school shirt.

The Principal went across to him at 10 a.m. and he said Warren's mum still hadn't been in to see him. When school finished, I rang the hospital. They said Warren hadn't had any visitors since the Principal that morning. I rang his mum. She told me she had been to the hospital nine times already that day!

I asked if she'd like to go once more and offered to drive her up there. I didn't go in to see Warren that afternoon. I knew he'd just be dying to see his mum and I hoped that maybe she'd be more focused on him if she went to visit him on her own.

My logbook ends there. Just like that. Warren never returned to my school. I don't know what happened to him. Sometimes I feel so bad that I ever prayed for him to be away. I feel guilty that my prayers were answered.

How to be a teacher

'*M*um?'

We are driving home from Sophie's tennis lesson. She is snacking on Burger Rings, one threaded on each finger, nibbling them off like edible jewellery.

'You know how my name's smart?'

I wait a beat, try to join dots. 'Mmm,' I say, still puzzling it out.

She has heard my uncertainty and clarifies: 'How my name means smart?'

'Ah, yes. Your name means wisdom. And Olivia's means peace.'

'So . . .' She crunches through another Burger Ring and I try not to think of the mess she is creating in the back seat. 'Did you call me Sophie because when I was born you looked at me and knew I was smart, or did I do something smart?'

'Well,' I tell her, flicking on my lights as the grey evening

transforms our world. 'Daddy and I both liked the name Sophie. But there was also a lady—you've met her. You know my friend Sophie? We visit her farm? She does puzzles and craft with you?'

I can hear her licking each finger, ten emphatic sucks.

'Yeah,' she says.

'You're named after her, baby. She's an amazing lady and I love her very much.'

Sometimes people are saving your life and they don't even know it. Sometimes *you* don't even know it. You're hanging by a thread. They're keeping you afloat, brightening your day. That was Sophie Kaye for me during that time I taught Warren in Belmora.

She was in the classroom next door, battling along with her own cohort. Like me, she had a Stage One, Year One and Two class, and just like me she had a child in there whose needs were limitless. Somehow though, she was coping, and even managing to support me. When Warren started hurling furniture, she would appear at my door, like an angel, a fairy godmother, and whisk away my class. I would find them later, when Warren was calmer or serving time-out in the office. Sophie would have them singing or crafting or literally running through hoops in a makeshift PE lesson. Forty-eight children and Sophie, laughing and encouraging and threading herself through hoops.

As I taught Warren, a deep fatigue set into me. I would stand at my classroom door at 9 a.m., while my class waited like cows for the milking. *I want to lie down,* I would think as I opened the door and children pressed into the room. Next door, I would hear Sophie singing to her class and reminding children to open the blinds and switch on the lights.

'How can you just walk in and teach?' I asked her one day. She had come out to join me on playground duty, wanting to observe her 'troubled student' in his natural environment. She was munching on strips of capsicum; she never resorted to chocolates and cakes and biscuits like I did. 'I get to school at 7.30 most mornings and I never leave before six.'

Sophie laughed. 'When you get to my age, Gabs, you come to realise that no amount of preparation is going to save you.' She paused, shielded her eyes against the sun and watched some students tussling over a skipping rope. 'Wait,' she said as I moved to mediate, 'they've got it sorted. Anyway,' she went on, tapping her head, 'it's all up here. And some of it's here.' She tapped her heart.

'A taste, Mrs Kaye?' Three hopeful girls stood in front of us, their hands out begging.

Sophie popped a piece of capsicum in each palm.

'It's capsicum,' she told them. 'You tell Mummy to pack some for you. Isn't it delicious?'

The girls nodded and ran away. Sophie scavenged in her pocket and produced an entire cucumber.

'What are you doing with that?' I asked, eyebrows raised.

Sophie took a gutsy bite and we doubled over laughing.

'You can't eat a cucumber like that!'

'Why not?' she said and took another bite.

Sometimes, when I came out to take Sophie's place on play-ground duty, the yard was like a ghost town. A few stray kids would be kicking a ball and the diehard sandpit kids would still be in position, but everyone else would be somewhere else. Eventually I'd find them wearing rubber gloves, snapping BBQ tongs and toting plastic bags.

'We're just clearing out a rubbish hotspot,' a proud child would tell me. 'Mrs Kaye has been noticing it build up. Look how much rubbish we got.'

'Hello, Gabs,' Soph would say as I approached the group of kids. 'I might stay out here and finish this area.'

I would watch as she headed back to the 'hotspot' with a tribe of children following. She lived the things she taught those children and I felt my fatigue compound: I could hardly survive a teaching day without collapsing in the staff-room during my designated break. But Sophie, twice my age, would voluntarily stay out weeding and rubbish-hunting with the kids and still return to her classroom with a smile and a song.

I was still using bribery and rewards to cajole my class into behaving well, and I realised it was a futile strategy and an exhausting cycle. It was like waving a carrot in front of a donkey: eventually you get sick of holding the carrot and the donkey says he doesn't care for carrots, anyway. No amount of sticker charts or certificates or prize box rewards would make any significant change for a student like Warren, but I tried them all nonetheless.

Sophie had a different approach. Her behaviour-management system was herself. When a child made an effort, showed improvement, had a go, reached a milestone, did something amazing, produced quality work or just asked a good question, Sophie would build them up with dollops of praise and feedback so specific that the child would clearly know why he was being applauded by his peers. Instead of using high-budget stickers from the two-dollar shop, Sophie rewarded her students with simple dot-stickers she called *genius dots*. If a child did something worthy, she would look in their eyes and say, *You are a genius!* before pressing one of those ordinary stickers right onto their face.

Sophie had such candour with the children. When she spoke to them she was never patronising, and sometimes her honesty shocked me.

'Mrs Kaye, Mrs Kaye,' sobbed a girl, racing up to her one day. 'Warren took my ball.'

'Well,' I heard Sophie say, 'you have every right to reclaim it. Warren can be a bully, but bullies are everywhere. So, you need to march up to him and say, "Stop it, I don't like it," and then you need to say, "Give my ball back."'

I watched the child hesitate. She was ready for the teacher to intervene, to be the acting solicitor on behalf of her, the injured party.

We watched the child confront Warren without success.

'He won't give it back,' the girl moaned. 'He called me a bad word.'

'Right, well, let's do it together.'

Soph walked down with the child, standing by her side as the entire drama was replayed. Warren booted the ball away, and Sophie said calmly, 'We will wait here while you go and get that, thank you, Warren.'

It surprised me, but he did it. Warren had taken Soph's measure a long time ago. As he meandered across the yard to retrieve the ball, Sophie told the young girl that she had been brave and strong and commanding and powerful. She told her that she should remember this moment.

Paperwork was not Sophie's strong suit.

'Come on, Soph,' I said during our first Stage One meeting. 'Let's work on our program. If we stay an hour extra tonight *and* again next week and if we do a bit on Thursday lunch when we're both off, then we'll have hardly any to do on the weekends.'

'Alright, Gabs,' she said, biting into a capsicum like it was an apple.

'So, let's see your Art program from last year,' I said. 'You do such amazing Art with the kids. It's my worst area I think.'

Soph scavenged around her desk, shifting seedlings growing in egg cartons and a pretty silk scarf. She moved stacks of paper, and towers of student books, piling them on her in-tray and then on her out-tray.

Eventually, she handed me three sheets of paper stapled together. They were photocopies. I looked at them closely.

'No, your *program*,' I said. 'These are just pages photo-copied from the syllabus.'

'Oh, I know, Gabs,' Soph said. 'I just think it's ridiculous that we have to re-write the syllabus as a program so I just photocopy the pages I need for the unit I want to teach.'

I paused. It made good sense.

'But,' I said, hating the words I was going to say, hating that I sounded like management. 'Where do you put the date and the class and show what you're planning to do and when?'

'Here,' Sophie said, and she leaned over my shoulder and pointed. At the top of the page she had handwritten in the date, the class and the school term. 'And here,' she pointed to where she had labelled each syllabus dot point: week one, week two, week three and so on. 'And here,' she flipped the pages and showed me where she had written down a few sentences to evaluate and register what she had taught.

'But,' I paused again. 'It's not typed up.'

'Does it have to be?' she frowned. 'Oh goodness, Gabs, we might be here all night.'

'And we're meant to set it out like this.' I slid my laptop over to her, so she could see the formatted table on screen.

Sophie slipped on her glasses and squinted. After a while she said, 'But Gabs, you've just typed up the syllabus and put it in columns.'

I laughed. 'I know, Soph, but see here I put some detail about how I'd teach the activities.' I pointed.

'Alright,' she sighed. 'You'd know more than me, love.'

'I don't think that's true, Soph,' I said. 'Okay, read this bit out to me and I'll type it in.'

She offered me a tub of nuts and then started reading. 'Outcome V. A. S. One point two. Making. Students experiment with a wide range . . .'

I typed and typed, tabbing across to different columns, copying and pasting where I could. Control B bold. Control I italics. And the whole time, Sophie's old 'program' was perched on the corner of her desk, folded up alongside the seedlings.

I watched the clock and kept on thinking, *I'd be home by now if we did it Sophie's way.*

Sometimes, on mornings when I woke up and couldn't face the thought of Warren, I would think about seeing Sophie. She always had something funny to tell me, a great idea for a lesson, a little strategy I might try with my class. We shared books, introducing each other to our favourite authors and discussing characters at length. She listened to my endless rants about Warren and all the things I found hard and frustrating. She was a colleague and a friend.

Whenever I was with her, I was learning. Sophie Kaye was showing me how to *be* a teacher.

'Mum?'

My mind telescopes back from my years with Sophie Kaye and into the car with my own little Sophie and her Burger Rings.

'Yes, my darling?' I say.

'Is that Sophie smart? Is she wise like me?'

I glance back at her, all long limbs in a booster seat, her thumb now stacked with fresh Burger Rings.

'Yes,' I say. 'She is wise. And full of joy. She is just like you.'

More rigorous, more standardised, more professional

I stayed on at Belmora school. I had realised that the massive workload of teaching could not be avoided, no matter where I taught. I was twenty-seven years old and just starting to feel like I had a handle on my teaching. Matty was still working at a local joinery, although he wasn't really enjoying it. We were making plans to renovate our little seaside cottage. We would be owner–builders, so Matty could work part-time and do most of the renovation himself. My reliable teaching income would carry us along through the process and, afterwards, Matty would return to work and we would enjoy our beautiful new house.

I felt very much at home at Belmora. The staff were experienced, professional, hardworking, compassionate and creative. They were also totally ridiculous. It was normal to walk into the staffroom and find teachers duelling with tennis racquets or demonstrating questionable yoga poses or eating chocolate biscuits before 8 a.m. Funny anecdotes from the classroom were shared, like jokes, over morning tea. Tunes from musicals were belted out as theatrical segues. At times, a simple 'goodbye' could lead to a stirring rendition of the von Trapp family's 'So long, farewell . . .'

I felt that I'd found *my* kind of teachers at Belmora. It was like my uni crew had reappeared, at different ages, and had met up to teach at the same school. These teachers got on board for dress-up days and school concerts. They were always ready to laugh and find joy and celebrate the fact that it was good to be alive. And they ate a lot of cake.

I felt valued at Belmora. Teacher opinion mattered. Suggestions made at staff meetings were considered. We supported one another as best as we could, sharing our time and resources, offering suggestions and advice. There were friendships within the staff but no dangerous cliques and political alliances. There was no Lilith lurking around a corner, waiting to trip you up.

The students at Belmora were happy, too. There was still the group of 'usual suspects'—kids who behaved like Ryan and Burt from my Paradise days—and of course we had a couple of Warrens. But there was a certain security for students at Belmora. The school was governed by a consistent, if somewhat draconian, behaviour-management regime that was policed with vigilance by the Assistant Principal. This rigorous system was tempered by the joy-filled teachers and, on the whole, the school was a happy and safe place for everyone.

By this time in my career, I had come to understand that staff meetings were a special kind of torture. Without a judicious Principal or Assistant Principal or middle management person to keep things on time, on track and on task, things could and would degenerate quickly. Teachers in a meeting will generally behave about as well as their third most disruptive student. (I am exaggerating, but only slightly.)

Staff meetings at Belmora were no exception and I came to think of them as my first line of attack. They were theoretical spaces where our future workload was bandied about, existing only as ideas and words and imaginings. Part of me was always on high alert during these meetings. I was fearful of a workload I couldn't sustain.

'Is there funding?' I would ask.

'Is it compulsory?'

'What research supports this?'

'Why do we have to do this?'

Somehow, over time, I became the person—the idiot—who voiced what everyone was thinking.

'Is everybody here?'

The staff meeting was about to begin and the Assistant Principal was doing a head count. I slid into my seat and produced a pile of Brenex squares—shiny coloured papers that are a staple for junior primary Art projects.

'What are we cutting?' asked Madge, slipping into the seat next to me. She took up the extra scissors I had brought and slid a blue square off the top of the pile.

'I need two hundred and fifty equilateral triangles ready for tomorrow's Art lesson,' I told her and held up a sample. 'See, here: they need to be equilateral so the kids can fold them like this.'

'Why so many?'

'My class,' I said, 'and Soph's class. That's forty-eight kids, plus a sample for each class—that's fifty projects. Each project needs five triangles.'

'You making the boat thing?' Lana slumped into the chair on my other side.

'Yeah,' I said. 'It always turns out well.'

I sat and snipped triangles with Madge as we waited for the meeting to begin. Teachers arrived and then left, remembering a phone call they had to make, racing back to their classroom for paperwork, dealing with children who had missed the bus, speaking to parents. By four o'clock we were ready to begin, but then the Principal discovered the digital projector wasn't working.

'You start,' he said to the Assistant. 'I'll try to fix this.' He crawled under the table to check the leads.

'Alright,' the Assistant Principal said. 'Item number one. We need to start meetings on time. We are officially twenty minutes late. Let's work on that for next week.' She pulled the lid off a pen and made a tick on the page. There was a grunt from under the table and the Principal inched his way out and sat down.

'Bloody cord had come loose,' he nudged the mouse and we all looked at the wall where images were supposed to be projected. 'What's wrong with it now?' He stabbed angrily at his keyboard.

'I'll go on,' the Assistant said. 'What we want to talk about today and what's going up on screen is the new model for reporting that's being implemented. We've agreed to be a trial school.'

'I never agreed,' muttered Madge under her breath. I tried not to snort. Last term, Madge and I had been banned from sitting beside each other. We were supposedly a bad influence on each other. The truth was we shared a low tolerance for bullshit and a chronic addiction to humour.

'From now on, A to E graded reporting is going to be the way we report to parents,' the Assistant Principal explained. 'It's being introduced to make things standard across the state so all schools are speaking the same language, and when a child arrives from another school we know where they're at.'

'Yes, yes,' said Lana, older and wiser than the Assistant Principal. 'I've been here and ridden this donkey. And you know how it ends? Eventually we realise that you can't quantify what a child knows with a single letter. So, let's short-circuit this and stick with what we've got and save ourselves a whole heap of work.'

'She's right,' Jule said. 'Been there, done that, got the T-shirt. A to E is a grand idea in theory, but how do we agree on what constitutes an A and a B and a C? And what about the poor bugger who tries his guts out but still performs at an E level? The thing I never liked about A to E was that we never acknowledged effort. Surely the student's effort is of as much value as his or her achievement.'

'I think that's one of the best moments in teaching,' Sophie said, looking up from the sample Art piece she was making for tomorrow's lesson. 'That moment when a child understands that they can exert effort on their learning, that they can try hard to learn.' She paused. 'It warms my heart.'

'No, no, no,' the Principal said. He flicked a switch on the projector and the thing blazed to life, filling the wall with an image so bright we couldn't see it. The Assistant fussed about with the curtains, creating darkness, and the first PowerPoint slide came into focus.

The Common Grade Scale will be used to report student achievement in both primary and junior secondary years in all NSW schools.

The state's education logo was plastered above the statement like a royal decree.

'So, this is going to be mandatory?' Jule asked.

'Yes, very soon,' the Principal said, stacking a wad of home readers beneath the projector's stumpiest leg. 'We're a pilot school. We'll trial it.'

'What if we don't like it?' Lana said.

'Then we'll put that in our review,' the Assistant said.

'And it'll all go ahead anyway,' Madge said, not under her breath this time.

'Well, at least we get an opportunity to have a say,' the Assistant replied. 'We might be able to make some recommendations that improve the reporting.'

'Who writes the review?' I asked.

'We'll do it together,' the Principal said and I groaned, loudly and rudely.

'Another hour of my life I'll never get back.'

A few people laughed.

The projector shat itself again and we were in darkness. The Principal headed back under the desk while the Assistant made for the lights.

'Why does *that* become my job?' Madge whispered, jabbing her scissors at the screen.

I shrugged. 'Here,' I said, handing her a red square. 'Just cut another triangle and try not to think about it.'

'Oh, before I forget,' the Assistant said, 'is someone taking minutes?'

This time there was a collective groan.

A roster was produced, a name called out, and someone threw a notebook in their direction.

'I can do it for you,' I suggested, but from under the desk came the Principal's voice—an emphatic *NO!*

I had been banned from minute-taking early in Term One after I wrote additional comments next to each minute. Honest, childish things like:

This will never work.

Bags not doing this.

This will probably suck.

I had been told off, publicly and privately: *These are official documents* and *We need an accurate representation.* The other staff had thought it was hilarious and my notes had been read aloud over recess when the Principal and Assistant were out on duty.

'I can't seem to get this projector to work,' the Principal admitted. Defeated, he plopped back into his chair. 'I'll just talk you through it,' he said, his finger hovering over the mousepad. 'I spent all afternoon preparing this . . .' He sighed.

He clicked through slide after slide, telling us about the need for standardisation and the A to E model that would level playing fields and bring clarity to our teaching.

'An important thing to understand,' he said, 'is that under this model, a C is like the new A.'

'What?' I paused my cutting, looked up to find most of my colleagues were bent over marking, preparing lessons and hiding behind computer screens. Only Jule, who was taking the minutes, appeared to be following the thread of the discussion.

'Go back,' I insisted. 'What does that mean? *C is like the new A?*'

'Well, under this model this kind of grading is about what the student has learned and how well they've learned it. A student scoring a C grade has'—he squinted at the screen— 'a *sound* knowledge and understanding of the main content.'

'So, what's an A?'

'The student has an *extensive* knowledge and understanding, and they can readily apply this knowledge.' He looked up. 'Make sense?'

'Yes and no.'

Something inside me wanted to rage against this imposition. I wondered what the letter E would mean for all the Warrens and Ryans of the world. I thought of a younger me flipping herself inside out to achieve an A and hating myself when I didn't get it. I glanced at the clock. It was nearly five. *Shut up, Gab.*

'Parents are going to struggle with this,' someone else said. 'The last time we had the A to E grades, A was always quite achievable. It doesn't sound like it would be with this model.'

'I'm struggling with the words "readily apply this knowledge",' Lana said. Up to this point, she had been marking books—the open pile on her left gradually shifting to a closed one on her right. 'If I teach a child how to measure out liquid amounts and how to weigh things, how can I be sure that child can apply that knowledge in different contexts? I can't follow them home and watch them bake a cake.'

'No, no,' the Principal said, his tone placating with an edge of patronising. 'And that's to do with how we're assessing students more broadly. We'll need to review that. We'll need to establish rubrics. Our assessment processes need to become more rigorous, more standardised, more professional.'

There was a quiet then. It happened most meetings when the Principal said something with such perverse ignorance that we were all offended. *So, what you're saying,* I wanted to rant, *is that what we do now isn't rigorous, isn't standard enough and isn't professional? How would you know? You never come into my classroom, you've never seen the way I assess.* I cleared my throat and swallowed down my inner scream. Only fifteen more minutes until we could all leave.

'Anyway, we can talk about all of that next week,' the Principal said. 'Let's have an early mark today.'

'No, we can't leave yet.' It was the Sports Coordinator. 'We need to run through the procedure for the carnival. It's this Thursday.' She pointed to a bunch of papers on the desk in front of her.

'And I have a few items I need to cover as well,' added the Assistant Principal. She pointed to the diary, tapping her finger against the page.

'Alright,' the Principal said. 'Let's move on to those.'

We didn't finish until 6 p.m.

'These are some examples of rubrics.'

It was staff meeting, the following week. The Assistant Principal had the PowerPoint screen working—she'd been in at lunchtime setting it up. Blazing on the wall was a grid with the values A through to E listed along the top. Down the side, in bold, were elaborate descriptions of task criteria. Every square included a note.

'If we look here'—she used the mouse and the little arrow trailed across the screen—'we can follow this criteria along the scale. This one's been designed for high-school students, but we can still get an idea.'

I followed the words on screen as she read aloud: *Task. Expository Essay. Criteria 1. Introductory paragraph. Grade A. The introduction is inviting, states the main topic and previews the structure of the paper. Grade B. The introduction clearly states the main topic and previews the structure of the paper, but is not necessarily inviting to the reader . . .*

'Now, Criteria 2,' the Assistant Principal continued.

'Oh, kill me now,' I muttered to Madge. 'I'm going to have a micro-sleep. Wake me when she says something important.'

I wiggled down into my seat, folding my arms. But then Sophie cleared her throat.

'I think we understand how the rubric works,' she said. 'I just can't imagine why we would need it. I mean, my little Stage One students, most of them are struggling to read, let alone wade through a grid like this. Pierre's just learned to write his name. He'd be overwhelmed with something like this.'

'Well, of course, you'd adapt it,' the Assistant said. 'You'd change it so that it was easy for them to read. Like I said, this is for Year Eight.'

'Yes, but we don't teach Year Eight,' Sophie said, and I loved her just a little bit more.

'Sophie . . .' The Principal intervened. 'We need our learners to understand what is expected of them. We need to make it clear what we are teaching to them.'

'Of course, Boss,' Soph said and I watched as she danced on ice. 'But that's why we model what we are teaching. Isn't it better to demonstrate to the children *how* they can succeed at a task? You know, how you break it down into steps and show them the first part and then they have a go, and *then* we do the second part. All of that immersion and approximation, modelling and scaffolding. You know, conditions for learning?'

The Principal looked at her blankly. The truth was that he probably did know once, but he'd been out of the classroom longer now than he'd been in it.

'Another thing,' Sophie went on, 'and this has always been a tripping point for me when it comes to assessment: how do we know when we know something? What I mean is how do we know when a student has really *got* something? Really understood it? Do they have to demonstrate that skill once? Or twice? And what if they can do it one day and I issue the C, but then the next day they can't do it, or they need help?' She shifted in her seat, but she wasn't uncomfortable; she was leaning in to her own discussion, considering aloud the slipperier elements of learning. 'And the flip side of that: what if I've issued a grade—say a D—and then I'm doing a completely different lesson and the child has cause to demonstrate in *that situation* the skill they couldn't demonstrate two days earlier? Suddenly they've got it, but the grade's already issued.' She frowned and shook her head.

We looked to the Principal, waiting for a reply. But his face had lapsed into incomprehension. It was as though Sophie had spoken in a foreign language.

'Well,' chimed the Assistant, 'we have to collect evidence. Every time a child demonstrates something, we make a note of it as an anecdotal record and we make photocopies of their workbooks and we collect samples of their worksheets.'

'That won't take long,' Madge muttered.

'The thing is,' the Assistant continued, 'it should never be a secret what we're trying to teach our students. They need to know the goal and how to get there.'

'But a rubric doesn't show them that,' Sophie said. 'It doesn't show them *how* to get there. A teacher shows them *how* to get there. And, let's be honest, not all kids are going to get there.' She pointed to the column marked *A*.

'Yes, of course. If a child wasn't here,' the Assistant waved the mouse over the *A* column, 'then we would issue another grade.'

'But don't you think that just consolidates for a student what they already suspect of themselves?' Sophie pressed.

There was a moment of silence, a beat, two beats. Then Sophie sighed. 'Oh, thank God I'm retiring soon.'

The meeting closed at 5.45 p.m.

'How did everyone go?'

Staff meeting, the next week. The Principal was standing at the head of the table, rubbing his hands together like someone was about to serve up Christmas lunch.

'How did you go, Gab?' It was Madge, pushing me forward with a glint in her eye. I elbowed her and then toyed with the page in front of me.

'Okay. So, this week I did a rubric for Art.' I passed a few copies around the table.

'Looks good, Gab,' my friends said encouragingly.

'Thanks,' I said with a nod, looking again at the work on the page. The grid had taken ages, transferring outcomes from the syllabus and slotting them into the tiny boxes, then creating descriptors of achievement, each slightly worse than the one before. *Excellent / good / satisfactory / unsatisfactory / poor.*

'And how did the lesson go?' the Assistant Principal prompted.

'Umm.' I thought back to the lesson. Painting a self-portrait. In the past, I'd started with mirrors and pulling faces and big posters of van Gogh and Picasso. I had let the children get excited about the task; had them thinking about ways they could represent themselves. But not this time.

'I started with the rubric,' I told the group. 'I gave a copy to every child and we read through it together.'

'Was that effective?' the Principal asked, his brow furrowed like we were unearthing a new method of teaching that was going to change the world.

I shrugged. 'Well, keep in mind I teach Stage One. They're only seven and eight years old. Bernie Bittman had his copy upside down for the whole time. Gordon rolled his up into a cylinder and was using it like a telescope until Pippa bumped him and I had to send him down to the office for an ice-pack. He got a cut under his eye here.' I gestured at my own face and the staff gave a collective 'ouch'.

'And after that?' prodded the Principal.

'Well, we didn't get to painting the first lesson. We spent the whole time going through the rubric, and then I wanted to do the introductory activities with the mirrors, but I found a few kids were hung up on how they could get an A. They had a million questions, like what if they went outside the lines, and what if a blob of paint accidentally got on their work, and what if someone bumped them, and what if we didn't have enough skin-colour paint, and what if they got a broken paintbrush. Then they were asking if they could bring in their paints and brushes from home, and then Jane-Anne asked if she could do it at home because she really wanted to get an A and she said she can't do her best in the classroom.'

The Principal rubbed at his forehead. *Good*, I thought. *Welcome to my world.*

'So,' I continued, 'a few days later we finally got around to painting the self-portraits and now they're pinned up on the back wall of my classroom. A few kids did their painting with the rubric right next to them and marked off all the items as they did them.'

I remembered the room, the chaos of painting, the desire I always felt for it to be over—so much cleaning and washing and rinsing. I remembered the productive hum, their concentration and the kids' pleasure. It was the same painting hum as usual—it wasn't any better for the rubric.

'Jane-Anne, who is a very good little artist—remember her work from last year?' I nodded at Joan, the Kindergarten teacher. 'She wanted to add some extra things on her picture, but she came and asked me before she did. She had the rubric in her hand and her painting in the other, and she said, "I want

219

to put my shadow down the side here, but will I get an E if I do that?"'

'And did you mark them against the rubric?' the Assistant asked me.

'I tried,' I said. 'But it was hard.'

The truth was that it had been depressing. Their faces had stared down at me from the wall, a garish, colourful mass that had given me great joy and amusement. Some looked like pirates, others like something from a police file. Anita had given herself glasses and Claude had given himself a huge scar from his right eye down to his chin. Maurice had painted his eyes different colours, while Todd, my slowest worker, had no mouth, one ear and half a nose. Every child had painted a representation of themselves and I could honestly say, having been in the room when they did it, that they had all tried their best. Some had got the new techniques I'd shown them just right, their features were in proportion and in correct position, but others weren't so great. They had tried, though, they had really tried. But you could tell there were some kids who just weren't there yet. Either developmentally or artistically or cognitively—they just didn't quite have the skills to nail it. Yet.

'The next day they all wanted to know what grade they had got,' I said.

Lana laughed. 'Like HSC results!'

I smiled. 'Yeah, something like that. I gave them back their rubric with everything highlighted and a grade at the bottom.'

'It sounds like a success,' the Principal said.

'Four kids cried,' I told him. 'Gordon threw a pencil at his portrait and Jane-Anne said she'd do an even better one at home that she would bring in for me to grade. Narelle's parents have made an appointment to come and see me tomorrow. They're concerned because Narelle only got a C.'

'Well!' The Principal rubbed his hands together as though he was ready for the second course. 'How did everyone else go?'

The meeting closed at 6.38 p.m.

'Look,' Lana said the following week at staff meeting. 'I've got to come clean with all this assessment stuff. It's so time consuming and I don't think the kids really understand it. They're getting hung up now on grades rather than thinking about their learning.'

We all made noises of support.

'All this collecting of evidence. Evidence for everything. I feel like I work for a crime squad,' Madge said. 'You know, yesterday I stayed here until 7 p.m. uploading photos of kids doing the bush dance, and then do you know what? I discovered that I'd missed taking pictures of two kids. Two kids!' She slammed her hand on the table. 'So today I made the whole class go back out and run through a bush dance again so I could get this one photo that I needed as bloody evidence. I think it's a load of—'

'This isn't about what we think,' the Principal cut in, aggressive for the first time. He had been on edge for days. It turns out that Narelle's parents were more than a little concerned about her C grade on the self-portrait. They had been in to see the Principal every day this week, demanding to know how we were qualified to give out As and Bs and Cs. I'd been made to attend the meetings too, defending a C that I'd never wanted to issue in the first place.

'Listen.' The Principal's voice was lower now, calmer. 'We are accountable to our students and to our stakeholders. They're our clients. We provide a service and they're entitled to receive good service. We need to provide evidence of what we are doing here. Every day.'

'You make it sound like we're a business,' I said, fatigue overriding my verbal filter.

'Well, what else are we?'

'A school?' But I could tell it was the wrong answer.

Meeting closed at 6.49 p.m.

Clem

It was my third year at Belmora. I was still teaching Stage One next door to Sophie Kaye. Rubrics and A to E reporting had become entrenched in our teaching lives and, with that, my workload had seemed to double.

In the staffroom, we heard the school bell clamour, announcing the end of lunch. On and on it went, three or four more clangs than was necessary.

'Who's on bell?' the Assistant Principal asked with a frown.

'Douglas Alexander,' Lana said wearily, rising from her seat. 'From my class.'

'Right!' The Assistant bustled out of the room determined to put an end to excessive bell ringing.

God forbid an eleven-year-old should give the school bell a few extra peals, I thought.

'What's on tonight?' I asked Lana as we grabbed notes from our pigeonholes and scooped up hats and keys.

'*All Saints!* Season seven starts tonight!' she said, slapping my arm. 'Don't tell me you'd forgotten?'

'Oh, my God!' I squealed. 'That's right. I can't wait. That's a reason to live!' I felt myself smiling at the thought of lying on my lounge in a near-catatonic state while the make-believe lives of other people played out on the television.

'Do you think it's bad that we get so excited about a TV show?' I asked.

'No,' Lana said simply. 'I think it's like therapy. It's our chance to switch off from all this.'

We stepped out through the office doors and she stretched her arms out, capturing the entire playground and every child in it. The students were racing in every direction like a nest of ants had been disturbed. Handball games ended abruptly and children scrambled from the sandpit as we passed.

'Bell's gone,' Lana announced. 'Playtime's over.'

A little one, named Guinevere, was racing towards me. Her huge brown eyes were alight with drama.

'Mrs Stroud!' she was shouting. 'Mrs Stroud!' Brown curls bouncing. 'Clem swallowed an aeroplane. Come quick!'

'Good luck with that,' snorted Lana as she peeled off in the direction of her Year Five and Six class.

Behind Guinevere was a posse of students, moving like paparazzi around a central individual.

'He's really swallowed it,' she said. 'You can see it.'

As the group of children moved closer, I could hear the bellowing: a primal, aching keen.

Clem.

Clem had autism. He had been placed in my class at the start of Term Two after endless meetings and consultations with his mum.

'But I haven't had much experience of students with autism,' I told the Principal.

I had taught one young man in England all those years ago. I remembered him being literal with everything I said. 'Pull your socks up, Toby,' and he'd pull his socks up, right past his knees. He had been fascinated with his own pre-pubescent body and spent much of his time with his hand in his pocket fondling and foraging and making discoveries. He had once hit a home run in a game of softball and run all the bases with his hands working his pockets. 'Get ya hand off it, Tobes!' the other boys shouted. 'You'll run a lot faster.'

This year, I already had a child in my class with Asperger's. Storm was a high-functioning guy who often hijacked my lessons with his wealth of knowledge and his ability to explain the most complex things in his seven-year-old vocabulary. I had listened with wonder as he had explained to another child why she should wear her hat. The explanation expanded from our playground rules right through to the effects of global warming, including the Earth's exact distance from the sun down to the nearest kilometre. The hat-less child had wandered away before Storm's explanation had finished, but I had stayed, enraptured and fascinated and overwhelmed.

I had been working with Storm on recognising emotions, expressing feelings and forming friendships. We had come a long way since the start of the year, but there was still the occasional outburst, the occasional punch for me or another student.

'He's not like Storm?' I asked the Principal as I leafed through the thick folder on Clem.

'No, he has autism. And as for how he functions with it . . . well . . .'

He paused just long enough for me to think, *Why me? Why my class?*

'Every child is different,' he went on. 'And you're doing such great work with Storm. It just makes sense to have him in there with you. You can use the same resources you're using with Storm, all those social stories and things like that.'

I raised my eyebrows. Those social stories took me ages to create: *Here's how we take turns. Here's how we wait at the tuck shop. Here's how we invite someone to play.*

'I just don't think—'

I had closed the folder, but the Principal cut me off.

'He can't go in Sophie's because she's already got thirty and you've only got twenty-seven. It's a numbers thing, Gab.'

I sat back in the chair. It was plusher and deeper than any seat in my classroom.

'Do I get more teacher-aide time?'

'You'll have Bonnie with you until twelve every day. That's an extra hour.'

An extra hour. Two kids diagnosed with additional needs. It was a joke, but one that wasn't funny.

Clem had sensory-processing issues, a limited fine motor repertoire and an obsession with Spiderman. He didn't like to speak. He couldn't hold a pencil properly. He moved around the room like he was Spidey himself.

His mum was a beautiful, loving, proactive lady who had been advocating for her son for so long that she had perhaps forgotten to advocate for her own needs, too. Her husband had opted out when Clem's needs became too demanding. Like every parent, she had a wealth of knowledge and understanding about her child, but she also had a fierce streak of protectiveness.

'Clem has rights,' she told me more than once. 'He is entitled to the same school experience as his peers.'

I always felt as though I was going to fall in a trap as I tried to create positive school experiences for Clem. If I adapted things too much it would be patronising, but adapting too little would ignore his needs.

'I know it's difficult,' his mum said one afternoon—we met weekly. 'And I know he's hard work.' Her voice quavered as the mask slipped, but then she recovered and pressed on. 'You're doing a great job, and if we work on a few more social stories, and if I bring in some resources from home, we'll soon see him settling in.'

As I watched her leave, I remembered my days at uni—our twelve-week course on Students with Special Needs (as it was called back then). Fragments of a poignant reading flittered into my mind: *Like arriving in Holland when you were planning for Italy* . . .

But after months of social stories and tailor-made resources and meetings with physios and doctors and speech pathologists, Clem was still the same as he had been that first day. Speaking only occasionally, spidering around our classroom and still unable to hold a pencil, let alone write his name. He hated disruption, loud noise, bursts of laughter, the flickering overhead light, the fan. He didn't like other children coming too close, touching him or his things, and he couldn't deal with pain—his own or anybody else's. If a child on the playground fell and skinned their knee, Clem would stand near the bleeder and moan and wail, his mouth slack with saliva, drooling. As many people would rush to Clem as to the injured party.

But I could always find something to love about my students and it was easy to fall in love with Clem. He always thanked me before he walked out of the classroom for recess or lunch or at home time. *Thank you for having me, Mrs Stroud,* he'd say, his voice mechanical. And sometimes he caught me off guard with a smile, a glimpse of emotion that spread across his face so rarely you couldn't help your heart melting.

'Come on, Clem,' I would say when the other children were reading at their desks after lunch. 'Let's work on your pencil grip.' We would sit together at a round table. 'Like this I would say,' nipping my fingers together as the occupational therapist had taught me.

Clem would copy, his fingers plucking at the air.

'Snap, snap, snap,' I would say. 'Like a crocodile!'

'Nap, nap, nap,' Clem would say, his fingers seizing the pencil I held out to him.

'Now we turn it.' I rotated the pencil. 'That's great, Clem. You're holding the pencil correctly.'

I would slide the paper in front of him and guide him to write.

'Let's write, Clem.'

I would print his name and he would watch, his face blank.

'Your turn, now. Move your pencil on the paper.'

But he would shift his hand, losing the grip and making a fist around the pencil.

'Nap, nap, nap,' he might say. Or mumble lines from the Spiderman movie: *The story of my life is not for the faint of heart.* Or he might say nothing at all and I would hear the gash of his pencil across the page and the low hum of student voices arguing over where Wally was.

I started attending workshops and in-services, trying to learn more about students with autism. But each time I was away it seemed to be a set-back for Clem and the class. The disruption of a relief teacher almost didn't seem worth the few nuggets of insight I might pick up at a day-long course in Canberra.

It didn't take many workshops for me to get a basic understanding of what to do. The message was clear: adapt everything you can to meet the learner's needs. But, after a time, it felt as though I had gone beyond adapting resources and worksheets and teaching activities. I had adapted myself and dragged my class along with it. We worked in darkness. We didn't sing. We avoided collaborative tasks. We never ever mentioned spiders or webs or Peter Parker, even though there were plenty of little ones in my class who also loved the action hero.

'I don't feel like I'm meeting his needs,' I confessed in the staffroom.

A few of us had gathered after a particularly hectic day. The students had been dressed in casual clothes to raise funds for a mother with cancer. The kids had been crazy with the simple change and a cabaret show put on by Year Six had tipped them over the edge. The last fifteen minutes of class had felt like hours.

'You're doing a great job,' Joan reassured me. She had shifted from Kindergarten and was now the Resource teacher.

She had been an amazing support, liaising between me and all the people who cared for Clem.

'But I have no idea what I'm doing! I'm making it up as I go along. It's trial and error. And the other kids—they're great with him, but sometimes I just wish we could—' I stopped, feeble with guilt.

'You know he's entitled to this education, don't you?' Joan spoke gently. 'This is about equity.'

'I know, I know.' I was almost slumped over the staffroom table, my head propped up by tired arms. 'I *get that*. I understand I need to make my classroom a place where everyone can succeed, but I'm just saying that sometimes I don't think *anyone's* succeeding.'

'And sometimes you just feel exhausted,' Madge said. She was also slumped in a nearby chair, her fingers looped around a giant mug of coffee.

'And sometimes you just wish you could turn up and do your best and have that be enough,' Lana added, twisting the lid off a bottle of Diet Coke.

I thought for a moment and then sat up straight— enlightened. 'You know, it *is* an issue of equity,' I said. 'That's why I'm frustrated. Clem's entitled to a teacher that is an expert in teaching children with autism, not some crazy idiot like me who did a few weeks at uni on this specialisation. If we wanted to provide an equitable learning experience for Clem and kids like him, that's what we should have on offer. There should be classroom teachers out there who know how to integrate a student with a particular need *alongside* the "mainstream" students. That might enable Clem to succeed alongside the other kids in our class.'

I fell back into my chair, exhausted by my speech.

'You're not an idiot, Gab,' Joan said, and she rubbed her hand across my back.

'No,' Madge said. 'But you are crazy. All the best teachers are.'

Guinevere ran from the entourage back to me.

'I'm telling you, Mrs Stroud, he swallowed an aeroplane!' Her voice was triumphant.

The children were clustered in a careful circle around Clem, orbiting like satellites; they knew not to touch him or he would howl and thrash.

'Okay,' I said, parting the crowd and moving towards the skinny, moaning Clem. His hands were shielding his face and I took a breath, my wild imagination making leaps between the words *aeroplane* and *swallowed*. I had already done a mental inventory of first aid. Clem was walking and his noises were familiar enough for me to know he wasn't choking. *But how could he have swallowed an aeroplane?*

I dissolved the crowd with a pointed finger and firm words. 'Go to the classroom,' I ordered. 'Everybody line up at our door.' The children scuttled like rubbish taken with the wind.

'Clem,' I said, crouching in front of him. I was always ready to leap in case he struck out at me. 'Hold Spidey.' I clipped the tattered Spiderman off my lanyard and handed it to him. It was a soft figurine that had literally been my hero since Clem arrived in class. He was down to one leg, though, after Clem bit the other one off during last Friday's assembly.

As he reached to hold the action figure, Clem's face was revealed and I found the aeroplane—a toy, matchbox size—wedged between his two front teeth. It was as though a tiny jet had tried to fly into his mouth before being snagged on the two white mountains of his central incisors.

'Told ya he swallowed it!' It was Guinevere, still at my side.

'Guinevere,' I said. 'Go up to our classroom and tell our class to come down here and line up behind Clem.'

She took two steps and bellowed in a voice that could be heard around the school. 'COME DOWN HERE MRS STROUD'S CLASS AND LINE UP BEHIND CLEM!'

She then inserted herself behind Clem, creating the line.

The children barrelled towards us, but they steadied themselves when they saw me. I was holding one hand out like a stop sign and a finger over my lips. It had become our signal for a quiet approach to any situation that might startle Clem.

We walked down to the office as a close-knit group of twenty-eight. I let Guinevere press the doorbell button that signalled to the office staff. Lou opened the window into the world of our school's administration. Clem stared at her, the aeroplane protruding from his teeth, as he moaned and rubbed Spidey against his hair.

'Clem swallowed an aeroplane,' I shrugged.

It's hard to know who to call when a child with autism has an aeroplane wedged between his front teeth. In the end, we called his mum and she came straight away. But Clem wouldn't let her touch him so she made the decision to drive him home.

'I'll figure it out from there,' she sighed. 'It's stuck pretty good, though.' She frowned. 'He's just started this habit of mouthing on things.'

'I've noticed. That's how Spidey lost his leg.' I pointed to the figurine Clem was still rubbing against his hair.

'Where's the rest of the class?' his mum asked.

'Umm . . .' I looked around, trying to remember where my crew had been sent. 'I think Mrs Kaye was taking them to the oval for Sports.'

'I'm sorry,' Clem's mum said, clutching my arm.

'It's okay,' I told her. 'Bye, Clem.' I turned to face him. 'You are going home now and your mum is going to try to take the aeroplane out of your mouth.'

He stared at me for a moment and then handed me Spidey. We had established rules that the figurine belonged to me.

'Thank you for having me, Mrs Stroud,' he managed to say around the jet. He looked exhausted.

'Let's go, Clem,' his mum said. 'Walk with me to the car.' When she offered him her hand, Clem just stood beside her, his own hand close to his body.

That night, in my beautifully renovated lounge room, I let myself drift off to the anaesthetising land of commercial television. I watched as two TV characters I had come to love smiled and kissed their way through the birth of their first baby. The background music was sweet and heart-warming and I dabbed at tears while Matty rolled his eyes. My phone twitched with a message. It was Lana.

Doesn't that make you want to have a baby?

I let my fingers hover over the buttons for a moment before I replied. I felt the weight of fatigue in my body, and the adrenaline that had sustained me all day now turned to lead. I remembered Clem's aeroplane and considered the bizarre dramas that might find me tomorrow. *How could I ever manage a baby while still being a teacher?*

NO! I typed back. *NO!*

Shared leadership

Another meeting. The projector blazing. Sophie trailed in late with apologies. Another teacher, Gretel, was stuck in the office with a howling Kindergarten boy who had missed his bus. Lana was eating the lunch that she'd skipped because a guest speaker had come to talk to her class about maintaining good dental health. Madge was filling out two incident reports for a lunchtime head clash that had been, in her words, monumental.

'Two boys, both of them just fixated on that ball in the air.' Her own eyes were raised skyward. 'And then—*KABOOM*! Lucky they didn't knock themselves out.'

'So, what's on the agenda?' I took my seat in the staffroom and read the screen. *Shared Leadership*.

The Principal was in his seat today, ready to command the meeting from his laptop. He flicked onto the second slide and read out a whole heap of stuff about teachers as professionals and how we demonstrate professional behaviour through additional responsibilities and working across various areas within our profession.

Slide, slide, slide. They moved across the wall like ghosts. The need for standards. The need to be professional. The need to distribute responsibility. The need for teamwork. Sharing the load. Understanding the work of others.

'This place shouldn't rely on me for it to run smoothly,' he said.

It doesn't, I thought.

'We are all managers of this school and, as such, we should share the responsibility of that management.'

I looked around at our staff. Madge had finished her incident reports and was helping Lana bag up activity packs for the Year Six school camp. Jule was cutting out teddy bears for Gretel the Kindergarten teacher. Joan was listening quietly, the basket beside her brimming with the staffroom's tea towels that she always took home to wash. Beside her sat Lou, taking minutes, and next to her Bonnie was putting newsletters into classroom bundles even though she should have gone home hours ago.

'Wait,' I interrupted. I could feel the rage flaming inside me, a feeling that was becoming dangerously familiar. I put my hand up like one of the kids in my class. The Principal stopped talking, his finger poised and ready to click over to the next ghostly slide. I let my hand drop.

'I get what you're saying,' I said. 'I mean, I get it and I think it's a great idea—sharing the load and working together, and *There's No I In Team* and all that . . . But I think we're already sharing leadership. Look at how we work together.' I pointed to Lana and Madge, Jule and Gretel. 'Joan washes all our tea towels for us. Lou takes the lost property home in the holidays and washes it. Soph's forever out there gardening and picking up litter. Every night I do a tour of duty down my corridor flicking off extra lights and locking extra toilets and stuff. We *already* share leadership.'

I took a breath.

'And bigger stuff too, you know? Joan's on the school board. Madge coordinates the school concert, Lana's got the student council and all those meetings. Jule does the school magazine—that's an obscene amount of work, and right at the end of the year, too. Jan does all those fundraisers. And now we've started that Lego club in the Library that I've been doing at lunchtimes. We all step up.'

An awkward moment followed until the Principal spoke again. 'You're expected to do all those things, Gab,' he said. 'I'm talking about things that are fundamental to the running of this school. The business end of things.'

I cringed as I heard that word again. *Since when?* I wanted to ask. *Since when did we become a business?*

He kept on. 'Policy documents. Student management. Curriculum management. Organisation. Logistics. Promotion.'

He was trying to take a stand, I could feel it—a desperate power struggle playing out in the staff meeting. He could have the power. I wasn't interested in that.

'Oh, *that* kind of shared leadership,' I couldn't stop the sarcasm. 'Well, for that we're gonna need to be paid extra.'

'Next slide,' the Principal said.

The truth of staff meetings plays out in the car park. Or in the pub. Or the coffee shop. Wherever teachers gather without management, therein lies the true staff meeting. Teachers need to talk without fear of judgement, criticism or added workload. And sometimes they just need to drop the F-bomb without someone gasping in horror and reminding them that they work with young children.

I walked out of the meeting with Lana, hauling luggage to our cars. I had a basket laden with books to be marked and laminated sheets to be cut and home readers that needed repairing. Lana had an actual suitcase, just cabin-baggage size, that she wheeled along behind her. We often joked about her flying off to Heathrow.

'I wouldn't be taking this for luggage,' she said, kicking the bag that was heavy with student work and a weighty program. 'Though I reckon these books might be some of the most well-travelled books around.'

'I just don't get it,' I said, flipping open the boot of my car and hauling my workload inside. 'Where do they think we're going to find the time to do all this extra work?'

'I don't know,' Lana said.

'That meeting has made me feel depressed,' I admitted.

'Why do you bother challenging him? There's nothing to be gained.'

'I dunno.' I slammed the boot shut. Hard. 'Sometimes I think he's got no idea.'

Lana laughed. 'It's not *him*, you know?' She straightened her luggage and fiddled with the handle. 'He's just the messenger. Like all the Principals, he's just delivering what gets set out for him.'

'From the department?' I suggested.

'Yes, or the Board of Studies or the media or the government or any of the other drivers behind education.' She smiled at me. 'I've been doing this a fair bit longer than you, Gab, so I feel like I've seen all this before.'

'Well, how do we stop it?'

A truck rolled past, its engine loud and gravelly and sinister.

'We don't stop it, we survive it,' Lana said. 'I think education is like this huge pendulum.' She dropped her arm out in front her, mimed the swinging motion. 'Over time it swings from this side and then momentum pulls it back to this side. But you've got to understand that this is the world's slowest-moving pendulum.' She clutched her luggage again. 'Sometimes you've just got to ride out whatever stupidity it was that pushed it all the way over to one side.' She tipped her suitcase and made to roll away.

'But what makes it swing—this pendulum? What gives it momentum?'

Lana shrugged, pulled a face. 'The government, ultimately. Take it up with a politician. Who's the Minister for Education right now?'

'I dunno.'

Lana sighed. 'Maybe that's our problem. Maybe we're not political enough.'

'You reckon *that's* the problem?'

She laughed, my tone of voice delighting her. 'I loved watching you in that staff meeting, though.' She wheeled away from me, waving to Madge as she approached.

'You were keeping it real in there,' Madge said as she stopped beside her car. 'I was behind you one hundred per cent.'

'Thanks,' I said. 'Hey, Madge, do you know who the Minister for Education is?'

'State or federal?'

'Either?'

'Nope,' she said with a grin. 'We can look it up tomorrow.'

'Yeah,' I said. 'Let's do that.'

'You gonna write to them about A to E reports and shared leadership?' She threw a tub of books into the backseat of her black hatchback.

'Nah. I just thought it was something I should probably know. Since we're teachers.'

Madge laughed. 'Don't bother getting to know their names, Gab,' she said. 'They're politicians. Just wait five minutes and the Minister for Education will be the Minister for Roads.'

Yes, I thought, starting up my car and flicking on the lights, *and meanwhile I'm left here, trying to teach.*

I teach Kindergarten

*L*ivvy and Soph are playing schools. Now that she's in Kindergarten, Sophie has become enchanted by Olivia's ability to pretend a classroom to life in our very own lounge room. Soph would dearly love to be the teacher, but Liv is older and always instigates the game. For these reasons, the laws of childhood dictate that she gets to play the leading role. Sophie settles on being the teacher's aide or sometimes 'the very naughty kid'. She plays that part with gusto, throwing herself on the ground and thrashing her arms around. I wonder at the behaviour she has seen at school.

Today, they are doing an assembly, complete with toy microphones. Both my girls enjoy the sound of their own voice and they like nothing more than hearing it amplified with volume.

Olivia gives an Acknowledgement of Country but then

realises she can't continue the format she knows from school without having awards to hand out.

'We need to make certificates,' she tells Sophie and they bustle into her bedroom. There's a few moments of quiet and then Liv asks, 'Who should this award be for?'

'Trouble,' Sophie suggests. 'Make it a kid named Trouble and they get the award for being good.'

'That's hilarious,' Liv says, and there's a pause as she writes the information down.

'The next one can be for Bum-Didley-Um,' Sophie giggles. 'He gets it for flushing the toilet.'

Olivia laughs. 'Okay.'

They go on like this for a while, amusing themselves with their own cleverness. Eventually they return to the lounge room. Olivia takes up the microphone.

'And now our voices go down!' It is a perfect imitation of her school Principal. 'Our voices go down,' she says again, lowering her voice. 'Our voices go . . . down.' She pauses and then thanks the boys and girls for listening.

Sophie stands beside her, looking up at her big sister, waiting for her cue. She is clutching the awards in her hand.

From the kitchen I watch the drama unfold. Sophie presents the awards and Olivia steps up, pretending to be each student with a funny name. They exchange the 'certificates' with ostentatious handshakes and cheesy smiles. It is a perfect parody of a school assembly and I wonder what their teachers would think if they could see it.

'What else do you think teachers do?' I ask as the game draws to a close. 'Other than assemblies and standing out the front to teach?'

Livvy draws in a breath, ready to give an extended response, but Sophie jumps ahead. 'They check the books and put ticks all over our work. You should know that, Mum.'

'Do you know my daughter just loves you?'

It was a parent–teacher interview at Belmora. The mother was relaxed, calm and ready to enjoy a conversation. I was not. My mind was jumpy, desperate to convey everything I could in the allocated time in a way that would be useful for the parent and the student. My eyes were on my notes, on the clock, on the list. I was wary of fatigue that could lead to lapses, a wrong name or a mismatched comment. I had twenty-five interviews in three and a half hours. Making each one of them meaning-ful, was draining.

'She just loves you!' The mother smiled at me.

'That's nice,' I said, and I launched into my spiel about her daughter. I talked about areas where she was performing well. I canvassed the things she was finding a challenge. I talked about her social skills, her effort, her friendship group. I leafed through a workbook, flashing samples of her daugh-ter's achievements like a movie on fast forward.

'She really does love you,' the mother said again, gathering up her handbag and keys. 'You know, she comes home and relays your lessons, word for word. My husband gets home and says, *Is that Mrs Stroud I can hear?*'

'Oh, that's sweet,' I said, without any real feeling at all. My mind was already on the next interview. I scanned the play-ground for parents. It was dark and the smell of wood smoke hinted through the air; other families were tucked up around the fire while I was still at school.

'She'll hate me for telling you this.' The mother stopped walking, pressed her hand against my arm. 'But she made me get curling ribbon and curl it up and attach it to bobby pins. She pins it in her hair so she can look like you when she's teaching.'

The mother laughed a little then, so I laughed too. Secretly I was wishing she would leave so I could call in the next parent.

'Thanks for all you're doing for her.' The mother made a gesture to the classroom that was meant to encompass everything I did. 'She's had such a good start to Big School.'

'Thank you,' I said. 'That's a beautiful story.'

'No,' said the mother, squeezing my arm again. 'You're beautiful.'

She stepped out into the evening, leaving me with a feeling that I was missing something.

Big School. That was what I did now. The Principal had shifted us around and late last year I'd found my name listed next to the word Kindergarten. The thought of it had filled me with a special bubble of joy—I would be ushering little ones into the world of learning. I would teach them to read! To write! We would count to one hundred and it would seem like such an impossibly huge number. Kindergarten. Such a crucial and important year.

But slamming hard against these ideals was the workload— paperwork and meetings and documenting and assessing, the planning and the recording and the preparing and the reporting. Big School still meant Big Work. The bubble of joy hadn't survived the first week.

In fact, I'd been shipped off to Canberra in the first week for a professional development day, leaving my uncertain new students in the hands of a relief teacher. The in-service had been on Kindergarten assessment. I'd been instructed on how to administer a battery of individual, diagnostics tests that would give me information on the student's abilities in reading, speech and Maths. Initially I'd thought the assessment regime would be informative and beneficial, but then I returned to school and started the testing. I watched as students struggled through the long and tedious tasks, growing weary and losing concentration. *Just a bit more*, I'd cajole them along. They would sigh wearily and count out some red counters. Each assessment took at least forty-five minutes, but funding only allowed around twenty minutes per child. I'd started calling kids in from their lunchtime play so I could get through all the activities.

Time had become my most valuable commodity and I had learned to guard it as though it was gold. I had planned these parent–teacher interviews down to the minute using a precision known only to teachers who have previously been held up for hours. I called the next parents in and began the verbal outpouring that summarised their child's school experience in a fifteen-minute sound bite.

'Do you have any questions?' I was almost breathless and certainly delirious. I kept looking at the father and thinking, *Your name's not Tom, but it's something like Tom.*

'Is she happy?' asked the mother. 'Do you think she's happy at school?'

'Yes,' I said, resisting the urge to glance at the clock. 'When she arrives at school she's always got a story to tell me and throughout the day she's busy with her work and with her friends. I think she goes home quite happy, too. She's often holding my hand as we walk down to the buses and she tells me little things about what she wants to do when she gets home. Do *you* think she's happy?'

I felt a flush of panic as I imagined these parents telling me a story of this child being utterly miserable and not wanting to come to school. The panic surged to anxiety as I imagined this meeting running overtime. I still had four more parents to see.

'Yeah, nah, we think she's happy.' The mother glanced at the father and they grinned at one another—the mutual satisfaction of parents who suspect they might be doing an alright job. 'I just wanted to know what you thought,' she added. 'We just want her to be happy.'

'Well, I think she is,' I said, standing up and immediately squatting to avoid a large painting of a hippopotamus hanging overhead. I moved towards the door, the politest way of suggesting the interview was over.

'These must drive you crazy,' commented the father, tapping his hand against a painting.

'The trick is to hang things at a height so that you don't decapitate yourself,' I said, and they laughed. 'But I certainly get a good workout: sitting on the floor and having to stand up . . . Oh, and getting up and down from those little chairs.' I rubbed at my thighs. 'It can be hard work!'

'Being stuck in a room with thirty kids would be hard work,' he said. 'I couldn't do it.'

They stepped out into the darkness and I could hear distant voices from other classrooms. A sudden burst of laughter. A car starting up. Next door I could see Sophie framed in her classroom window. She was talking animatedly to a set of parents while a swag of other parents loitered outside her door. Sophie always ran overtime.

I powered through the last four interviews. By 7.30 p.m. I was in my car, flicking the dials to hot and full blast. The dark country road waited ahead of me and I pushed away the gritty, sleepy feeling that was sticking on my eyelids.

As I drove, I listened to my mind rattling through the things to be done, the things forgotten, the things neglected.

What's with the Frederickson family and the McBirds? Why didn't they come to interviews? You never meet the parents you really want . . . I'll have to chase them; I'll call them tomorrow . . . I'm so worried about Sarah, she's still not writing her name . . . Damn! I didn't change those books in the reading boxes, I'll have to do that in the morning . . . Did I swap duty with Gretel? Am I on lunch tomorrow? . . . Shit! It's week eight. My class has got to do the assembly item on Friday. I need to get that organised. We could do that song about the farm animals and they could each wear a headband . . . Will we have time to make headbands?

I curved my car along the solitary road, my mind still fifteen kilometres behind me, in my classroom but already in tomorrow's dramas. A feeling of being overwhelmed seemed to seep into the space around me, like the darkness of the night was closing in. The feeling grew, consuming the air in the car until I thought perhaps there was nothing left to breath. I touched on the brakes, flicked on my blinker and pulled over to the side of the road.

It was an effort to let go of the steering wheel. My hands were clutching at it, fingernails stabbing into my palms. I was sitting forward, too, like I was leaning into the future, trying to arrive and get everything prepared before it had to be done in real time. My breath was loud and fast.

I sat back, pressing my spine into the seat. I let go of the steering wheel and opened my hands, stretching my fingers and shaking them. I took a deep breath and took in my surroundings, noticing the night and the dangerous place I had chosen to pull over. Inside my car, I saw the tub of books on the seat beside me, spilling onto the floor. I had planned on marking them this evening. That wasn't going to happen.

I teach Kindergarten.

The thought filled me up and I recalled the face of each child in my class. I thought of Dale's freckles and Steve with his two front teeth now missing and Azhar with the news of his new baby brother and Sally with that pretty feather she had brought to show me and how Fiona seemed to grow ten centimetres when I told her today how proud I was of her reading . . .

I teach Kindergarten. It was a revelation. I'm not a heart surgeon. I don't have to take everything so seriously. People won't die if I don't get everything done. It won't matter if the green group read the same books tomorrow. It won't matter if the kids don't have headbands for their assembly.

I teach Kindergarten. They just need me to turn up every day and let them know that learning is a great thing. Let them know that they are special and amazing and that they are important in this world. They just need me to read them a book and sing them a song and give them time to write and count and be curious about their world.

I teach Kindergarten. And it's a blessing and a privilege and a joy.

Hold onto that, Gab. Don't forget.

I smiled, a deep, rich grin, as I thought of that little one pinning curling ribbon in her hair. *She would remember that,* I thought as I returned to the road, hands loose on the wheel. When she was older she would remember that she loved me and that she played schools at home and pretended to be me. She would remember my curly hair and maybe the things I said. She would remember the way I made her feel.

'Long day, huh?' Matty asked. 'There's dinner on the stove. Just spag bol.'

'Sounds great! Guess what? I had a revelation,' I told him. 'Just then, as I was driving home.'

'Right.' Eyes still on the TV.

'No seriously,' I said. He looked over and I went on, 'I realised *I teach Kindergarten.* I mean—it's *Kindergarten.* I'm not a rocket scientist. It's just . . . Kinder.'

'Mmm.' He nodded.

'But then,' I slumped on the lounge next to him with a brimming bowl, 'it's, like, I teach Kindergarten, you know? The most important job in the world: creating lifelong learners. The way I teach these kids could impact the way they feel about school and learning for the rest of their lives. The work I am doing is *so* important!' I shovelled spaghetti into my mouth. 'But mostly the revelation was that I teach Kindergarten and I'm not saving lives.'

'Right,' he said. 'Well, good for you.'

'But, in a way, I am.' I added. 'Saving lives, I mean. Because I teach Kindergarten.'

He looked at me.

'I think you're tired. You should eat that and get to bed. You've done a solid twelve-hour day.'

I sucked up a strand of spaghetti and grinned at him.

'I think you have to be a teacher to get it.'

I held onto my truism, my *I teach Kindergarten* revelation. Despite the barrage of supposedly important tasks that tried to knock it from my hands, I held fast knowing it would help me stay the course. I meditated on it often, *I teach Kindergarten*, recognising the weight and weightlessness of each word. *I do the most important work in the world and I must remember to work at it as though it is completely unimportant.* When I held on to the polarity of these ideas without discord, I found a clarity in my days that I hadn't known before.

Whenever staff meetings ran overtime and the to-do list grew to indeterminable lengths, I reminded myself, *I teach Kindergarten*. When new acronyms wandered into my profession—'*Gab, you need to look at ARC on BOSTES for ILPs on COSA*'—I allowed myself an acronym of my own *(WTF)* and calmed myself with my personal mantra. Whenever something else landed on my desk—the assessment data spreadsheet, the new form for documenting a playground incident, the English policy that needed updating, the instructions for the installation of interactive whiteboard software—I placed them into my inbox and said, *I teach Kindergarten*.

I let myself fall deeply in love with my teaching, carving out time for the things I knew to be beneficial. I read to the children every day with funny voices—sometimes for half an hour or more. It was as though I was casting a spell on them, bewitching them not only with stories but with my voice, my eyes, my passion. I watched as they grew still, became entranced, and forgot about the world around them. We ventured together into dark, dark rooms, met hippos on roofs, danced like wild things, found magic for possums and took tea with tigers.

We started going outside more often, looking for Maths in the real world and becoming curious about things like dripping taps and the length of shadows and the height of trees and the number of bricks it might have taken to build the walls of our classroom. We used chalk on concrete and put water in buckets and carried clipboards and worked with pencils tucked behind our ears.

When a parent knocked on my door and suggested she bring in some baby chickens that had recently hatched, I smiled and said, *Yes!* And when a child asked if he could bring his puppy in to show the class I said, *I can't wait!* And when another child brought in a book that she had read at home and handed it to me saying, *I think our class might like this,* I dropped whatever I was doing and sat the children down to read. I sensed with a deep, marrow-knowing understanding that the most important thing I could do for these children was to leave room for *them*. For their stories. For their lives. For their chooks.

I found myself leaning less on external rewards like stickers and prizes and points. I was connecting with the children in unique and meaningful ways. When their work was good, their effort improving, their questions insightful, their comments amazing, I would say, 'Get up there!' and point to the nearest desk. 'Let's all look at this learner! What you just did was *ahhhh-mazing!* Ten big claps for this clever, clever person.'

I found a joy in my teaching days that I had missed, and I let myself take delight in each moment. I laughed with gusto when things were funny and explained the joke to the precious little ones who were so keen to know, to learn and to grow. I discovered that a space was created where I could *see* the children. I found myself able to almost step inside their way of thinking, to understand where they were coming from and how they were seeing the world—how they were learning.

In that space, between me and my learners, an almost sacred bond was formed. These children revealed to me their vulnerabilities. We talked about things we worried about, things that gave us a funny feeling, and raging feelings that could consume us and cause us to panic. Together we created a panic chart, scaling from one to ten these feelings that were so puzzling and unreliable. 'Calm down,' I'd hear them say to one another when a bag wouldn't zip or a drink bottle had leaked. 'It's not panic day! This is only like a three out of ten.' I saw resilience and persistence start to take up residence in their dynamic chests and I watched them grow in ways I had never anticipated.

Liberated though I was with my *I teach Kindergarten* revelation, I was still tethered to my workload and the endless mandatory requirements of accountability. While my days were spent teaching with wild abandon, my nights and weekends and 'holidays' were spent hunched at the desk documenting, recording, reporting. I was forever chasing up work that I hadn't completed during my working day. I drew up belated programs and individual learning plans that never quite captured what really went on. I met with colleagues, rewriting and updating documents so they would now be in line with the new policies that sat in layers of bureaucracies above us. I did my A to E reporting and created evidence that showed how I had refined every formal assessment task to make it meaningful and accessible for my students.

As each term rolled to a close, I delivered token lessons to my class that would give a nod to anything—such as concepts and topics—that I had chosen to neglect.

'Why are we doing this?' a bright little button might ask, their wise young mind aware of the discord.

'Well,' I would say, 'I have to write report cards soon and we haven't done anything in the strand of Health, but I have to mark a grade in the little box next to the word Health. So, for the next two weeks, we're going to learn about making healthy food choices.'

'Why can't you just leave the box empty?' they would ask.

'I don't really know,' I would confess. And together we would shrug, knowing that these things just didn't make sense.

It was a beautiful, beautiful, exhausting time in my teaching career. I was surviving on a mantra. On the euphoria of watching children learn. On the patience of my husband.

I knew it could never last.

Getting a baby

'**M**rs Stroud?'
        'Yes, Miss Melody.'

'When are you gonna get a baby?'

I paused, midway through pegging the children's *My Family* painting to an overhead wire. Bonnie caught my eye and raised a single eyebrow in her unique way, as if to say, *Answer the question, Gab.*

'Hmm,' I said, turning on the stepladder to watch them working at their desks. They looked beautiful from above, a collective, industrious family, creating finger puppets for a retelling of *Red Riding Hood*. 'I think,' I said, slowly and carefully, 'I think I'll get a baby when they start selling them at the shops.'

Piper roared with laughter, loud enough to make others glance up from their work.

'Mrs Stroud,' he said through his guffaws. 'You don't get a baby from the shops. You gotta get them from the hostabill.'

Later, as we relayed the story in the staffroom, Bonnie said, 'He would know. He's one of seven.'

'Soon to be eight,' Lana added. 'I saw Mum at the parent–teacher interview before the holidays and she said she was pregnant again.'

'Eight kids,' I said. 'How do they afford it?'

We asked all the questions and marvelled at the idea of eight. Then Gretel came in and trotted out her often-told personal account of life in a family of twelve.

As I wandered up to the classroom, Bonnie fell into step beside me. She had two daughters herself, both in high school. One of them set to endure the HSC in a few months' time.

'Do you think you will have children, Gab?'

She asked it gently and I made the decision to answer honestly. Since turning thirty, I'd become a disconcerting anomaly for particular friends and family. I'd been dodging *When are you going to?* with agility, but not much grace.

'I don't know,' I shrugged. I'd been teaching at Belmora for several years, dealing with the Clems and Ryans and Warrens as they came my way, and negotiating constant demands from higher up that we work in more standard and professional ways. The thought of a baby in my life seemed impossible. Ridiculous even. I hardly saw Matthew as it was: *When would we conceive a child, let alone care for it?*

'Because I just wanted to say,' Bonnie went on, 'there's never going to be a good time to have kids, you know? You'll never afford them. You'll never be fit enough for them. You'll never have the house perfect for them.'

'But will I have enough time for them, Bon?' I was standing in front of my class, their precious faces shining as they waited for me to move them inside. 'Or enough energy?'

I felt the sting of tears at my eyes and realised with a fright that I was about to cry. Bonnie saw it too and she touched her hand on my back and leaned in close.

'Take maternity leave,' she whispered. 'Then teach part-time. Just do a few days a week. Don't put it off if it's something that you want.'

'Mrs Stroud?' It was Melody, with a glob of snot congealing in her nostril. 'If you get a baby, you should call it Princess.'

My little Olivia arrived in my life within a year of that conversation. It shames me to admit it, but part of my motivation to have a child at that time was the lure of those beautiful words: *teach part-time*.

It was 2008 and the landscape of education changed while I was on maternity leave. I watched from the comfort of my lounge room as new valleys were forged. Breathing in the delicious smell of my newborn's downy hair, I watched national news broadcasts where Prime Minister Rudd and The Honourable Julia Gillard (Deputy Prime Minister and Minister for Education) declared new goals for young Australians and promised a world-class education. As I watched, I realised with a jolt that these were promises not just for me as a teacher but for my child too. There would be equity and excellence. Successful learners. Creative individuals. Informed citizens.

Are these new ideas? I wanted to ask these politicians. *Don't you think teachers have held these goals for decades? Centuries, even?*

But there was to be a difference, the politicians explained. It wouldn't be right to just promise equity and excellence. We would test for these things. We would test for equity and excellence. Because these were things we could measure. And the tool we would use to measure with would be standard because, well—equity. And the results would be published and compared, because, well—excellence. We needed transparency. A system of accountability.

It would be a revolution. Apparently.

So, under the guise of equity and excellence, standardised NAPLAN* testing and the My School website infiltrated classrooms around Australia. Infiltrated the profession I loved. Infiltrated the classrooms my baby would one day attend. And no matter which way I looked at it, I just couldn't feel good about it.

I returned to teaching back at Belmora for two days a week, when Olivia was six months old. We found her a place at a family day-care close to my school so I could pop down and breastfeed during recess and lunch. I had been allocated middle primary, Stage Two—a Year Three and Four class. I would be sharing the class with Jody, a new teacher who had moved to the area from Canberra. I was ready to work hard and then go home.

* National Assessment Program—Literacy and Numeracy

'I'm not staying late,' I told my husband. 'I'm not going to do work on weekends. We should plan for a holiday this year. I won't have to do staff meetings or parent–teacher interviews or all the extra things like discos and the fete and all that. I'll probably still have to do some assembly items, I guess. Maybe an excursion or two. But I'll only have half the planning, half the reporting. Two days a week. It's going to be great.'

'I hope so,' Matty said. 'Our family should come first.' His tone was layered. Over the years, his commentary on my teaching life had developed strong, repetitive themes. How I worked too hard. How school expected too much. How I was too nice. How I should just say no!

I started that year with firm and determined intentions. I would put boundaries around my family time, keeping it discrete and protected from the demands of school. But I found that it wasn't as simple as just making a decision to separate school and home. Becoming a mother had made something come loose inside me as teacher. When I returned to the classroom, I saw every child as someone's Olivia. In each of my students, I saw a beauty and a value and a precious-ness that I hadn't been able to recognise before. I was now aware that mothers arriving at my classroom door to discuss their child were asking something deeper than 'How's their Maths?' or 'Have they made new friends?' They were wanting to know if I had really *seen* their child.

I had softened somehow; not that I was ever a teacher with sharp edges. But I heard my words become rounder, my demeanour more patient, my judgements slower. I was acutely aware of the miracle each child was when they came before me in the classroom. But I also worried in new and heartbreaking ways about those children who arrived hungry or who seemed miserable or who made disclosures about their dad being in prison. *You are someone's baby,* I would think, *and you should be looked after.*

But despite this looseness and love that motherhood had brought to my teaching, the workload remained. It only took a few weeks before I felt overwhelmed again. I had been wrong about the meetings and the interviews and the planning and the endless paperwork. The expectation was that I would *liaise* with the other teacher; that we would make decisions together, write reports together, program together, plan together.

'It's the best thing for the children,' I was told.

'What about *my* child?' I wanted to ask. 'In day-care before eight—first kid there—and the last to leave. Do I really need to be at a meeting discussing the location of future garden beds?'

It wasn't long before my teaching partner made changes to her workload and I was asked if I could pick up an extra half day. Then it grew again to a full day. Three days a week.

'Just say no,' Matty said. He shook his head as I tried to explain why it was better for the students and better for me that we stick with two teachers on a class. Introducing a third would be disruptive for the students, creating all kinds of behaviour-management issues and the logistics of meeting to *liaise* would become impossible.

'If I work three, it's easier,' I said. 'If I stick with two, I'll end up working three anyway by the time I deal with all the meetings and send out all the emails and chase up all the behaviour issues.'

But I don't think he was listening by then and I knew I was really just trying to convince myself.

The IWB isn't working. Sorry about that. Sad face.

It was a note from Jody, my partner teacher. It was scrawled on a gaudy pink Post-it, waiting for me on the classroom desk. We communicated endlessly through emails and text messages and bright sticky notes that we dotted around the classroom.

I sighed and crumpled the note. Interactive whiteboards, or IWBs, had arrived while I was treating nappy rash and pureeing vegetables. The blackboards and whiteboards had all been removed and the Principal—a new guy who loved IT—told us it was his goal to have our school go paperless. He reminded us constantly that the IWB was not to be used as a glorified overhead projector. We were expected to create dynamic, interactive lessons that used the IWB in unique and engaging ways. But, as an aside, there was no money for professional development; no one was coming in to show us how. All the money had been spent on these shiny new things that nobody knew how to drive.

Outside, the sounds of heavy machinery starting up reverberated; persistent deep, droning motors had become a fixture of our days. A new school hall was being built. It was part of the politician-promised education revolution. At Belmora, a hall was certainly needed and would be well utilised, but I couldn't help thinking of all the other things that could create a revolution in education: full-time school counsellors for every school would be a great start.

I stared at the useless IWB and took a mental inventory of the lessons I had planned. Did I need the interactive white-board today? I did the juggle in my mind, trying not to think of the hours I had spent on the computer last night preparing slides and activities that would never be seen . . . I decided I could wing it, get through with some worksheets and a Maths game. Maybe a few kids would learn something.

I was at the photocopier running off sheets when the Principal walked by. He had an iPad in one hand, a mobile in the other, and his computer bag slung over his shoulder.

'Morning, Gab,' he said. 'You couldn't think of a way to make that activity paperless?' He nodded at the photocopier.

Fuck you. The thought startled me. Where had it come from? I took a breath. 'Nah,' I said. 'This activity is an oldie but a goodie. It's just got to be done with pen and paper. The kids love it.'

'Right.' He glanced at one of his screens.

'By the way,' I added, 'my interactive whiteboard isn't working. I'm pretty sure Jody told you about it yesterday?'

'Oh, that's right,' he said, tapping something onto his phone. 'I'll get that sorted for you.'

He went into his office. Didn't speak to me again for the rest of the week. Didn't fix the whiteboard, either.

The class I shared with Jody that year was a cruisy group. They got along well with one another and were usually keen and curious to investigate and learn. There were some who tried a few tricks every now and then, but nothing like Ryan or

Warren. They loved hearing about my baby Olivia, and each week I'd bring in some new photos and I'd beam them up on the IWB (when it was working) so they could see how she was growing and changing. Livvy even came in one morning for a special Maths lesson on measurement where the class compared their abilities with hers. They laughed and laughed as they realised how little she was—how far she couldn't jump, how fast she couldn't run, how much she couldn't lift.

It seemed that Livvy was cruisy, too. She went to family day-care, leaning into her carer's arms without a backward glance. She slept well. She ate well. She learned new tricks. Her lovely body grew and changed.

It seemed everyone was fine—except for me. I was the only one being eaten alive by anxiety.

'I'VE HAD ENOUGH!'

It was a shout, loud and aggressive, from Benjamin, a student who was usually quiet and unobtrusive. I glanced across the room, my attention leaving the group I was working with. I watched as Benjamin leaped up, abandoned his group and stamped across the classroom.

'I'VE FUCKIN HAD ENOUGH!' he shouted again and he yanked at the bookshelf, pulling it down hard so that books thundered to the floor, and students ran for cover as the shelf fell in slow motion, like a tree that had been felled.

Benjamin left the room, slamming the door behind him, as I stood up and assessed the damage.

'Is everyone okay?'

I watched as the kids—as shocked as I was—nodded at me with round eyes. I glanced at the clock. Fifteen minutes before the home-time bell.

I crossed the room and propped the shelf back against the wall.

'What was that about?' I asked the children who Benjamin had been working with—a group of girls I would describe as conscientious and reliable.

'We were just having a joke,' one girl admitted. She had tears in her eyes.

'We were laughing at his shoes,' another girl said. 'They were peeling away at the toe here.' She showed me on her own shoe. 'And we were saying it was like a mouth.'

'At first, he was laughing about it,' the last girl added. 'He was making his shoe flap around on purpose and doing a funny voice, like it was talking.'

'Then I asked why he didn't buy some new shoes,' the first girl said. 'I'm sorry, Mrs Stroud. That's when he went crazy.' She started crying and I felt an ugly desire to sigh with impatience. A can of worms had obviously been opened and it would be up to me to wrangle the lid back on.

'Okay.' I rested my hand against the girl's shoulder. 'You didn't do anything wrong. I think you just said something that Benjamin feels sensitive about.'

The crying girl nodded and sniffed.

'Okay, everyone,' I announced. Several good Samaritans had already started stacking the mess of books into neat piles. 'Just leave those books now guys, thank you.' I gave them a smile and glanced at the clock. 'It's home time. Just stay away from this area.' I gestured towards the bookshelf. 'It might not be safe.'

I opened the door and looked around for Benjamin. He could be miles away by now, I realised. A quick scan of the playground: nothing. Then I heard a noise and I looked down to find him squished into a corner just outside our classroom. I left the door open and approached him gently.

'You okay, mate?' I asked and sat down beside him.

'Yep.' He sniffed and it was a rotten, grotty sound. His eyes were wet and his arms locked tight around his legs. He looked like an egg.

I sat for a moment, filtering possible questions. *I should find out what it's about. I should sort this out.* But then another voice—*It's five minutes until the bell. Just get these kids home.*

Then Benjamin spoke, his voice low. 'You know how Dad's, you know, in jail?'

I nodded.

'Well,' he said, 'I don't think Mum's coping, like with all us kids.'

'What makes you think that?'

'She just went crazy last night.' His head drooped to his knees. 'She was angry cos the dog was barking and Tasha hadn't fed it and Jay Jay was being an idiot and wouldn't unpack his lunch box and then the baby—he vomited all over the lounge. And Mum went mental and sent us all outside and,' he looked at me with sad eyes, 'she didn't let us back in. Not even this morning.'

The school bell went then, pealing and pealing with news of the weekend. A few of my students tumbled out of the classroom.

'Can we go, Mrs Stroud?'

'Yes,' I told them, standing up and trying to shield Benjamin. 'Have a great weekend, guys. See you Monday.'

As the yard emptied out, Benjamin and his siblings—all five of them—clustered at my classroom door. They all seemed to be waiting for direction from Benjamin. I took a breath, glanced at my watch. I was due to collect Olivia in fifteen minutes.

'What do you want to do?' I asked Benjamin gently. His face had changed; I couldn't see sadness there anymore. He was just Benjamin again. 'You want me to walk home with you? You want me to ring Mum and check she's okay?'

'No! No!' Benjamin's eyes were wide. 'She'll kill me if she knows I said anything. It was just a bad night. We'll be right. C'mon guys.' He corralled his brothers and sisters together and made to leave the yard.

'Wait,' I called and dashed into the staffroom, grabbing a box of muesli bars. 'Here, eat these as you walk.' I busted open the box and handed out the food.

'Thanks,' said a sister. 'I've bin starvin'.'

They moved away from me, Benjamin herding them along while the angsty young brother kicked a stone and the starving little sister dragged her bag. I looked at my watch. I had missed Olivia's pick-up.

'It's fine, Gab.' Livvy's day-carer was always sweet and understanding. 'I'd love to have Liv a bit longer.'

'I'm so sorry,' I said again. 'I'd ring Matty to collect her but he's installing a kitchen way out past Paradise so he wouldn't be there any sooner than me.'

'It's fine,' she said again. 'Go do what you need to do.'

I went to the school office and relayed the afternoon's events and Benjamin's disclosure to the Principal and again to the Assistant. We rang the Department of Family and Community Services to seek advice. They told us that the family was known to them and that an online form should be filled in immediately by the classroom teacher who witnessed the event and who heard the disclosure.

'I'll help you,' the Principal said, clicking through websites and linking into portals and creating applications.

I felt the tug in my chest, my boobs inconveniently filling with milk. I looked at my watch: 5 p.m. It figured. Livvy would be getting hungry. Missing me. I took a breath, long and slow and tried not to think of her, tried to make the weight of every-thing go away.

I was still worrying about Benjamin at 6.30 p.m. when I arrived at day-care. As I approached the house I could see the family framed inside their window, the soft glow of evening television lighting up the room. There was the mum, the dad and their two kids all bundled in the lounge room. And there was Livvy. Freshly bathed and in her PJs, mouthing a toy as she clam-bered across their laps—being loved and cuddled and made to belong.

I smiled to see her so happy and content. But something felt wrong—like discordant notes on a piano or brakes on a car screeching to a halt. *I wanted to bath her.* I was tired of loving other people's children, especially now I had a child of my own.

As the weeks passed, a sense of defeat came to sit alongside that of being overwhelmed. I had this constant dreadful feeling of being unable to go back to school. I couldn't undo Olivia and I couldn't undo my commitment to teaching. My life seemed to yawn out before me—long and arduous and without relief. I could only see a constant juggling act with endless demands placed on my time, my energy and my heart. I was all aboard the working-mother train, steadily ignoring the shadowy feeling that the wheels were about to fall off.

On the days I wasn't at school, I tried hard to enjoy my baby. I ignored the school work piled up on our table and the nagging feeling that I should be getting something ready for the following week. I took Livvy to the park, to swimming lessons, to baby music—I tried to cram all the mothering into the days I wasn't teaching.

As I pushed my baby on swings at the park, I tried to talk to other mothers about it, but the consensus was that I wasn't special. Every woman goes through this when they return to work, they told me. It's the other agony of childbirth: letting them go before you're ready.

'But I think it's different when you're a teacher,' I tried to argue. 'I think if you have to leave your child and care for other people's children . . . that's really tough. I feel conflicted.'

'Yeah, I'm the same,' my friend said.

But you're not, I thought. *You're an accountant. You don't have to care for others and you aren't with an audience of thirty schoolkids every single moment. When your boobs start to leak, you can excuse yourself and take a break—probably in some designated workplace breast-milking room. I've got to wait until recess, until I've done playground duty and then miss my morning tea while I pump in someone's office, listening to two kids fighting over the bubbler just outside the window.*

I pushed Livvy in her pram. Made recordings of her first words. Read books to her each day. But whenever I was with her I kept thinking about what needed to be done for school. And whenever I was at school my heart was longing for my beautiful little girl and her soft, chubby chin.

The revelation didn't work anymore. Because *I teach Kindergarten* or *I teach primary students* now sat alongside *I am a mother*. Each was an all-consuming role. *If I am the mother I want to be, I can't be the teacher I know I should be. And if I am the teacher I'm capable of being, then the mother I should be is diminished.*

So, now we have to think about NAPLAN

Earlier this year . . . New Year's Day. I wake, grateful for the choices I made the night before, grateful to wake without a hangover. Livvy and Soph bundled into bed with me. I think for a moment about Matty and how his morning might be—it's tough now we're divorced and sharing the girls. I'll send him a text later, wishing him well. We're still friends despite everything.

The girls sink into pillows, burrowing beneath the sheet, looping themselves under my arms until we are tangled together in our own familiar way. We talk about the new year ahead.

'This year, you'll start Big School, Soph,' I say.

'I can't wait!'

'And you'll be in Year Three, Livvy.' I squeeze her body close, still soft from sleep.

'I don't want to go up,' she says and I feel her body change, her spine straightening. Her shoulders shift.

'Hey, baby,' I say. 'Are you crying? What's wrong?'

'I don't want to do NAPLAN.' She sniffs. 'When I think about it I get this stressed-out feeling.'

'Aww, Livvy,' I say. I'm surprised that she's thinking of this, worrying about it. 'You won't have to do NAPLAN.'

'But won't I get into trouble?'

'No, my darling, you won't. You don't have to do NAPLAN; it's not compulsory. And in Mummy's opinion, it's pointless.'

'What does pointless mean?' Sophie asks.

'Mmm, it means "not important",' I suggest. 'It's something that has no meaning, no point, it's not needed.'

'It's stupid,' Livvy hiccups, still swiping at tears.

'Don't cry, Livvy,' Sophie says. 'It's a happy new year.'

I tickle them both, finding their weak spots, until Olivia's crying with laughter and Sophie begs me to stop. They leap out of my bed, ready to face the day, the year, the next adventure.

After they've gone, I lie back and wonder at what just happened; how the power of politics could infiltrate my child's love of learning, her love of school; how it could infiltrate my bedroom and our happy new year morning.

But I know. I was there when it started. And I had been powerless to stop it.

'So, now we have to think about NAPLAN,' said Jody, flipping to a new page in her notebook. It was the Term One holidays and we had agreed to dedicate a day to planning Term Two. We were *liaising*. But I had been glancing at my watch as the hours moved by. One day wasn't going to be enough.

We would need at least two, plus all the individual follow-up work the planning days created. I thought of Olivia, spending the day at my mum and dad's, and felt a pang of longing that took my breath away.

'Are you okay?' Jody paused, glanced at me with concern.

I nodded, trying not to seem grim. 'Talk to me about NAPLAN. I feel like I missed that while I was on maternity leave.'

'Okay,' Jody said. 'Standardised tests for Years Three, Five, Seven and Nine in Literacy and Numeracy. Tests run over three days. Results come back to school *and* parents, with individual feedback for each child.'

'Fair enough,' I said. 'We've had tests like that before. We used a standardised in-class test at the start of the year. Why are we worried about this NAPLAN?'

'Well,' Jody shrugged. 'My School.' She flipped open her laptop and clicked through websites. I studied the My School page over her shoulder; felt the weight of something I had felt before. At that moment I remembered Nathan from England.

Things have gotta be standard.

This is just the way they do it.

They survive.

'This is really dangerous,' I said to Jody, tapping my finger on her screen. She had left the table and was making us each a cup of tea.

'What do you mean?' she asked, swishing the teabags around before drawing them up and dropping them into the sink with a sodden thud.

'This idea that we can compare schools based on test scores. It buys into an idea that parents can shop for schools like they're shopping for insurance. I mean, the tests only cover two subjects. This My School website can't tell you the well-being of the students, the experience of the staff, the context of the learning.' I took up the cup of tea and felt myself frowning.

'It's just a means of providing information,' Jody said. 'The idea is that it makes comparing schools more equitable. You can get the results in the context of the broader socio-economic demographic. See here?' She pointed things out on the screen and I tried to feign interest.

'I get how it works,' I said. 'I just don't like it. Schools are not about this. Schools are not businesses. Schools are schools. You can't put them in a graph. You can't capture them in a test.'

'But that's not what this is about,' Jody said, pointing at the screen. 'This is about how the students performed on the test.'

'Nobody's going see it like that, though,' I said. 'People look at that and say, *Good school, bad school. Good teachers, crap teachers.*'

'I don't think so. You're being a bit extreme.'

'What about remote Indigenous communities?' I challenged. 'What about taking on kids with special needs? How are their results going to look on this website?'

'Well, not everyone has to do the tests,' Jody said, and I laughed.

'That's *equity*? That's *excellence*?'

Jody sat back in her chair, her head cocked to one side, considering the screen and me—the devil's advocate, arrived in person.

'I guess this reflects where each school is at and it's a chance to look for growth,' she said.

'I think it reflects socio-economic status,' I returned. 'If we were serious about students' progress and growth, we wouldn't spend money publicising test results on a website.'

'Yeah, but if you think about it,' Jody pushed, 'this website reflects our school and our students. It reflects us.'

'It doesn't reflect me,' I said stubbornly.

'Anyway,' Jody sighed, putting her mug down on the table and picking up her notebook, 'we still need to prepare these kids for the test. We can start in week two—that gives us plenty of time.'

She started drawing up a grid, slicing the page into weeks and then into days. I watched her and tried to dismount from my high horse. Meanwhile, Jody was probably wishing she didn't have to work with such a cynical bitch.

Staff meetings were no longer held in the staffroom. The Library was considered a more professional location, plus it was equipped with an interactive whiteboard so we could be anaesthetised by slide shows without anyone having to crawl under the desk and plug in a cord. Every Tuesday at 3.40 p.m. I would find myself sitting in near movie-theatre darkness ready to watch a screen, while my exhausted colleagues suffered alongside me.

'NAPLAN results today!' The Principal was cheery as he stood up the front and touched the whiteboard, navigating his way through files to bring up a graph on screen.

I felt myself wilt into the seat, my arms crossing tight over my chest. *Bloody NAPLAN.* I was sick of it. We had planned for it. Prepared for it. Practised tests ad nauseam. The Assistant Principal kept throwing preparatory tasks my way saying, *We're not teaching to the test, we're just getting them ready for it.*

I was glad I didn't teach on the days it was administered. Jody said two kids had cried, but most had managed well.

'Steady improvement,' the Principal was saying as he pointed to the graph. 'Our spelling is still our worst area. I'm starting to wonder if we need to review our whole school policy on spelling. Next week at staff meeting, I want everyone to bring their spelling resources to the meeting. I think it's time we agreed on one commercial program and we all use that.'

Commercial program. I rolled my eyes. *Reading,* I thought. *Reading is the single most effective way to improve spelling. We need to devote more time to reading if we want spelling to improve. But you can't fit reading in when you're working through practice tests . . .*

'And this is a credit to Gab and Jody,' the Principal said. He had flicked on to a new graph. It compared the results of our Year Three cohort with the state. We were slightly above in almost all areas. 'This is great, isn't it?' He pointed to various plot points as though he was forecasting weather. A few staff members murmured agreement but the Principal was watching me, his expression wary.

'No, I'm sorry,' I said, shaking my head and tightening my arms across my chest. 'I can't get excited about this. I don't even know why we're looking at these results. We keep telling the kids, *Just try your best* and *It doesn't matter how you perform,* but if we're going to sit here and analyse this, then it does matter. I'm really confused about how we look at NAPLAN at Belmora.'

'Gab, it's a brief snapshot of how our school's performing at a moment in time,' the Assistant said. Placating. Patronising.

'I know what it is.' My voice firmer than I intended. Darker. 'My question is why do we buy into it? What do we gain?'

'Data,' the Assistant said.

'No,' I pushed. 'That's not, that's not . . .' I fumbled around for the words. 'Do we really need data? This data?' I waved a hand at the screen. 'I have pages of work samples and projects created by those students. I have tons of comments and observations I have written about them. I can tell you so much more than that little dot right there tells you.'

'It's just a snapshot,' the Principal insisted.

'But it's dangerous,' I went on. Something was stirring inside me. I had made impassioned speeches at staff meetings before but this time I genuinely felt as though I might cry. 'I mean, listen to what we've just been talking about—you gave credit to me and Jody for these results. That's a joke really, because we'd only been teaching them for a few weeks before they sat the exam. Credit should go to the teachers they had in Kinder and Year One and Year Two. Credit should go to their parents and their preschools. Credit should go to the students. I can't be sure I'm responsible for these results.'

An awkward, uncomfortable feeling had infused the Library. I was painfully aware that none of my colleagues were chiming in to support me. I was out on a limb and filled with doubt but memories were flooding back to me: league tables in England and news reports on performance-based pay.

'Fair point,' the Principal said, 'but I think we should take a minute to feel some pride in our collective results as a school. Further to that, we can use these results to support the students to make additional progress.'

'That's what we do every day,' I snapped. 'That's teaching. We shouldn't just be focused on improving results that can be collected through high-stakes testing of two subjects. Doesn't that go against what we believe about education at Belmora? Don't we have a statement pinned up in the office that pledges we teach the whole child?'

'I'm not sure you're making a very clear point,' the Principal said delicately. 'And perhaps it's something you should think about and then bring back to a future meeting so we can consider it together.' He was trying to diffuse the situation, giving me an escape hatch.

'Okay,' I said my voice low and conciliatory. 'I just worry about performance-based pay and things like that. Imagine if Jody and I were about to get a ten-grand bonus based on that graph.'

'It doesn't work like that,' the Assistant said quickly, but I felt Madge shifting in her seat beside me. She had taught those kids the year previous, so those results were arguably hers to boast about. That fictitious performance pay should land in her account.

'I just think it'll be interesting to see what NAPLAN and My School does to education,' I used a lighter voice, trying to make it seem like the last few minutes had been nothing more than light-hearted professional discourse.

'Mmm,' others murmured. 'Yes, you're right, Gab,' they agreed. 'Very interesting.' They were token words, niceties and politeness. We were restoring equilibrium to the room, finding our way back to the benign world of compliance and calm.

'You might feel differently when Olivia's older, Gab,' the Principal said absently, clicking forward to a new slide. 'I can imagine you'd be very interested in her results on a test like this.'

'Olivia won't do NAPLAN,' I said.

'But her results will be so good,' the Assistant said.

I thought of Olivia, twelve months old, chewing through books and scribbling on things whenever she could. Already they wanted her score, her results, her data. These teachers had decided she would be smart because I was smart and Matty, too. She was from a loving home where both parents worked, her mother had a tertiary education. They could guess that there would be more than one hundred books in her home and that she had been read to almost every day since birth. Her 'good' results were a foregone conclusion.

I turned the idea over again in my mind. *No!* The school *didn't* want her results, I realised. They wanted her cultural capital, the data her socio-economic status would bring.

'You don't need Olivia's results,' I said lightly. 'You need her energy and her curiosity and her questions. You need her willingness to learn and her humour and her ideas.'

'I dunno, Gab,' the Principal said with a goofy grin. 'It'd be good to have her results as well.'

He was trying to make a joke, but nobody laughed.

That afternoon, I collected Olivia from day-care. We sang songs together until she fell asleep and I was left to replay the staff meeting in my mind. I blushed as I thought of the things

I had said. I had been ranting without anyone backing me up. Not for the first time I missed Sophie Kaye, who had retired the year before. Sophie would've told me if I was making a fool of myself.

I sighed deeply and looked at Liv through the rear-vision mirror. *Potential,* I thought as I studied her face. *A child is pure potential. So why do we need to test that? And why start so young? Was it really that important?* I worked the questions around in my brain, trying to find clarity.

We can already estimate Olivia's results, I thought cynically. *And if that is the case, why don't we start testing earlier? Test the shit out of them the moment they're born. We could start with the Apgar and go on from there.*

I flicked on the radio, adjusting the volume so it didn't wake Liv. The sounds of Triple J filled the car. *Gab,* I told myself, *you need to get out of your head.*

I text Matty: Hey, Happy New Year! Hope it's a good one.

He replies: Right back at ya! *With a string of party emojis.*

Livvy's freaking out, *I type.* Cried this morning. Doesn't want to go to Year Three. Doesn't want to do NAPLAN.

Not cool, *he writes.* What do we do?

Reassure her. Write a letter to the school. Object on ethical grounds.

Can you do that? I mean are we allowed?

Yep.

Alright. You're the teacher so I'll follow your lead. Poor Livvy.

Thnx. *I flick out of the screen feeling grateful that Matty gets it, that he's vicariously experienced enough of the teaching world to know that the child must come first. And I'm grateful that we're still friends, raising our beautiful girls together.*

Relief

'We had Mrs Lindard today,' Livvy says.
    We are driving to her swim squad session. I am confi-
dent we will be late.

'Is that a relief teacher?' I ask.

'Yes.'

'Do I know her?' Sophie asks.

'I'm not sure,' Liv replies. 'But everyone is so annoying when
we have a relief teacher.' She makes a noise, a frustrated growl,
a sound that says, Why can't everyone take school as seriously
as I do? 'You know what Jock and Miles were doing? Right while
Mrs Lindard was teaching?'

'Tell me,' I say. 'What were they doing?'

'Trying to pull each other's pants down. Right in the middle
of the classroom!'

She gives a horrified sigh and I'm glad because it covers the tiny giggle that escaped from me.

Liv is right to be horrified—and I shouldn't be giggling.

A scratchy, snaky, cynical streak had found its way into my teacher psyche. The glass was still half-full, but the water didn't taste right. I was still able to enjoy my time in the classroom, was still able to connect with my students in ways that were profound, but there was an edginess to me that hadn't been there before. Everything I was doing seemed to be driven by something beyond me. We were implementing new spelling programs in an effort to improve the NAPLAN results. We were formally testing the students more regularly just to keep them in the habit. We were gathering more evidence than ever to justify the grades on report cards. The word 'accountability' dogged my working days. I had lost all sense of autonomy and had learned to stop asking 'why'. I had never been one to play much sport, but I still knew the feeling of defeat.

It was the end of 2009, Livvy was fifteen months old and I was rounding out the year of job-sharing Stage Two with Jody.

'I don't think I want to do this anymore,' I admitted to Matty one night as I was ticking books and making notes against a checklist. It was late—Livvy had taken a while to settle.

'Pack up,' he said. 'Call it a night.'

'No,' I said. 'I don't mean this. I mean teaching.'

'Aww, every job's the same,' he said.

'Please don't say that,' I sighed. 'Teaching is not like any other job. Remember how you felt on those days when you came to my classroom in Canada? I'm still working in that environment, Matthew. Teaching is not like cabinet-making or banking or waitressing. I mean when you do *your* job, there's nobody trying to stop you. When you're installing a kitchen, you're installing a kitchen. But when I'm teaching, there's a kid trying to interrupt and another kid looking for a pencil and a parent knocking at the door and a Principal ringing up and demanding evidence for my report cards and an email from the government wanting signs of improvement.'

'An email from the government,' Matty scoffed.

'You know what I mean,' I said irritably.

'You're just tired,' he replied gently.

But I wasn't tired. I was in the space beyond tired.

'I'm going to do my Masters,' I announced a few days later. 'Take a year away from teaching and do some study.' My voice was bright with hopefulness, bright with the idea of being *away from teaching*.

'I'll do some casual work,' I told everyone. 'Relief teaching. A day or two each fortnight while I study. Livvy's older now. I can do assignments while she sleeps, read while she plays.'

I signed off the paperwork—twelve months of leave without pay—and I went through the process of becoming registered to relief teach in public schools, Catholic schools and independent schools. It was March before all the systems agreed that I was competent and qualified to teach on a casual, day-to-day basis. Apparently, the fact that I had taken leave from a permanent position I had held for several years was irrelevant. Different hoops. Different jumps.

Study was enlightening—gruelling, but enlightening. I came back to ideas I hadn't thought about since my first degree, and now, with my classroom experiences, I could understand things on a level that was almost cellular. *That's why this works in a classroom* and I would smile with the realisation. *That's why this never works* and I would chuckle at the idea. I specialised in Children's Literature and Literacy and let myself wallow around in the miracle of reading and writing and speaking and listening. There was so much to know! So much to think about. Digital literacies. Multi-modal texts. The definition of Literature. So much I could bring to my teaching—I felt excited at the thought. *Almost.*

The trick was to remember that there were two worlds: the theoretical world, where great ideas could gain leverage and take flight; and the real world, where whiteboards didn't work and Warren threw chairs and standardised tests were the measure of your success. As long as I didn't fall for the idea that theory and reality could live together happily ever after, things would be okay.

Relief teaching was hard work, a different kind of teaching to anything I'd ever done before.

'It's like they're paying you danger money,' a friend and long-term casual told me. 'It's like you walk into a hostage situation every day. And you're the hostage.' She laughed, throwing her head back, and I thought, *You're slightly mad.*

I had none of my usual supports as a relief teacher. The classroom was different, the kids were unknown. I didn't know when bells went, or where my class would line up.

'Who the fuck are you?' one kid asked me on my second day.

I glanced at my watch. *It's not even 9 a.m.*

I couldn't rely on an established reputation. I had to prove myself to the students, to my colleagues and to the parents who would also ask, *Who are you?*, with the same cutting candour as the kids. I couldn't just raise my eyebrows at a child as a means of calming behaviour—because these kids didn't know that raised eyebrows from Mrs Stroud meant she was getting kind of grumpy. I couldn't call out a name in a warning tone because I didn't know their names. I couldn't say, *Detention* or *Pink slip* or *Time out*, because every school had different systems and it was hard to keep track. I felt forever on the back foot.

'What's your name?' I was always asking.

'And do you usually sit here in this cupboard to read?'

'Does your regular teacher let you use permanent marker in your Maths book?'

'Are you really allowed to use the computer on the teacher's desk?'

It was challenging and exhausting in ways unlike full-time teaching of your own class. You had to be quick, witty, a step ahead, but always ready to backtrack and fact-check and chase up.

In my mind, I started labelling different classes. The Zoo. The Asylum. The Slaughterhouse. I became tactical when schools phoned in, always asking what class I would be on, any special events I should know about, if the work was just for a day or if there was a chance it would be more. I came to realise that in some schools the relief teacher was considered the general dog's body. You were expected to do extra playground duties and you were allocated the tasks that nobody else liked: *Before you leave today, would you mind cleaning this / photocopying those / filing this / sorting that?* And you had to say a keen *Yes* if you wanted to be invited back. It didn't matter that you'd been sworn at by a twelve-year-old or laughed at when you didn't know the iPad password or lost your voice trying to stop two boys who had spent the afternoon pulling pants down while other kids sniffed textas in the corner.

It wasn't all bad. There were some beautiful classes where the teacher had left a few plans and given the class the 'heads up' that a relief teacher was coming in. Those kinds of classes were fun—the kids enjoyed the change in routine without losing the plot—and I felt as though I'd achieved something beyond basic babysitting. It was interesting to step into other teachers' domains and see how they operated. But it wasn't really teaching. It wasn't the lengthy discourse and exchange of ideas and observation of growth that happens when you're the regular teacher. It wasn't sustained teaching. It wasn't real learning. I wasn't making a difference.

'Just enjoy those days,' my mad friend told me. 'God knows, you've earned them. Makes up for the danger-money days when you're in a terrorist situation. When you fear for your life.'

'I don't think I want to do this anymore,' I admitted to Matty one night as I was preparing games and activities for students in the Zoo. The call had come at 5 p.m. and I had wanted to say no, but I also wanted to make our mortgage repayment.

'Pack up,' he said. 'Call it a night.'

'No,' I said. 'I don't mean this. I mean relief teaching.'

He sighed and, quite rightly, rolled his eyes. 'So, go back to your job. Finish off the Masters, but ring your Principal and tell him you'll be back next year. Relief teaching's too unreliable, anyway. All those early-morning phone calls and never knowing if there's work coming or not.'

I groaned at the thought of returning to full-time teaching.

'I know it's hard,' he said. 'But every job's the same. You're just tired.'

But I wasn't tired. I was pregnant.

A glimpse

'Wonderful,' the Principal said. 'I'll put you on Kindergarten.'

I gripped my mobile tightly, felt the baby kick and churn inside me.

'Wait a minute,' I said with a laugh. 'Did you hear what I said? I'm coming back next year, but I'm also pregnant, so it'll only be for Term One.'

'Oh, sorry,' the Principal said. 'Congratulations.'

'What I'm trying to say is that I don't think it would be good for Kindergarten students to have a teacher that won't be with them for the whole year.'

And it wouldn't be good for me.

'But you might come back,' he said. 'You'll probably want to come back by Term Four. It could work out perfectly.'

I sighed and the baby moved again; it felt like something clawing inside me, and I pressed my hand against the bulging shape. *Maybe that's not the baby*, I thought. *Maybe that's desperation come to life inside me.* I had made the phone call hoping for a job, but also hoping for some sense—the offer of a few days on Library, a day covering this class, a day covering that. I didn't want all the responsibility of reports and programs and assessments and interviews and meetings. Oh, the bloody meetings!

'Gab,' his voice was quieter, perhaps his version of cajoling. 'You're one of our best teachers.'

Then stop punishing me.

Being pregnant and teaching Kindergarten felt weighty. And I don't mean that in a funny way. I was forever hauling myself up off the floor, up off the tiny chairs, up from the squatting position.

'Don't go into labour,' the other teachers quipped when they saw me trying to straighten up after a chat with a tiny one, and they would hoist me up by the elbow and offer to finish my playground duty, though I always declined.

It was easy to think that I was doing it tough at that time— racing through the mornings, dropping Livvy off at day-care and lugging my heavy, pregnant frame through the school gates, ready for a day with twenty-seven five-year-olds. By 8 a.m. it felt as though I'd already done a whole day's work. I knew, though, that all the other teachers had their own struggles. Pip's husband was dying—adult-onset leukaemia—and she had adjusted her workload to care for him, but still needed an income more than ever. Jule's granddaughter had just been born, but there were complications; the baby was likely to die. And Jan was only just back at work after recovering from a heart attack that had struck last year. Madge had two new kids join her class, two unknown quantities that turned out to be Warrens, and she looked exhausted. There were sick and elderly parents, daughters transitioning to uni, partners out of work, marriages on the tilt . . . We were all of us just ducks on the lake, keeping our heads up while our legs kept treading—hoping and hoping and hoping for calm water and good weather.

I had arrived at school earlier than usual, signing a form at day-care agreeing to pay the extra fifteen bucks for an early drop-off. I needed to prepare an activity for my class. We had been reading *Where is the Green Sheep?* by Mem Fox and Judy Horacek, and today we were going to search the school for a lost green sheep. It would be a chance for students to get familiar with the layout of the school as well as engaging them in a rich literacy task. Boxes ticked. One day closer to maternity leave.

On coloured paper I had drawn and laminated sheep—a blue sheep, a red sheep, a yellow sheep, an orange sheep—and I was dotting them around the school. One had been taped to the underside of the slippery dip. Another had been pinned to the tuckshop menu board. I would deliver a couple to classrooms as well. The green sheep himself, a plush soft toy, would be waiting for us in the Principal's office. The Principal seemed bemused by the entire activity, but had agreed to play along.

I hustled into Gretel's class and explained the activity while she started up the bank of computers against the back wall of her classroom.

'Sounds great,' she said, never looking up. 'Sit it on my desk and when you bring your class down to find it. I'll do the whole shocked and surprised routine.'

'Thanks.' I dropped off the orange sheep and lumbered out the door. I glanced at my watch. Twenty minutes until show time. One sheep left to deposit.

'Hey, Lana.' I knocked on her door, but didn't wait for her welcome. 'Can I please leave this sheep in here with you? And then later this morning I'll come down with the Kindies?'

'I can't do this,' Lana said, and for a moment I thought she was talking about my activity.

'Okay.' I took a step backwards. 'I can ask someone else.'

There was something about her face I didn't recognise, even though I'd been teaching with her for years. But then it clicked and I did recognise it and I was terrified. It was stress. And defeat. And possibly desperation. All brought to life on the pale, frowning face of my long-time colleague and friend.

'No,' she said and slumped forward in her seat. 'I can't do *this*. I can't do this anymore.' She shoved at the paperwork in front of her. 'None of it!' She shook her head.

I moved towards her, abandoning the red sheep and putting my arm around her shoulders. Outside a child shouted, *Too bad, so sad!* and there was the tattoo of school shoes across the concrete.

'I know, it's so exhausting,' I said, rubbing my hand across her back. 'Let's just take a minute and have a cry and then we'll get our shit together, hey?'

'No,' she said. Her stare was defiant. 'I can't do it anymore.'

Tears started streaming and I felt panic grip me. I glanced at my watch. Fifteen minutes.

I've got to get her together. I need another teacher in here, but I don't want to leave her. Shit! She's got car keys in her hands. She is really sobbing. This isn't a brief breakdown, this is something else.

'Here's what we're going to do,' I said with a voice that was warm and confident and reassuring. It was my teacher voice— Lana had one too—but she looked at me in the same way a little one does when they've spilled an entire tub of yoghurt down their front. 'I'm going to call Pip because her class goes to Library this morning and she'll come and take your class. So we can stop worrying about that.'

Lana looked at me, nodded, and asked for some tissues. I found the box and passed them to her.

'Then I'm going to ring the Principal. I'm going to tell him to get a relief teacher for your class for the rest of the day.'

She nodded again.

'Thanks,' she whispered.

'You're probably just really tired,' I said and squeezed her arm.

'No!' Her voice was loud. Wild. 'This isn't tired! This is something else. This is . . . This is . . . I can't do this anymore.' New tears came and she leaned over her desk, over the books and the papers and the laptop and the awards and the stickers, and sobbed.

I made the phone calls and our teaching community rallied. Madge offered to take my class for a bit and I sat with Lana until she had stopped sobbing and shaking.

'I'm so sorry,' she was saying. 'I don't know what's wrong with me.'

The Principal came to her room, sat beside her and found his teacher voice, too. He talked about stress leave and mental health and going home right now and not to worry—we would sort out the details later.

'I'm sorry,' Lana said again.

'It's okay,' he said. 'And don't apologise. Happens to the best of us.'

I found her bag and phone and I watched her go, bent over and frail like someone sick, very sick, about to die.

That's me, I thought. *That's going to happen to me.* And the baby rolled inside, uncomfortable under my skin.

'I can't believe it,' I said.

We were in the Library after school, waiting for the staff meeting to begin, debriefing about Lana and wondering how she was feeling now.

'I mean, Lana's so steady and calm and bomb-proof. She never seems stressed or frazzled. You never see her busting someone's arse at the photocopier because she's left things to the last minute and needs to jump the queue.'

'Appearances can be deceiving,' Jule said.

'We all wear stress in different ways,' added Madge.

'She'll come good,' the Principal said. 'Eventually.'

'You reckon?' I could still see her face—that was the face of a teacher having a breakdown.

'I've seen it before,' he said. 'Plenty of times.'

Something about the way he said it, that nonchalant, casual manner, made me feel like exploding all over the room. I wanted to see my body fly against the walls in wet, red, meaty splatters. I closed my eyes for a moment, wondered at this anger that kept flaring inside me. Then, I took a breath and asked, 'So what are we doing about it?'

He shrugged, opened his diary. 'Nothing we can do. Okay— let's start this meeting. First up, funding cuts.'

'Are you okay?'

I was lurching out of my car, willing my body to move faster to get to my friend, to hold her and hug her.

Lana nodded and watched me, framed in her doorway. She was in trackies and uggies, and her face was bare.

'I've never seen you in trackies,' I said.

'Or without makeup, probably,' she said. She tried to force a laugh, but it turned to a sob, and I stood there and hugged her as close as I could with the buffer of a baby inbetween us.

'Thanks for coming around,' she said, ushering me inside.

'I'm worried about you,' I said. *About me,* I thought.

'It's stress,' she said simply, flicking on the kettle and pulling mugs from the cupboard. 'I've seen the doctor; even saw a psychologist today. I just can't seem to find a way to make my work and my life manageable.'

I nodded, watching as she moved about her kitchen. There was a weariness to her, like she was just out of hospital and recovering from surgery.

'Let me,' I said and took her place in the kitchen, making tea and finding biscuits.

'I mean, I've got some hormonal stuff that needs sorting out,' she said. 'At my age, that's pretty normal. But I just can't see how I'm meant to go on being a teacher for another twenty years. I think about those professional teaching standards coming in and I just think, *When am I going to get those done?*'

'I try not to think about them,' I said. 'Or the national curriculum.'

'Oh, my God,' Lana said. 'That as well. I'm a teacher with over twenty-five years of experience, but these past few years none of that seems good enough. I've got to learn this new teaching technique and integrate new technology and promote the school at this thing on the weekend and help that student manage his emotions . . .' She sniffed. 'I just wonder where it's all going to end?'

'Me too,' I agreed.

'I bet you're getting excited about the baby.'

'Yeah,' I said, touching my belly. 'Probably for all the wrong reasons though.'

'Maternity leave?'

'Yep,' I admitted.

'I get it,' she said. 'I get it.'

I stayed until Lana's husband came home from work, watched as they embraced and she found fresh tears. Driving home, I couldn't shake the feeling that I'd just had a glimpse of my future. This baby would buy me time away from the classroom, but then what? I would have to return and continue the battle, slogging it out day after day with big dark shadows of standardisation lurking over my head.

Part of me felt like sobbing, just like Lana.

A long, long way from normal

'What did you say when I was born, Mum?'

Sophie is avoiding her dinner and thinking up endless small talk that could distract me from the vegetables growing cold on her plate.

'She said, "Now I've got a spare kid,"' Olivia stabs at a carrot with a grin.

'No,' Soph insists. 'What did you really say, Mum? When I was born?'

'I can't remember,' I confess. 'Eat some potato, Soph, come on.'

There is a moment of eating and then a memory comes floating back to me with a rush of feelings.

'I can remember that you didn't make a sound when you first came out,' I say. 'I just wanted to hear you, to know that you were okay. But I was tired and I wasn't thinking straight. And I said,

"Why isn't she talking?" And then you gave a huge cry and you've been talking ever since!'

Sophie laughs. 'Babies can't talk, Mum.'

'I know, but I couldn't think of the right word.'

Sophie takes a breath and I sense that she is going to launch another topic, another distraction from corn and zucchini.

'No more talking, Soph. Eat your dinner.'

While I was pregnant with Sophie, Matty and I made the decision to buy a business. He had been cabinet-making since he was eighteen and wanted a change.

'I want a job that's fulfilling for me,' he said. 'Like teaching is for you.'

'Are you joking?' I asked. 'I don't think teaching's fulfilling. It's draining. It's exhausting.'

'You don't always feel like that,' he said. 'Do you know that you never call it work?'

'What do you mean?'

'Like you say, "I've gotta go, I'm late for school" or "I need to get this done for school". You never call it work. I think there's something in that.'

I considered what he said. 'That's interesting but, make no mistake, teaching *is* work. Hard, continual, never-ending work!'

'I know, I know,' he said. 'I'm just saying, I need a change.'

'I get it,' I nodded, sliding a hand along my belly to receive a kick. 'I get it.'

We sold our home and bought into holiday apartments, quickly falling into a life that was alarmingly similar to *Fawlty*

Towers. We lived upstairs in a two-bedroom apartment that had a stellar view but no yard, no spare room and no bathtub. I shifted furniture around, gradually selling things off so we could all comfortably fit. Matty was certainly happier, finding his stride as a small business operator. He took bookings and cleaned units and chlorinated the pool. But he was busier too, literally living at work and finding it almost impossible to 'switch off'.

'I think I finally know how you've felt,' he told me on the first Saturday afternoon after we moved in. He had stretched out on the lounge after a morning of cleaning. Layers of book-work were stacked nearby, ready for him to work through. 'There's always something to be done.'

'Yep,' I said. 'Now do it for ten more years and get back to me. Oh, and Matty?'

'Yeah?' He was already distracted, leafing through the reservations book and tapping a pencil against his lip.

'I don't think the cot's going to fit.'

Something strange happened to time after Sophie was born. The days could feel interminably slow, starting early and finishing late, dragged along by playgroups and community nurse appointments and trips to the park. ABC2 became perpetual background noise while I mashed food and folded washing and listened as Olivia pretended to read a tattered old copy of *Charlotte's Web*. Hours yawned by as I tried to get the pair of them to sleep simultaneously, while minutes passed as I closed the bedroom door with the stealth of a woman engaged in international espionage.

But, somehow, through the molasses of these mundane events, my calendar seemed to be accelerating. I kept checking and counting that I still had time—still had time to be at home, still had time to enjoy my kids before I had to go back to school. Our new mortgage needed my income and permanent teaching positions cannot be suspended indefinitely.

As the weeks reduced, twenty, sixteen, twelve, eight (*that's only two months!*), all those feelings of defeat and desperation started to shadow in my chest. Anxiety and dread became my constant companions and I found my temper flaming when a piece of Duplo crunched underfoot or a plate of mush was left to harden in the sink. *How will I do this while I'm doing that?* I kept asking myself. *How will I manage two kids and all the household crap while I'm teaching full-time?*

I spent my last weeks of leave planning the weeks ahead. I wrote my teaching programs and my timetables and my assessment schedules and my rubrics and my welcoming letters and my global statement about my year-long learning goals for this group of kids. Then I planned the schedule for our household: the meals, the drop-offs, the pick-ups, the lunches, the shopping days, the cooking days, the washing days, the cleaning days.

As long as nothing goes wrong. It was a fragmented thought, needing a clause at the end, like, *I'll be alright* or *This could work*. But I knew, deep inside, that I was building a house of cards. A strong wind, a dose of flu, a case of head lice or an accidental sleep-in and the whole thing would tumble down.

Again, I was allocated Kindergarten. An unusual class, weighty with boys—twenty in total, with five girls.

'One more thing . . .' The Assistant Principal had rung to check dates for the Kindergarten assessment routines.

'Yep?' I was looking out the window. A beautiful summer's day was waiting, waiting for me and my girls to be at the beach.

'You're going to have a prac student, too. They'll arrive in week four, I think. From the University of Newcastle or Sydney or somewhere. I thought you could do with the extra hands in that first term. I hope that's okay?'

'Okay,' I said and tried to see the extra helping hands, rather than the extra reporting, documenting, paperwork and emails.

I tried hard, but when I returned to school after being on leave with Soph, something about me had changed. I felt like a flickering fluorescent light. Like uninsulated wires. I had no patience. No compassion. And a strange thing had happened. I couldn't cry. And I couldn't laugh.

It was in this second week back at school that Grayson threw his shoe at me. I responded with rage. 'Teacher-me' was broken.

Somehow, moments after the shoe-throwing, I managed to compose myself and prepare the class for afternoon dismissal. Grayson hopped theatrically around the room, conspicuously demonstrating that he only had one shoe. One of the cicada hunters had offered to retrieve it and, before the afternoon had closed, Grayson was wearing two neatly laced black leather school shoes. The class had bundled out the door looking as tired and raggedy as any other day, seemingly unaffected by my outburst.

I took myself straight down to the Principal's office.

'I have done a bad thing,' I said.

'Sit down,' he said. 'What happened?'

'I threw a shoe.'

He laughed. 'That's okay.'

'No, it's not okay,' I said and wished I could cry, wished I could squeeze out some visible sign of the emotions that had been brewing within me. *But you're almost numb*, I realised.

'I took this kid's shoe and hurled it out the door and into the yard.' I took a breath and described the afternoon, giving context to the situation.

'Hmm, I see,' he cocked his head to the side and studied me for a moment. 'It's not a big deal, Gab. Teachers face a great deal of stress. You saw Lana that day she went out on stress leave. We've all been there. I've slammed down books and raised my voice so loud I've frightened myself.'

'Yes,' I was clutching on to what he was saying. 'I frightened myself.'

'It's okay,' he assured me. 'You're settling in after being on leave and from what I've observed they're a pretty busy class. Plus, you've got two kids of your own now. That's a fair bit on your plate.'

'But it's not like me,' I insisted. 'I don't throw things.'

'I'm not worried about it. So, you threw a shoe. Next time, just send the kid down to me. I'll handle it.'

'Thank you,' I felt my face change, relaxing a tiny bit, but there was no flood of feelings. The numbness remained. *I might be sending kids down to him all the time*, I thought. *I'm not coping.*

'Now, Gab, before you go . . .'

'Yep?'

'Those Kindergarten assessments? Where are you at with them?'

Are you kidding? I wanted to say. But I dug deep inside, found a shred of professionalism and said, 'I've started but they always take a lot longer than the time allocated.'

'Get on to them,' he said. 'ASAP.'

At home that afternoon, I told Matty about the shoe.

'Well, the kid wasn't wearing it, was he?' He smiled at me. 'He probably deserved it. When I was a kid I got chalk thrown at me by one of the nuns. I turned out alright.'

'That's not helpful, Matty.'

'I don't know what is helpful,' he shrugged. 'I honestly don't know how I can help you.'

I nodded, agreed with him. 'I don't know either.'

'Let's get away,' he suggested. 'I'll book us a little trip, try to sneak it in before the apartments get busy.'

'Okay,' I said. It was a nice gesture, but it wouldn't change anything.

Term One went on but there was a scratchy feeling that gnawed at me each day, and I knew that I was facing the beginning of the end.

'I can't do this for much longer,' I started saying to my colleagues, and they would smile and say, 'We all feel like that, Gab. You'll be right.'

Only Lana seemed to understand. She was back—just two days a week.

'I'm being rehabilitated,' she said. 'Like that's a thing.'

My heart had started to ache—like Grayson's shoe had left a bruise. It was an ache that was never painful enough, only a perpetual weight that I now carried. It flared at staff meetings, when new students arrived, when paperwork was called for, but what would I tell a doctor about this shadowy bruise in my chest? This pain that ached when I was asked to work harder?

Throughout the term, Matty kept suggesting I take a day off. 'Have a break,' he'd say. 'Have a rest.'

But it wasn't worth the effort—all the organising of lessons and worksheets and activities and writing out instructions on how to log in to the whiteboard. Not to mention the clean up the next day, dealing with the debris of a class out of sorts and unfinished paperwork.

'I need more than a day,' I told him. 'I don't even know what this job is anymore. There's just so much to get done and now we're implementing a new national curriculum, but there's no time to stop and get your head around it, just a two-hour staff meeting where the Principal bumbles his way through the website and then it's like, 'Good luck with that'. And all this testing we've got to do—these poor kids.' I sighed, wishing I could cry, wishing I could let the pain seep out.

'Why don't you take stress leave?' Matty pressed. 'Lana did it.'

I made a face. *Stress leave.* I wanted to be tougher than that.

Term One was over and Matty had planned a trip away. We packed up the kids and the car and drove south, away from Belmora, through Paradise and then beyond until we were far, far away and nobody would recognise us in the supermarket.

We found the best coffee in town and, then, the best playground. Matty bought a newspaper and I opened my laptop to a screen of school work. We settled in as the girls played.

I started drawing up the Term Two program for English and found myself paralysed.

'Matty, I think I need to get out of teaching.'

He closed his paper and studied my face. Didn't say anything.

'I'm not myself, Matty.' I felt my voice falter and wondered for a fascinating moment if maybe I *could* cry, but then I went on and my voice was the same. 'I don't feel right—I feel numb and it's because of teaching.' I watched as Sophie tottered towards the swings.

'Okay,' he said. 'What about if you just worked part-time? Did a job share?'

I shook my head slowly, remembering my year with Jody and all the *liaising*. Matty left for a moment, helped the girls to clamber on to the see-saw.

'Yeah, we have tried that,' he said, sitting beside me. 'How about if you finish this year and then take another year of leave without pay?'

'And study?' My expression horrified.

'No!' he said. 'No, just a year of leave. You could help me with the apartments. It'd be tight financially but we could manage it.'

'Yeah?' I felt a flutter of hope. 'And then what? After the year of leave?'

'Well,' he considered the situation while we watched the girls, each one bobbing up and down in turn. 'How about you go back, but just for a year. What if you did a year on and a year off for a while. Then see how you feel once the girls are a bit older and all these national curriculum and teacher standard things have settled down.'

'Maybe,' I said. 'Maybe I could do that. I mean it's like going part-time really isn't it? But less disruptive for the students.' I sat with the idea a moment longer. 'This would be an amazing job-share experience.' I could feel something like muted enthusiasm stirring inside me. 'Imagine if I could find another teacher who wanted to do the alternate year. We could have one position but share it on a yearly basis.'

'You should at least ring up and ask if you can have leave for next year. That's a starting point. You could ring up today. Your human resources people would still be at work. They're not on holiday like you teachers.'

'Matty!' I growled. Anger was never far from the surface. 'Just because I'm not at school doesn't mean I'm on holidays—do you not see the work I'm always doing?' I snapped my laptop shut.

'Gab, relax,' he said. 'Let's get the girls and walk back and you can make the phone call. Okay?'

'Okay.'

I shut myself in the bedroom of our accommodation, made the phone call, and listened as it rang. A whitewashed sign on the wall promised *Life's A Beach*!

'I've found teaching has really changed for me,' I explained to human resources. 'I just feel like there's so much to do.

I find myself wishing the students would stay home so I can get all the work done.' I paused, looked out the window and saw rain clouds gathering. 'And then, when I *am* teaching, I'm morally and ethically conflicted. I don't think we're devoting enough time to the actual teaching—we're racing them through a crowded curriculum, testing them when they're not ready, using methods they're not ready for.'

'Why don't you go part-time?' human resources asked. Her voice was polished and patronising.

'Because I don't think that's great for the kids I teach. Or for the teachers, really. I've tried it before and it's a lot of work.' I paced the bedroom, tugged gently at a curtain. Darkness was coming.

'Are you requesting stress leave? Because, if you are, there's a form you complete online and . . .'

'No,' I cut in. 'I was wondering if I could plan to have next year off? Leave without pay. I'm thinking about maybe just working every other year or two years on, one off. In my head, I . . .' I paused. 'I need to know there's an end in sight. That I'll do all this work and get a chance to rest and fill the cup, you know?'

'Oh, we're not awarding leave without pay anymore,' HR said. 'It's too disruptive for the school and the students.'

'But you just suggested I work part-time. Don't you think that's disruptive?'

'Not if it's well managed.'

I paused and for a moment I thought about all I had done for this employer—all the Ryans and Warrens I had nurtured. All the Clems. All the Spidermen I had bought, only to have their legs chewed off. All the times I'd worn costumes and fed children and stayed at work when I should've been at home. All the meetings. All the forms and spreadsheets and programs I'd completed. All the skinned knees I'd tended. All the stories I'd listened to. All the hands I'd held. All the wood-chips I'd dusted from jumpers. All the yoghurt I'd hosed off concrete. All the vomit. All the snot. I thought of all of it. All of it in that single moment.

'What do you suggest I do?' I asked.

A heartbeat.

Another one.

'Resign.'

'Oh, thanks for that.'

I swiped at the screen and curled up on the bed.

Too bad, so sad.

'What's going on, love?' Dr Bentley tilted his head down, inspected me over the rim of his glasses.

'I'm not sure.' I shrugged. 'I just . . .' I shrugged again, by way of explanation.

We sat together for a moment, watching my girls, who were sitting on the floor. Dr Bentley had given them a handful of tongue depressors. Olivia was lining them up along the carpet, counting them carefully while Sophie watched on, absorbed and adoring. It was the last Friday of the Term One school holidays and I physically couldn't bring myself to even think of returning to the classroom.

'Something happened yesterday,' I began, and the words tumbled out of me while I was looking at the kids and not the doctor. 'I was down the street and I was putting the girls in the car and Sophie was wearing this ridiculous tutu dress. The tulle was everywhere and I couldn't get the seatbelt into the clip, and I was so hot—it's been so hot, you know? And the heat was burning me up and the bloody tulle was making it impossible. When I finally got the stupid seatbelt done up I shut the door and turned around and there was a bus coming and'—I lowered my voice—'I just thought I'd like to walk into that bus.'

I glanced at Dr Bentley and he was nodding like it was completely understandable. Like what I had told him was perfectly normal. Like *I* was perfectly normal.

'And there's more,' I said, my eyes on his face now, watching for horror, watching for surprise. 'I can't laugh. I can't cry. Even if something's really funny, or really sad. Even if I hurt myself. I've just got this numb, hollow feeling inside me. And my temper's like a bloody firecracker. I don't even know I'm about to go off. I frighten myself.' I glanced at the girls and then kept talking. 'I've tried talking to Matty,' I lowered my voice again, 'not about the bus, but about the numbness. He tries to help, but he doesn't understand. He thinks I just need a few days off work.'

'Open wide,' Olivia said suddenly and we turned to watch as she poked the stick into Sophie's obliging mouth. 'Very good! Let's do that again. Open wide!'

We watched her do three more rounds and I heard Dr Bentley chuckle so I put a smile on my face, too.

'What do you think is wrong?' he said after a while.

'I think I'm depressed,' I said and he nodded again, like he still thought it was perfectly normal.

But that night, as I slipped a prescription for anti-depressants and a psychologist's number into my diary, I felt a long way from normal. A long, long way from it.

Some weeks later, in the filtered afternoon light of the psychologist's room, my depression and the reasons behind it seemed muted and insubstantial. I had been taking the medication for several weeks and the feeling of numbness had been displaced by indifference. My head felt like it was clogged with cotton wool and I didn't care about anything that was happening around me. I was just showing up and going through the motions. There was no fiery anger flaring within me, my last remaining emotion had seemingly ebbed away. *Give it time*, Dr Bentley had said. *Give it time.*

I sat in a beautiful wicker armchair and felt the lacings of it, smooth and round, beneath my fingers. I noticed the swirls patterned within the carpet. I breathed in the gentle scent of jasmine tea and floral perfume that hinted through the air. In this space, my teaching life might not exist.

'Nurses feel it too,' the psychologist was explaining. 'People in armed services, doctors, anyone who works in a profession where there's a high chance of sudden change. There are so many variables in your workplace. A child can vomit. A child could collapse. An angry parent could arrive at the door. All your equipment can suddenly not work. A boss springs a sudden assembly on you . . . You start to exist in a state of high alert.'

'Yeah.' Though I was reluctant to agree. 'But it's not life and death, is it? I mean, a kid suddenly wets his pants—that's not the same as a person having an aneurysm. The staff meeting runs over time—it's a bummer, but nobody's going to die, are they?'

'But your brain doesn't know that,' the shrink said. 'If a kid starts swearing at you and you start feeling a stress response, your brain responds just the same as if a tiger was in the room with you. Cortisol starts dripping into your system and your body prepares for fight or flight. In your situation, your body has been resisting the urge to fight or flight for too long.'

I smiled at her, not quite a smirk, but something like it. I didn't want her to explain teaching to me, I wanted her to take it away from me.

'That's what teachers do,' I told her. 'They resist the urge for fight or flight.'

She nodded, her head to one side and the expression on her face so gentle and sympathetic that I felt myself shift in my seat.

'I see your pain, Gabrielle,' she said.

And that's when the bloody Zoloft kicked in and I was finally able to cry.

With the medication and the psychologist, I made it to the end of year. But I woke up every morning feeling scared.

Did I have enough energy?

Could I make it through the day?

What was going to happen?

I stopped taking school work home and tried to leave the classroom as early as I could. I spent my Sundays planning—building that house of cards that might ensure a peaceful, productive week. I took my tablet, talked to my psychologist and wondered if I would ever feel normal again, or if this was the way I would be for the rest of my life: slightly stoned, perpetually exhausted and relying on a monthly conversation where I tried out positive affirmations and talked about making time for yoga.

One afternoon, Matty rang me at school. The admin staff put the call straight through to my classroom. It was unusual for him to phone, especially via the office line.

'Gab!' His voice sounded desperate and I pressed the phone against my ear, trying to block out the sounds of Kindergarten in the throes of an independent Maths activity.

'What's up?' I thought of Shirley, our aging dog and then of my folks. 'Matty?'

'It's my computer,' he wailed. 'It has literally died. I've lost everything. All our end-of-month. All our templates. Guest information. It's all gone. I can't even turn the computer on.'

I rolled my eyes, felt relief, turned around to see a boy running with scissors. 'I can't help you,' I snapped. 'Call a computer guy, pay whatever you need. It won't be lost forever. Get them to back it up. Then go and buy a new computer.'

'Okay,' he said, oblivious to my flippant tone. 'Who should I ring?'

'I don't know, Matty. Figure it out.' I hung up on him.

At lunch, the admin staff were anxious to know if everything was alright. *Matty had sounded quite upset*, they said.

'His computer died,' I said, biting into an apple. 'He's alright.'

'Oh, that can be so stressful,' Gretel said, overhearing our conversation.

They chattered on, my colleagues more sympathetic to Matty's situation than I had been. *It's not my problem*, I thought. *It can't be my problem.*

That afternoon as I drove home, I couldn't shake the feeling of guilt. *Matty deserves a wife who gives a shit, deserves someone who has the energy to care.*

'Hey,' I said arriving home, finding him out the front and watering the lawn. I unloaded the girls from the car, hauling out enough bags to suggest we'd returned from a trip overseas. 'I'm sorry if I sounded abrupt on the phone today. Are you okay? Did you get the computer sorted out?'

'Yeah,' he grinned at me. 'I got this guy to come around and he brought it back to life and retrieved everything. Come and look,' he turned off the hose and led me towards the office. 'Plus, I went and bought a new computer. Check out this beast!' On the desk was a new laptop, connected to a large screen. A portable hard drive hummed nearby. 'Everything from the old one has been installed on here and backed up here.' He tapped each piece of equipment as he spoke.

'That's great,' I said. 'Good job.' I offered him my palm for a high-five.

He slapped it and then fiddled with the mouse, watching with delight as the screens burst to life.

Nearby, two invoices were printed and stamped *PAID*. The whole thing had cost us my month's pay.

The boogeyman

When I was a little girl, my much older siblings collaborated to craft a very living presence of the boogeyman
in our hallway.

'Watch out for the boogeyman,' Phil would say, his voice
urgent and breathless every time I approached.

'Oooh, I just saw the boogeyman!' Jacqui would exclaim,
drawing the hall door shut behind her. 'I'll trap him in there.'

They would wink at me, as though I, too, was a co-
conspirator in this world where boogeymen inhabited hallways.
I tried to return their winks, pressing my hand over one eye for
a brief moment, but I knew, deep in my being, where children
know such truths, that I was terrified of the boogeyman. In
my wild and creative imagination, I knew that he was big and
brown and shadowy. He was dangerous. He would hurt me if
he caught me.

I never walked down our hallway. I *fled* that strip of brown-patterned carpet with terror nipping at my heels. My heart would thunder as I crossed the boogeyman's territory.

'Don't! Slam! The door!' Mum would say every time I arrived in the lounge room, breathless and flushed. I would try to play it cool, arranging my face to hide all fear. My brother would raise his eyebrows at me—his question clear: *Did ya see him?* And I would press a trembling hand over my eye in an effort to wink.

I managed one more year. Kindergarten. Olivia was in that class—my beautiful little Olivia. She was going to Big School! My school! And I would be her teacher.

Term One and Olivia and Sophie were in the back seat, as I drove us in to Belmora. Olivia in her smart, new uniform and Sophie in play clothes, ready for day-care. Their car seats almost filled the back seat. Up front, layered beside me, were schoolbags and library bags and piles of books and tubs of resources. I tried not to notice it all as I drove. I tried to stay present and mindful—like the shrink had taught me. But when I approached roadworks and tapped the brake, my left arm went out instinctively. I needed all those things to remain in place. I didn't want the tower to tumble.

'Olivia,' I said as we paused at the *Stop* sign, 'look at all those spider webs. Can you see them glistening in the sun?' I tapped the window, pointing to the lacy webs that were beaded with dew and clinging to the tall grass on the roadside. 'I wonder if a spider like Charlotte made any of those webs?'

I glanced in the rear-vision mirror to see Olivia smile at my idea. We had been reading *Charlotte's Web*, a few pages every night. As the *Stop* sign changed to *Slow* we moved forward.

'Bye-bye,' Sophie called, waving to the traffic guy.

'Mum?' Livvy asked.

'Yes, darling,' I negotiated around the traffic cones. They were resealing an old road. It was messy work. I could hear the loose stones grabbing at my tyres.

'Do different types of spiders make different types of webs? Like a long-legged daddy spider makes something different to a red back?'

'I don't know,' I said. 'That's an excellent question, Liv. We can look that up tonight on the computer.'

'Hmm,' she said, thoughtful. 'Or I could ask another teacher at school. Because you only teach Kindergarten so you probably don't know much.'

They were a lovely class. Such beautiful learners. It's a bitter-sweet memory for me.

'Eyes are watching, ears are listening . . .'

The tune was *Frère Jacques* and I pointed to each body part as I sang. The children copied my actions, their tiny bodies finding space on the mat to sit. My mothering heart surged with love as I watched Olivia dash to the front, but then wriggle aside to make space for another child.

'Mouths are closed. Hands are still.' I placed my hands in my lap. 'Feet are very quiet, you should really try it. Listening well. Listening well.'

The song had a lullaby effect. They were almost silent and watching me earnestly like dogs waiting to be fed.

'Today, boys and girls, we're going to read a poem.' I perched forward on my seat. 'A poem can be like a story, but it's often told differently—it can be shorter, the rhythm of the words can feel different, and there can be rhyming. Are you ready to hear this poem?'

'Yes!' they chorused.

'But where's ya book?' a boy called out. Jock.

'I don't need a book for this one,' I told him. 'I just need . . . *this*!' I grabbed at the air, as though catching something that was flying by. I cupped my hands and peeped inside. 'Yes!' I confirmed. 'I've got everything I need.'

'There's nuthin' in there,' Jock said.

'Shoosh up,' a girl said. Sarah—she was always hungry and often stole the other kids' food. 'Let her do the pome.'

I smiled at them and ignored Isla, who was deftly undoing the buckle of my shoe.

'I found a little beetle . . .' I began and I looked again into my cupped hands, before looking back at the children. 'You find a beetle now, too. Quickly. Oh, my goodness, look at them! There's lots of them in here right now. Grab that one right next to you, Owen. And there's one near you, Isla!'

The children embraced my magic and captured imaginary beetles, then sat patiently, waiting for my next trick.

'I found a little beetle, so that Beetle was his name . . .'

On I went, miming and acting and reciting the great tragedy of Alexander until the bell rang for recess and they rushed out the door, still clutching imagined beetles in their capable, sweaty palms.

Later, after I returned from duty on the seniors' playground, I was thinking about the incident I needed to document, the worksheet I forgot to photocopy, the lunch I'd need to make for Sarah. I was ignoring the weight in my chest, the feeling that my heart was bruised.

My students waited outside our door, telling me they'd released their beetles, that they'd watched them fly away. But then there was a new drama because Allan lost his tooth—really lost it. It had fallen out and gone missing. A *lost* lost tooth. A great tragedy.

The children consoled Allan and admired his bloody mouth. They had learned to wait patiently because my classroom door was still difficult to open. New locks had been installed. New keys had been cut. A half centimetre had been planed away from the top and the bottom. But, still, it remained a hard door to open.

Eventually we found our way in, the door grazing against the carpet, my key refusing to slide out. We assumed our positions in the room, though Allan loitered near me up the front. I drew him close to me as I took my seat.

'Let's have a look,' I said and I studied the red, gummy flesh of his mouth. I gave him a tissue and he sucked on it for a moment before revealing his mouth to me again. There was a perfect gap where the tooth had been. I could even see the tiny hole of the root. Allan's face was sad. What good is it to lose a tooth and have nothing to show for it?

'I think you look so much older now you've lost a tooth,' I said, turning him slightly so his peers could confirm.

'You look like a old man,' Owen told him.

'A bit like a vampire,' another one said. 'With all the blood.'

'I haven't lost any teeth,' Olivia said miserably.

'Will the tooth fairy still bring me a coin?' Allan asked, his face pale and stressed.

'Yes,' I said. 'This has happened before; the tooth fairy understands. But what we should do is write a letter to let the tooth fairy know about your tooth.'

At that moment I decided to abandon my Maths lesson. I moved to the computer and brought up a blank document and projected it onto the screen. Together, as a class, we wrote to the tooth fairy and explained all about the lost lost tooth.

'You should write: *We don't know if he swallowed it,*' said Jock and I was surprised. Jock was yet to write a word for me. 'Write that, Mrs Stroud. We don't know if he swallowed it or dropped it.'

I typed their ideas and their words. It was new magic in my classroom and I saw the stress leave Allan's face. Saw the engagement in my students' eyes.

'Will we email this?' someone asked.

'No,' I said. 'Allan will take this home and leave it out for the fairy.'

'I don't think the tooth fairy does email, anyway,' Isla said. 'But maybe Facebook?' She looked to me for confirmation.

'I'm not sure. The tooth fairy's probably too busy for Facey.'

Allan took the printed letter. 'I'm still a bit sad,' he confessed as he sat down.

'It's a bittersweet feeling,' I told him. 'It's sweet because your first tooth has fallen out. But it's also bitter because you lost that tooth and you can't find it.'

The children understood immediately. *Bittersweet,* they echoed.

'Like sweet and sour,' one said. 'But mixed together.'

'Like chocolate and lemons.'

'Like crying and laughing.'

'Like ya dog dying, but ya get a new one.'

Bittersweet. It became our favourite word.

When I look back at that year, touch the memories like a bruise, I can see the beauty in my work, the sacred bond I had created, the learning that occurred, the teaching I was doing. The magic that was there.

'I think it's a book!' each child would say as I gave them a present on their birthday.

'How did you guess?' I would ask as the neatly wrapped package was ravaged by impatient fingers.

'Read it?' the child would demand, and they would stand beside me, beaming with the joy of ageing, while I read from their brand-new book that they got to take home. To keep!

Towards the end of Term One, somewhere near the Easter break, I delivered the lesson I had developed that had grown to become my favourite.

'I have something special for you today,' I told them.

'What is it?'

The kids popped up onto their knees and trailed their eyes around the room as though I might be hiding a pony.

'You have to wait and see,' I said, smiling as they moaned and collapsed on the mat with sheer anticipation.

I waited until later in the day and called each child out from their Library lesson, invited them to sit in the sun with me, and showed them a small brown box.

'In here,' I told each of them, 'I have the most precious thing in the whole world.' I let my eyes grow round and my voice stretch out and my face fill with the excitement of such a prospect. 'What do you think it is?' I asked and I shook my head at their suggestions—money, treasure, a magic spell!

'Do you want to have a look?'

They would nod, leaning forward and gently unclasping the box.

'Mrs Stroud,' they all said. 'It's empty!'

'No,' I told them. 'Look here,' and I tapped the mirror enclosed in the box.

'But that's just me.'

And I would nod and hug them to me and whisper into their ear, *That's right. You're the most precious thing in this world.*

When I touch those memories for longer, press that bruise harder, I recall the pain. The struggle.

The national curriculum was being rolled out like a steamroller flattening us into conformity and the Australian

Professional Standards for Teachers were looming like the boogeyman in my childhood hallway. I could almost hear him coming, screaming at me, *'You're accountable, you're accountable, you're accountable!'* I was creating new folders of paperwork. Collecting evidence to show that I was competent—feeling tempted to 'create' evidence that showed I was competent. Staff meetings became devoted to completing paperwork for professional standards. More meetings were held in the name of standards. The whole thing felt like an insult and a threat.

'Gab, do you have that data regarding Kindergarten Maths assessments?' The Principal was flicking through screens, preparing for another marathon meeting.

'I didn't get it done today,' I admitted. 'Allan had a *lost* lost tooth and so I—'

'Tomorrow,' he said and his eyes followed the artificial light, the staff meeting agenda glowing bright against the screen.

No! I wanted to argue. *What I did today was important. You didn't see the magic, you didn't see the things I did.* But then my chest began to ache and I thought, *I'm not sure I'll be here tomorrow.*

We started up our laptops and followed the Principal's gaze, light from the screen spilling over us as the machine hummed overhead.

'You've got to get this done,' he was saying. He was leading us through professional standards, dragging us towards a finishing line. 'It's part of being a professional, maintaining your accreditation.'

'I did my Masters not that long ago,' I said to him. 'I'm five years trained with over ten years of teaching experience, internationally as well as here in Australia.'

'Doesn't matter,' he said, but I could hear that his voice was weary.

'I've got thirty years of teaching experience,' Lana said, 'and here I am printing out this excursion note as "evidence" and writing a reflective summary of the excursion to show that I can ... what is it again?' She looked at the screen. *'Plan and implement well-structured learning and teaching programs or lesson sequences that engage students and promote learning.'* She shook her head. 'You'd nearly laugh at that if you weren't already crying.'

'Look at that,' Madge added, pointing at the screen. 'Look at all the things you're meant to aspire to; the standards you should now be trying to achieve.'

'Why can't they just value what I *am* doing? The things I *do* achieve?' Lana stapled sheets of paper together.

'Because,' I said, reaching to take the stapler from her, 'it's a deficit model. Our system examines what's lacking rather than valuing what's achieved.'

The system doesn't understand a 'lost' lost tooth, I thought. *It's never met Warren and it doesn't trust me.*

But, as the meeting continued, I watched as newer staff members listened, crouched and twitched their tails, ready to leap. Some were already earning more than me, gaining financial leverage from these standards. They devoted their time to the accreditation paperwork and were rising up, climbing those standards and becoming leaders. Soon, they would be Principals.

'What can I give the kids for dinner?' I asked Madge as the meeting ended.

'It's late,' she said. 'Be kind to yourself. Just drive through Maccas.'

'I can't,' I said. 'I did that last night.'

Madge laughed. 'But Gab,' she said, 'it's only Tuesday!'

I collected the girls from day-care at 6 p.m., finding them tired and ragged. Staff meeting day was a long one for all of us, especially Livvy who had arrived early at school, put in her day and was then bussed off to care. We stopped at the super-market, where I hit the frozen section, grabbing things I could shove in the oven with minimal preparation.

As I drove home, both girls fell asleep and I flicked on the radio for company. The news was full of talk about education and the impending release of the Gonski funding review. I wondered briefly what that was all about, considered how many more hours I would need in a day if I were to follow the news and read about these things that kept coming in and affecting my workload so dramatically.

The news moved on and my mind returned to the staff meeting. The professional teaching standards were sucking my will to live. They required me to produce evidence to show that I was meeting various requirements and write mini-essays that demonstrated how this evidence aligned with standards set down by the state.

A teacher could literally spend their working week creating the documentation required to teach, I thought, and laughed out loud at the idea. *What is it for?* I wondered. *Who benefits from all this red tape?* I was agitated with fatigue and devastated by the thought of my to-do list that now featured things like *Write a paragraph that addresses standard 1.3.2.* I sighed and loosened my grip on the steering wheel. *What they should do,* I thought wildly, *is install closed-circuit television monitors in every classroom, like they have in casinos. Parents and politicians and policy makers could log in and watch everything that was happening. I wouldn't have to document what I was going to do, what I did and then how I'd do it better. I wouldn't have to note down who got a bandaid and who got an ice-pack and who applied sun screen. It would be compelling viewing.*

It was nearly 7 p.m. by the time I got home. I woke the girls and hauled our luggage into the apartment. Matty arrived just as I was sliding trays of nuggets into the oven.

'Nuggets again?' he asked.

'Cook something else if you don't want it.' I stalked out of the kitchen and immediately felt guilty. 'Sorry,' I said, turning back.

'It's okay,' he said, unpacking the girls' lunchboxes and filling the sink with water. 'Nuggets are fine.'

I took my Zoloft every day. Talked to my psychologist regularly. Wrote in my journal each night about things I was grateful for. But, by Friday evening, I would be on our lounge in the foetal position, incapable of conversation and barely able to follow the TV. I was sinking. I could feel it.

You're accountable. You're accountable. You're accountable.

Too bad, so sad.

Bittersweet.

It was an ordinary moment, the moment I knew I was finished; that I knew I had to walk away.

A Thursday afternoon, four weeks shy of the end of year— that year I taught Olivia. At my classroom desk. While I was pushing a child through a test I knew he would fail and the rest of my class ran wild.

Chest pains. And a fundamental certainty that this was it. I wasn't teaching anymore.

I fumbled in my handbag and found my phone, sent a text to Matty that read: *I can't do this anymore.* It was an unremarkable end, without the theatre of shoe-throwing. Without tears.

I saw the Principal and said, 'Something is wrong.'

I saw my psychologist and said, 'Something is wrong.'

I saw Dr Bentley and said, 'Something is wrong.'

He said, 'It could be a heart attack or it could be your heart is broken.'

Walnuts

'**M**um! Do you know why a walnut's called a walnut?' Soph bounds into my bedroom keen to question me at 6.17 a.m.

'Why?' I ask, through the bleariness of sleep.

'B'cos if you throw a walnut against the wall, it'll crack open.' She climbs onto my bed and snuggles in. Her fringe is standing up at crazy angles and the sweet smell of sleep still clings to her.

'Who told you that?' I ask, and she names my dad, her grand-father, the 'one-hundred-year-old' Calathumpian, owner of rare and expensive macaroni.

'Hmm,' I say with a giggle. 'When did he tell you this?'

'Yesterday, when we were at their house. 'Member? I was on the deck with him, cracking those nuts we got him for Christmas.'

I smile and watch as she stretches and yawns ostentatiously, as though being six is really quite hard work.

'Do you get it, Mum?' she asks after a while. 'A walnut is really a wall nut?' She pronounces the words carefully.

'Yeah. Did you test it out?' I ask. 'Like did you throw a nut against the wall and see if it cracked?'

'Nuh, we just used the nut cracker.'

'Right,' I said. 'I think he might've been telling you a story. You know how he likes to tell a yarn.'

'Maybe,' Sophie considers the suggestion. 'It's a good story though, isn't it? Wall nut?'

We can hear Olivia, waking in her bedroom next door. Sophie fossicks her way out from under the covers and scrambles into Livvy's room.

'Hey, Liv,' she says, 'do you know why a walnut's called a walnut?'

I listen as they talk and I'm amused by their chatter; a plan is hatched to throw a walnut against the wall next time they're at my parents' house.

And for some reason I'm infused with a feeling of hope. My life has felt so unfamiliar in recent years but my dad is still telling yarns and my little girls are listening. It gives me a feeling that things will be okay.

When I left the classroom on the day that something was wrong, I drove straight to Dr Bentley. He requested medical tests to rule out a heart attack or cardiovascular condition. Then he reached across the desk, put his hand on mine and suggested it was likely my heart was broken.

'I think you're just burnt out, love,' he said, and I saw myself as embers in a fire, fading to grey, losing heat and becoming ash.

'But I have this pain,' I insisted, 'right here.' And I pressed again at my chest where it was hurting the most, my fist knuckling into my heart.

Dr Bentley nodded. 'Yeah,' he said. 'That sounds about right.'

The tests were clear and Dr Bentley rang my psychologist himself, made three appointments for the following three weeks.

I went home and crawled into bed.

Matty looked at me like I was a stranger, used a different voice to talk to me, closed the door and kept my girls away.

And I slept and slept and slept.

I will not forget my mother's face the first day she came to visit me. Like she was looking at a wounded dog.

'Oh, love,' she said, and I felt like a failure. My mum had endured the tragic loss of her son and she hadn't taken to her bed. *What was wrong with me?*

Olivia brought a card home, a giant thing made from yellow poster board. *Get Well Soon Mrs Stroud!* was printed on the front and all my Kindergarten students had signed inside.

Friends sent flowers. Like I was sick. *Was I sick?*

'I need to get up and move around,' I told Matty at the end of the second week. 'Can you call the gym? Tell Simon I want a Personal Training session.'

'I don't think you're up for that,' Matty said gently. He looked tired. It was obviously exhausting keeping things afloat while I was melting down. I wondered when his patience would end. 'What about some walking?' he suggested.

'No,' I said. 'Ring Simon.'

The next morning, I arrived at the gym.

'Hey, stranger,' Simon said. 'Matty says you haven't been well. It's good to see you back here.'

'Thanks,' I said. I had been coming to this gym on and off since Soph was born, trying to squeeze in workouts that would supposedly make me feel better about everything. In the past few months my attendance had dropped off.

'So what are we doing today?' Simon asked. 'What do you want to get out of this session?'

I shrugged. 'I think I'm broken,' I told him. 'I can't even answer that question.'

Simon studied me for a moment. 'You been to the docs?'

I nodded. 'He says I'm burnt out.'

'We're gonna do some boxing,' he said, sliding gloves over my hands and pushing his own into large, cushioned pads. 'Hit me,' he said and I did.

I crossed and jabbed, hooked and kicked, focusing my brain on Simon's instructions. He created a rhythm, consolidated the moves until I didn't need to hear him saying it out loud. Then he goaded me, urged me to fight and punch harder and harder and harder. *Is that all you've got?* He kept saying. *Is that all you've got?* until I was slamming myself against him and he was having to take a step back against the force of my blows.

When we stopped, I was wet with sweat, my body spent but I could feel my brain firing up—energetic synapses of connection seemed to be sizzling again after weeks of being dormant.

Simon watched as I stood there, panting. 'We all fall down, Gab. Our true measure is in how we rise up.'

I returned to school for the final week. The final week of the term. The final week of the year. The final week of my teaching life. Matty didn't want me to go back.

'Just stay at home,' he said. 'You've got the doctor's certificate.'

'I have to go back,' I said. 'To say goodbye.'

I wrote a letter of resignation which my Principal wouldn't accept. He had somehow managed to have human resources grant me a year of leave without pay. *Take the time to think it through*, he said. *You don't have to resign.*

I knew though, that last day I walked out of Belmora, that I wouldn't teach again. I couldn't.

The following year I worked at our business, cleaning apartments. It was satisfying work and physically demanding.

The best thing was that it was mindless work. *Perhaps that's the answer,* I thought, as I pushed the vacuum over carpets and reflected on things my psychologist had said. *Mindlessness not mindfulness.*

Guests that stayed regularly at our units asked why I wasn't working.

'I *am* working,' I would say. 'I'm just not teaching.' I struggled to explain my reasons.

'Well, you look great,' one lady told me. 'I thought you must've had Botox.'

I laughed at that and then took stock of myself. *I was laughing again. I could laugh.*

As the year wore on I started to feel more like myself. I laughed when my girls showed me tricks in the pool and I cried when our beautiful dog Shirley died. With the doctor's guidance, I took myself off my medication and spent a few months just remembering what it felt like to be me.

In October I re-dated my original letter of resignation and handed it in. The Principal, clearly harried and stressed the day I dropped the letter off, accepted it without question.

'I think I might be next,' he said.

After leaving teaching, life continued to roller coaster along, bringing unpredictable highs and lows. My marriage degenerated, not because of teaching, although my years as a teacher certainly took a toll on our relationship. I devoted myself to my writing and an essay I wrote for the *Griffith Review* on the state of education in Australia was shortlisted for a Walkley award. My teaching skills proved an asset and I worked at many different jobs, trying to keep the wolf from the door. Even so, I was wary of taking on too much. I was scared of fatigue, scared of being burnt out again.

I miss the classroom. I miss the kids. I miss the feeling that I was making a difference. But I don't believe that I left teaching. Teaching left me.

Epilogue

In Australia today, there's an expectation that our primary school teachers can be all things at all times for all people. And there are a lot of teachers out there trying to do just that. But the fact is, like the students we teach, teachers are not empty vessels. They bring something of themselves to the classroom every day. And they're affected deeply and irrevocably by the things they experience in their classrooms. As a teacher I am the product of all that has gone before. I bring my life to my work.

Trying to lay a blanket of standardisation over education shows a complete lack of understanding for the humanity required in this important job. Teaching, good teaching, is both a science and an art. In Australia today, we are confining education to a standardised model that values data and results and, in turn, conformity and productivity. We do not value the art of teaching and I suspect that the 'science' guiding our teaching at this time is faulty at best. We need to understand and accept that there is nothing standard about the journey of learning. Our schools are not businesses. Our students are not clients. They are individuals learning at their own pace, in their own way, with their own circumstances framing their experiences. Imposing standardisation on our students, on our teachers and on our schools only serves to stifle creativity, curiosity, progress, self-belief and autonomy.

I am often asked what the solution is for the problems we face in Australian education today. And I usually respond quite tritely, shrugging and saying something like: *I don't know. Education's so complex, like a tangled web, when you pull at an idea down here, something rattles up over there.*

I need to come up with a better response. One thing I can be sure of is that things will not change until we divorce politics from education. Australian schools, teachers and students are relying on a fickle, government-driven education system that gives and takes whenever the political winds blow. Over the past decade the changes in education have been exponential and every change has political roots, implemented and/or consolidated by both sides of the government. And our teachers and students suffer for that. I believe we need educators driving education, not politicians.

The best answer I can give when I'm asked to suggest solutions is that Australia needs a dramatic re-imagining of what education could be in this great country. Fundamental to that re-imagining is time spent dreaming and considering what is possible. We need to contemplate not only what we should teach our children, but also *how* we should teach them. And we must start valuing our teachers.

A note from the teacher

Dear Reader,

The recent implementation of a national curriculum, known as *The Australian Curriculum*, was a federal government commitment that would supposedly bridge geographical boundaries and reduce 'duplication' of time, effort and resources. However, each state still governs their own education system, which means that there are significant differences from state to state. For example, each state and territory has a different name for the first formal year of schooling, such as 'Reception', 'Kindergarten', 'Pre-Primary' or 'Prep'. Each state and territory also develops their own syllabus documents which are aligned with the national curriculum but contain local variations.

For the sake of clarity, it should be understood that this story is set predominantly in New South Wales. In New South

Wales the first formal year of schooling is known as Kinder-garten. To be eligible to enrol in Kindergarten, students must turn five by 31 July, although some parents delay enrolment until their child is due to turn six within the school year.

In New South Wales, Kindergarten is also known as Early Stage One (ES1) and the curriculum is organised as a twelve-month course of study. Beyond Kindergarten, the curriculum becomes organised into two-year courses of study that are referred to as Stages, although the students themselves remain organised in Year levels.

Stage One is Years One and Two, Stage Two is Years Three and Four, Stage Three is Years Five and Six, and Stage Four takes us beyond primary and into the realms of high school.

I trust that this explanation will clarify your understanding of the text, although I am sure it also raises some questions such as *Why do we have a national curriculum at all?*

Yours in education,

Teacher

Acknowledgements

I have dozed through enough Principals' speeches to know that this section needs to be short and to the point.

To Meg Mundell, whose outrage was infectious, thank you for lighting a fire beneath me when I felt my own was out. Also to Kate Maher, who is the gentlest, most supportive and honest critic that I have.

Thank you, *Griffith Review*. What a ride it's been! Julianne Schultz, your indomitable commitment to my story gave me the courage to write it. And thanks to Susan Hornbeck, who helped my essay find its audience.

Massive, ginormous, huge and epic thanks to Jane Palfreyman of Allen & Unwin, who read my piece in *Griffith Review* and rang to ask if I had more to say. I always have more to say, Jane! Thank you for inviting me to say it. Thank you to the professional and patient team at Allen & Unwin who have taken such care of *Teacher*.

Thanks to my editor, Rebecca Starford. Your honesty and praise helped me return to this manuscript and make it shine. Also to Curtis Brown and my agent Grace Heifetz, thanks for all you have done to bring this book to life.

Deep gratitude also to Varuna, The Writers House, and the Varuna Fellowship that was offered through the *Griffith Review*'s Contributors Circle. This manuscript grew stronger at Varuna and I am sure I grew stronger too, writing in the home of Eleanor Dark.

Big bear hugs to my mentor, Peter Bishop, who has had such faith in me. Peter, you reassured me that this story will know what it's doing. And it does.

Thanks to the vampires in my life. To Kate Forsyth who showed me how to begin, Zacharey Jane who kept me going when I wasn't sure, and Jesse Blackadder who gave me suggestions on what to do next. I love and despise you in equal measure.

Thanks to the amazing people of Protecting Childhood, especially my friend Kathy Margolis, who have rallied around my ideas and advocate so strongly for change. I am honoured and humbled by your commitment.

Thanks to all the unicorns in my life—you know who you are! Special thanks to Janet Lee, Jo Johnson, Kasia Drzewiecki and Sally Pike-Venner-Pointon. Your ability to love me in the way I need to be loved has been astounding.

To my Print Posse I say thank you. You gals are the best little writers group a girl could hope to have. Your ongoing support and encouragement has meant so much to me. Let's meet up again in real life one day.

Acknowledgements

Huge massive shout-outs to my friend Christine Doig, who has been my calm, deep, blue ocean during the final stages of this project. Thank you for always answering the phone, even when you'd probably had enough of me. Also to Azhar, who kept me accountable but in the best possible way. Thanks, too, to Leanne Bateman for finding the typos I had missed.

Thanks to all those fabulous teachers and students who agreed to let me 'write them in'. It has been an honour. Special mentions to Payton, Troy and Aiyman. My life is richer for having taught you. Thanks also to Dr Frank, Bonnie and Nadine. You kept me afloat. And big, fat, massive thank yous to all the students who I've ever taught and who still want to chat with me when they see me out and about. You were the best part of my teaching life.

Finally, thanks to my family for allowing me to weave their stories through mine. To my first and lifelong teachers, Mum and Dad, for all you have taught me and continue to teach me about being a good person in this world. To my sisters, Jacqui, Cheryl and Anni, who always seem to know when to lift me up. Thanks also to Matty, my friend and co-parent, who continues to walk beside me.

And, of course, to Livvy and Soph, my favourite characters in this book (and in real life)! They believed in me when I doubted myself. Thank you, my darling girls, for teaching me so much about life.

About the author

G ABBIE STROUD is a freelance writer, novelist and recovering teacher. After years of juggling the demands of the primary classroom, she became disenchanted and disillusioned, eventually making the painful decision to leave the profession she had loved. In 2016, her critical commentary of Australia's education system was published in *Griffith Review*'s Edition 51 *Fixing the System*, which went on to be shortlisted for a Walkley Award. Her first novel, a Young Adult fiction—*Measuring Up*—was published by Scribe in 2009. Gabbie lives on the far south coast of New South Wales, where she co-parents her totally awesome girls—Olivia and Sophie, aka Yaya and The Boph.